Application Development for Distributed Environments

James Martin/McGraw-Hill Productivity Series
Pieter Mimno, Series Editor

McGraw-Hill and world-renowned computer/communication technology expert James Martin team up to provide IS managers with the information they need to meet the application development challenges of the 1990s.

Organizations worldwide are under great pressure to achieve strategic corporate objectives, meet increasing global competition, get products to market faster, respond faster to competitive challenges, increase the quality of products and services, and reduce cost. Traditional IS technologies are no longer adequate to meet these challenges. IS managers need to learn a new set of technologies that can be used to rebuild the enterprise information system.

This unique series has been designed to present a comprehensive view of the new technologies that are required to rebuild the business. These technologies include business process redesign, client/server computing, downsizing, open systems, client/server development tools, CASE tools, relational database management systems, object-oriented techniques, and rapid prototyping methodologies. The Series provides a consistent view of how these technologies can be used within an integrated framework to meet the strategic needs of the organization.

Other Books in the Series

DEWIRE • *Client/Server Computing*

*To order or receive additional information on
any other McGraw-Hill titles, in the United States
please call 1-800-822-8158. In other countries, contact
your local McGraw-Hill representative.*

Application Development for Distributed Environments

Dawna Travis Dewire

McGraw-Hill, Inc.

New York   San Francisco   Washington, D.C.   Auckland   Bogotá
Caracas   Lisbon   London   Madrid   Mexico City   Milan
Montreal   New Delhi   San Juan   Singapore
Sydney   Tokyo   Toronto

Library of Congress Cataloging-in-Publication Data

Dewire, Dawna Travis.
    Application development for distributed environments / Dawna
Travis Dewire.
        p.   cm.—(James Martin/McGraw-Hill productivity series)
    Includes index.
    ISBN 0-07-016733-8   :
    1. Client/server computing.   2. Application software.   I. Title.
II. Series.
QA76.9.C55D47   1994
005.26—dc20
                                                        93-26522
                                                          CIP

1 2 3 4 5 6 7 8 9 0   DOC/DOC   9 9 8 7 6 5 4 3

ISBN 0-07-016733-8

*The sponsoring editors for this book were Neil Levine and Jeanne
Glasser, the editing supervisor was Jane Palmieri, and the production
supervisor was Donald Schmidt. It was set in Century Schoolbook by
Decision Tree Associates.*

Printed and bound by R. R. Donnelley & Sons Company.

To Andy, Travis, and Gregory

Contents

List of Figures

Chapter 4. Analysis Phase

Chapter 5. Top-Level Design Phase

Chapter 6. Detailed Design Issues

Chapter 7. Construction Issues

Chapter 8. Integration

Chapter 9. Production

Chapter 10. 4GLs for Distributed Environments

Chapter 11. Client/Server Products for Distributed Environments

Chapter 12. CASE Products for Distributed Environments

Chapter 13. Future Trends

Foreword

The James Martin/McGraw-Hill Productivity Series provides Information Systems professionals with objective information about the rapid changes in computer technology. This second book in the Series describes the techniques required to build applications faster and at lower cost for a distributed environment.

Application development techniques are evolving rapidly. Business managers are no longer willing to accept solutions from IS that take too long to deliver, cost too much, and fail to support the strategic requirements of the business. To meet increasing competition, organizations must introduce new products quicker, improve services to customers, increase quality, and reduce the cost of computer operations—simultaneously.

To respond to these business imperatives, Information Systems organizations must move rapidly to implement more cost-effective computer architectures, development methodologies, and tools. Major savings in the cost of computer facilities may be achieved by implementing distributed networks of micros and database servers. Substantial improvement in development productivity and quality may be gained through the utilization of rapid prototyping methodologies based on the use of small, self-directed teams, close end-user involvement in all phases of development, Joint Application Development workshops, and automated tools. New generations of automated tools are now available that can be used to generate 100 percent of the code for a distributed application from high-level specifications. Automated development tools for distributed environments include CASE (computer-aided software engineering) tools, client/server tools, and object-oriented tools.

Automated application development tools for a distributed environment are improving rapidly. Early versions of these tools were oriented toward support for pilot projects and used to demonstrate the technology. More recent versions of these tools employ object-oriented technology and provide substantial improvements in resource utilization.

Tools for the development of distributed applications have reached a critical stage in their evolution. They are being called upon to generate transaction-based mission-critical applications running in a distributed environment. Transaction-based mission-critical applications typically require high system availability, high transaction processing capability, and high data integrity.

Integrated CASE tools are being used to support the analysis, design, and construction of complete client/server applications for a range of target environments. Many organizations have successfully used integrated CASE tools to generate all components of mission-critical applications, including the graphical user interface, client procedures, server procedures, database access, and the communication of data between the client and the server.

Client/server development tools, an alternative to CASE tools, use an intuitive, windows-based development process for specifying applications. These tools are object-oriented and utilize a simple event/response development methodology that does not require using the structured diagramming techniques found in CASE tools. These tools are attractive because they can be used to develop applications for a distributed environment rapidly and at low cost. However, until recently, client/server development tools were limited in their ability to support requirements for transaction-based mission-critical applications, such as high online transaction processing volume, high data integrity, and rigorous analysis and design techniques.

Client/server development tools are evolving rapidly to overcome these limitations through the use of middleware—software that sits between the application and the operating system. Support for middleware has allowed client/server development tools to be used to build applications that support online transaction management and provide security, global naming, version control, and network management. Middleware has also been used to provide interfaces between the client/server development tools and CASE tools.

The tools available to build distributed applications are evolving rapidly, providing Information Systems managers with many choices for development technology. It is important for managers to make intelligent choices of enabling technology and use this technology to build applications much faster, at lower cost.

James Martin

Preface

Information technology is changing the way organizations do business. Local area networks and graphical user interfaces allow small groups, such as departments and divisions, to access information with ease, accuracy, flexibility, and speed—all at a fraction of the cost of mainframe-based systems with their dedicated staff and special environmental needs.

Some organizations are jumping into distributed environments, also called client/server architectures, in a big way. They are reengineering their mainframe-based applications to this new environment and doing away with the mainframe altogether. Other organizations continue to use the mainframe for legacy systems and design any new applications for the new environment.

It is important to understand why organizations are looking to distributed environments in the first place—to cut costs while improving reliability, availability, and user satisfaction. Distributed environments do not come cheap and the actual tangible savings (if the environment is actually replacing a mainframe, for instance) may not provide a comfortable cost/benefit ratio. Organizations need to factor in the efficiency of the new environment and its effectiveness. Another factor is the ability to conduct business in ways they were unable to do before, such as E-mail and electronic data interchange. Yet another factor is the expanded productivity of the users of the system, both the business user and the developer.

Distributed environments require a new focus, new skills, and new methodologies to maximize their effectiveness. One new area is the idea of clients and servers and how they interoperate. Another new area is the network—the intrastructure that links every node together to form "the system." The clients, servers, and networks have individual hardware and software requirements. Getting the intrastructure operating reliably is the first hurdle (and a large hurdle) for most companies. The area that seems to get short attention is how to best build (design and install) applications for this new architecture.

An organization needs to understand the ramifications of this new environment. It isn't as black and white as centralized versus decentralized, or application A's data versus application B's data. Data, the intrastructure, and the ability to easily access data wherever it resides become the life-blood of the organization. Every group in the organization has to participate in this new philosophy and work together to reach agreement on the meaning of data objects, who owns the data, and how data will be treated by each group.

Data becomes the major design issue. The applications themselves are quickly and easily generated using the development tools available for this environment. Consequently, the time it takes to build an application is minimal—if the data structure is correct.

As relational databases are becoming the *de facto* database structure for new development, this book will use it for all examples. It provides an easy-to-understand reference point. Bear in mind, however, that not all data structures are necessarily relational in nature and may be best implemented in another structure.

This book is broken into five parts. The first part covers what is meant by a distributed environment and how technology has evolved to this point. The advantages and disadvantages of this environment are also discussed.

The second part is a summary of the components of a distributed environment: the clients, servers, and network. It also covers some of the pertinent issues in a distributed environment, such as transaction management and distributed databases. Those readers familiar with client/server architectures may wish to skip over this part.

The third part covers the analysis and design of applications for distributed environments. The steps in the design process are discussed and issues unique to this process are identified.

The fourth part discusses the implementation and operational phases of applications in this environment. These phases are contrasted to mainframe-based applications and unique elements are identified.

The final part covers the application development products and contains a look at the future. Each category of products—fourth-generation languages, client/server development, and CASE—is dealt with in individual chapters. The final chapter in the book looks at where this evolution is going, what is impacting it, and how an organization can take advantage of the next generation of development products.

At the end of the book are four lists and the index. One list provides a reference for the many abbreviations used in the book. Another lists the trademarks referenced in the book alphabetically, not in order of appearance. The third list contains the addresses for the vendors whose products are discussed in detail. The fourth list contains additional readings.

This book assumes that the reader has some knowledge of client/server computing. It is intended to be a guide for those who have decided to embark on this new technology tide and recognize that it impacts more than just the hardware and operating software of an organization. It requires that the Information Systems group and the users work together for the good of the company. It requires that they agree that the *right* decision is the one that is best for the company, although it may not be a perfect solution for either group.

With such a quickly changing technology, it is difficult to predict what technology will bring down the road. But a review of where it has been and how quickly it has advanced makes it very clear—if you wait too long, your competitors will pass you by.

The bugs are pretty much worked out. The costs are coming down. Now is a good time to find that pilot area and install a distributed architecture. But be sure the applications on that architecture are designed to optimize its features. File away the dinosaur mainframe mentality. It's on to GUIs, LANs, DDBMSs, RPCs, APIs, middleware, and open systems. Have fun!

Dawna Travis Dewire

Acknowledgments

Special thanks to James Martin and Pieter Mimno, the editor of the James Martin/McGraw-Hill Productivity Series, for giving me the opportunity to write this book on developing applications for a technology which so strongly benefits those organizations that embrace it and for their continued support and encouragement.

Thanks to the staff of Decision Tree Associates for their seemingly never ending energy and support.

And, as always, a very special thanks to my family—Andy, Travis, and Gregory—and all the others who gave me the time and support necessary to complete this book.

Application
Development
for Distributed
Environments

Distributed Environments

Organizations are changing the way they use information technology. Conventional, mainframe-based computer applications that rely on proprietary hardware and software architectures are expensive and inflexible. Faced with shrinking product cycles and increased competition, organizations are looking for ways to cut costs, improve customer service, respond quicker to competitive challenges, and get their products to market faster.

To meet these strategic business objectives, organizations are looking to Information Systems (IS) for improved support, but at the same time, many organizations are reducing the IS budget. Business managers are expecting IS to reduce the cost of computer operations and work with fewer resources but build better applications faster and at lower costs.

To meet this challenge, IS departments are turning to distributed networks of low-cost computers in an open systems environment. This architecture provides a flexible and scalable environment that is supported by development products which allow higher-quality applications to be built faster at lower costs. By implementing this environment, IS can support the strategic requirements of the business as the organization redesigns its business to improve its competitive advantage.

This new environment incorporates new development methodologies that rely on major commitment and involvement on the part of the application's users during all phases of application development. By getting the users involved as important members of the development team, the requirement specifications, the designs, and the final production version of the applications are of a higher quality.

But there is no free lunch. A successful implementation of applications in a distributed environment requires a great deal of support from upper management; a cultural change for the users and IS staff; a commitment to "our" data rather than "my" data; a budget that covers hardware, software, and training; and enough time to get it all completed—and completed right.

Application Development Strategies

Information technology has been used as a competitive weapon by organizations to improve product quality, improve customer service, and establish global presence. It has allowed organizations to react—to adjust quickly to shifts in the market, to introduce new services and products to the market quickly and efficiently, and to strengthen their competitive position by improving internal processes.

Successful implementors have approached the use of information technology from an enterprise-wide point of view. New and existing applications are integrated. Data is shared among all areas of the company. The network infrastructure supports the enterprise—the entire organization.

Cigna, the third largest insurance carrier in the United States, began its information technology (IT) evolution by moving from 3270- and mainframe-based environments to client/server environments that could access data across the company. The IT structure was then converted to a fully distributed system using a mainframe as a database server, OS/2-based CICS servers for online transaction processing, and PS/2 client machines which optimize queries before they are sent to the servers. The GUI (graphical user interface) front-end uses color and pop-up menus. The entire distributed processing system runs on a token ring local area network (LAN).

The Information Systems division of Cigna made strategic use of information technology and reduced the department's annual budget by $30 million. At the same time, the division assisted one internal group in showing a 95 percent improvement in the time required to process a customer's claim. Savings of $11 million in one group and $8 million in another group have been attributed to the ability to look at data from a company-wide perspective and to access data from multiple sources.

The results: Cigna has reduced its size and is providing new services to its customers as the company continues to cut the processing cost of a claim.

1.1 Evolution of Distributed Technology

The last few years have brought major changes to information technology. Even the definition of an application has changed. Most Information Systems professionals think of an application as a set of programs that work together to complete a task, such as interactive user input routines (using a screen), validation routines, and an update procedure with audit trails. Now, a front-end GUI, such as Microsoft Windows, to a database can perform all these functions. Information Systems has to start thinking about applications and information technology in a new light.

1.1.1 Host to Micro/Server Platforms

One of the strongest forces pushing the IT evolution has been the increasing processing power of micros, which now rivals the processing capability of mainframe (host) machines. A host is no longer the only alternative for data- or compute-intensive tasks. The host is becoming less of a work-horse and more a storehouse for data, executing only those processes best performed with host capabilities.

The concept of a server was developed as a response to the need to share expensive peripherals, such as laser printers and pen plotters. The concept has evolved into that of a machine that services the needs of client machines. Such needs include:

- All processing and data needs with only the GUI micro-based
- Some processing needs and most data needs with the GUI and some processing micro-based
- Data storage and data management with all GUI and processing done on another machine or machines
- Some processing needs and no data needs with the GUI and some processing micro-based and the data on another machine

Some servers are mainframe or midrange computers. Other servers are micros that have been optimized for server functionality. Micro-based servers, called micro/servers, support multiprocessing and multithreading, have large disk arrays, and improved memory subsystems. They also offer optional redundant components, such as disk drives, power supplies, I/O (input/output) channels, fans, and automatic recovery features, that provide a high level of fault-tolerance capability.

Superservers are specially built micros with multiple processors, lots of memory and disk space, high-speed I/O channels, and fault-tolerance via redundant components. These machines support multiprocessing with either symmetric multiprocessing, where tasks are dynamically assigned to any processor, or functional multiprocessing, where processors perform an assigned set of tasks. Multiprocessing is discussed in Section 3.5.3. Superservers can support hundreds of workstations, handle heavy traffic, and are robust enough to handle mission-critical applications—all for substantially less cost than a mainframe or midrange computer.

1.1.2 Distributed Processing and Distributed Data

The days of centralized processing or decentralized processing are disappearing fast. Today there is a hybrid. Processing can occur anywhere in the enterprise network, such as:

- Under the control of **the operating system,** which looks for under-utilized resources and assigns tasks to them
- Under control of **the central processing unit** on the machine, which assigns certain tasks to specific processors
- Under control of **the application,** which codes assignments into the application

Data can be distributed throughout the enterprise network as well. By locating data on or close to the node that uses it most often (usually the update source) but still allowing the data to be accessed from any node, islands of data disappear. In addition, copies of data can be located at multiple nodes and synchronized by a distributed database management system. (A node is any processor on the enterprise network, such as a client machine or a server.)

1.1.3 Standards

There are many competing standards for micro- and LAN-based environments. Standards groups, such as Open Software Foundation and SQL Access Group, develop and publish standards. These standards are referred to as formal or *de jure* standards.

There are also *de facto* standards that are based on market share and market demand. Examples of these are Novell's NetWare for networking, Intel for processor chips, and Microsoft for operating systems and GUIs. By adhering to both formal and *de facto* standards, organizations can minimize the risk of incompatibility among the hardware and software components in the enterprise network.

1.1.4 Open Systems

Organizations can also minimize the risk of incompatibility among the components in the enterprise network by adopting open systems. Open (non-proprietary) systems allow organizations to mix-and-match hardware and software from a variety of vendors. The resulting enterprise network is not dependent on any one vendor for features or support.

In addition, applications specifications for open systems can be developed independently of the target environment. Developers focus on the application, not the technology.

1.1.5 Event-Driven Applications

Applications running in mainframe and midrange environments are process-driven. They are easily described by their input, output, and processes. Applications running in client/server and distributed environments are event-driven. Event-driven applications are described by their interfaces, data, and events, as illustrated in Figure 1.1.

Events are initiated by when a user selects an area on a GUI screen, such as a button. Each area is associated with a response (e.g., open a file) or the execution of a processing task (e.g., update). The application development process consists of defining the screen format and the event areas. The responses for each event area are then specified using

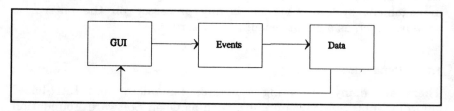

Figure 1.1 Event-driven applications

a high-level scripting language supplied by the development product or a source-level procedural language, such as C.

1.1.6 Automated Development Products

One of the major benefits of this evolution has been the introduction of micro-based, automated development products. These products automate the development of complex applications, as well as simple applications, such as the "new" type of application described in Section 1.1. Developers use these development products to define GUI-based screens, processes, and data structures. These development products are instrumental in some of the newer development methodologies, such as rapid application development (RAD), joint application development (JAD), and prototyping.

Compared to computer-aided software engineering (CASE) and fourth-generation languages (4GL), these products are easy to use, require minimal cultural change, and require less training for effective use. However, they may not be robust enough for developing mission-critical, transaction processing applications.

These three categories of development products—4GL, client/server, and CASE—are discussed further in Section 1.7, Overview of Development Product Evolution, and Section 5.1, Available Design Products. Individual products are discussed in the three chapters in Part 5, Application Development Products.

1.1.7 Middleware

This new term is used to classify the software that sits between the application and the operating system. Middleware includes:

- GUIs
- Databases
- E-mail applications
- Software development products, such as CASE
- IS management products, such as encryption and recovery routines
- Transaction managers
- Products for managing distributed computing
- Network management software

To provide a flexible migration path for future decisions regarding data sources, it is better to provide data access functionality at a higher level than database management software (DBMS) and, ideally, independent of the database vendor. Currently, products that provide this level of middleware include Ellipse from Cooperative Solutions, Inc., Encina from Transarc Corp., Tuxedo from AT&T, and TOP END from NCR Corp.

In a distributed computing environment, the management of networked systems, regardless of their hardware and software platforms, becomes a necessity. Networks and systems should be viewed as a single entity and their management handled as one process, not multiple processes. This management function is easier handled by software that sits between the two operating platforms. Such products are discussed in Section 8.4, Network Computing Environments.

Products that provide management facilities for the interconnected information technologies are primarily in the specification stage, although components are currently available. These products are discussed in Section 8.3, Enterprise Network Management.

1.2 Significance of Distributed Technology

Organizations cannot ignore the evolution going on in information technology. Benefits of this evolution include:

- Ability to meet the strategic needs of an organization
- Faster response to competitors' actions
- Faster product introduction
- Improved customer satisfaction
- Increased flexibility, scalability, and expandability
- Transparent access to data
- Reduction in processing costs
- Increased profitability
- Generation of distributed applications
- Development of enterprise-wide solutions

1.3 Strategy for Adopting Distributed Technology

Organizations must have a strategy for adopting this new technology. One aspect of this evolution is a three-tiered infrastructure, as illustrated in Figure 1.2. Centralized mainframes in the top tier are used to support high-speed transaction processing and provide access to very large databases. Shared servers in the middle tier store departmental data. Business rules are stored as triggers and "stored procedures." Business-specific processing is performed in the bottom tier on LAN-based micros and local servers.

This evolution allows organizations to:

- Rethink, reengineer, and redevelop their business
- Implement new business structure/design
- Rebuild the computer architecture
- Make the transition to the new environment
- Select from many choices, by adhering to open systems and standards
- Create an automated development environment

Organizations need to understand where they have been in the IT evolution and have a plan and vision for the current evolution.

Organizations must also have a strategy for how applications will be developed for this new technology. Customer-related applications are being targeted for LAN-based environments and developed with client/server development products. Mission-critical applications that support new business structures or reengineered processes are being developed with object-oriented CASE products. Existing applications are being downsized to micro-based processors.

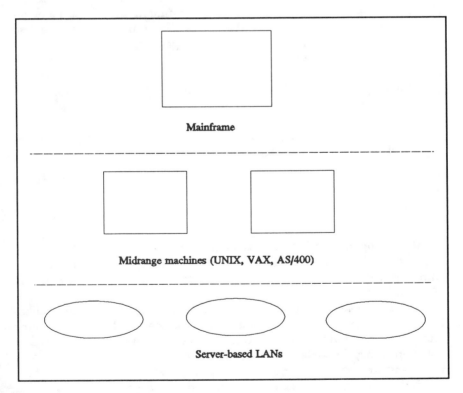

Figure 1.2 Three-tiered distributed architecture

New development methodologies, such as Information Engineering and rapid application development, stress the importance of user involvement through the analysis and design phases of the development life cycle. Prototyping products assist developers in generating mockups of an application and enhancing the prototype to generate a production version of the application.

1.4 Categories of Traditional Applications

Not all applications need to be distributed. Applications that share data or processes benefit from distribution. How large a benefit is derived from distribution is a function of the type of application.

1.4.1 Transactional versus Informational

One of the goals of distributed computing is to locate the data closer to the users who access it the most. The implied benefit is faster access times. But designers of a distributed environment must also focus on the use of the data at each of the nodes. Structures (hardware and DBMS implementations) that are optimized for efficient and fast transaction processing are rarely optimal for informational reporting needs. In addition, transaction applications usually do not maintain data for long periods of time. Informational applications require data that covers a wider window of time. The concept of *data warehouse* addresses this disparity.

A data warehouse recognizes four levels of data and processing in an organization. These levels, from low to high, are:

- Operational level
- Data warehouse level
- Departmental level
- Individual level

At the operational level, a single line of detail is of primary importance and summary data is secondary. At the higher levels, the summary calculation is of primary importance and the line of detail is of secondary importance.

For example, during the month-end closing of the accounting books, the trial balance lists all the transactions for the month and summary totals, which should agree, although the actual amount of the total is not of primary importance. If the totals do not agree, the individual line items are reviewed to identify the error. Once the books balance, the individual line items are summarized and a balance sheet and a profit and loss statement generated. These summary numbers become the important items and the line items, which make up each summary number, become secondary.

However, as an organization moves toward the concept of a data warehouse, access to data can actually become worse. As more data is stored in the warehouse and more users try to work with the data in the warehouse, manipulation of the data becomes cumbersome and time consuming. At that point, the warehouse distributes data to departmental machines and possibly to individual machines for storage. Those users who infrequently access data located at another node will still experience some time degradation, but the trade-off—speed for those who access it most often—is worth it.

1.4.2 Operational versus DSS

The idea of sharing data becomes more clouded as one reviews how data is used, as illustrated in Figure 1.3.

Operational applications access data in a procedural manner and the data to be accessed can be identified in advance. The process might be to first access data element A, then data element B, and so on.

Users of decision-support applications (DSS) access data in a nonprocedural manner. A user might review data element A, then access some portion of data element C, then access a different view of data element A, and so on. In some cases, the user might not be able to determine in advance what data elements will be needed for a particular session, task, or time. Depending on the business climate of the moment, data element A might be more important than data

	Operational	DSS
Volume	High	Low
Time Span	Short	Long
Updates	Frequently	Rarely
Access	High probability	Low probability
Access Style	Programs One or two records	Interactive language Multiple records
User	Clerical	Business users

Figure 1.3 Comparison of operational and DSS applications

element B. As the business climate changes, data element C might become more important than either data elements A or B.

Since most of the data accessed by DSS applications is generated by functional areas of the organization, the required data will most likely not be on the connection nodes of the DSS users. To provide as much speed as possible to these users, data is often replicated at their connection nodes. Replication is discussed in more detail in Section 6.6, Methods for Distributing Data.

1.4.3 Workflow Applications

Workflow through an organization is documented by forms. This process is one of the last information areas to benefit from computer technology. Forms are completed, sometimes manually, sometimes online (such as an order taken over the telephone). Multiple copies of manually prepared forms are made (or printed) and routed—and usually stored—by different departments.

In contrast, electronic forms—the image can include the form's graphics and fonts—can be routed electronically like E-mail messages. But automating an ineffective process will yield a faster ineffective process. Workflow software can streamline processes but the greatest benefits from automating work processes are realized when the processes themselves are effective. Organizations first need to study the processes to determine where improvements can be made and take appropriate actions. For some organizations, a minor fix is all that is required; for other organizations, a major overhaul.

Electronic forms can go beyond mail-like messages—they allow users to electronically sign the form. Such a signature might indicate approval or that the form has been read. To support workflow, routes could be automatic. For example, when an employee "signs" an electronic timecard, it locks in the hours and automatically forwards the timecard to the employee's supervisor. The supervisor reviews it and "signs" it, signifying approval, which automatically sends it to the payroll application for processing.

Electronic data interchange (EDI) has formalized how forms are processed among businesses. EDI is the transmission of data for standard business transactions, such as orders, order change requests, invoices, and requests for quotations, from one firm's computer to another firm's computer. The transmission is almost instantaneous. In the case of purchase orders, the receiving application can check for availability and respond quickly with a confirmation and an invoice. There is no manual intervention between the transactions that are exchanged among the various applications.

Standards are beginning to be accepted for EDI formats and communication protocols within industries. Currently, the United States and Canada use the ANSI X.12 protocol and Europe uses a standard called EDIFACT. Until these standards converge, multinational organizations will have to support both.

EDI was originally adopted for competitive advantage but is quickly becoming a competitive necessity. For large companies, the benefits of speed, reliability (the data is keyed only once), reduced past-due payments, and reduced cost per purchase order far outweigh the implementation and operation costs. Smaller companies that need to support EDI in order to stay competitive are using commercial value-added networks that provide EDI services.

1.5 Types of Distributed Applications

Distributed applications can be categorized by what is distributed: processing, data, or both. A set of data may be replicated on multiple nodes for quick access by a variety of users. The copies would be kept in synchronization by a distributed DBMS on a coordinating server. A set of data could be split among multiple nodes (fragmented). The coordinating server could make the set of data complete in virtual memory if needed. These two alternatives are shown in Figure 1.4.

Applications could be distributed in similar methods. A copy of the

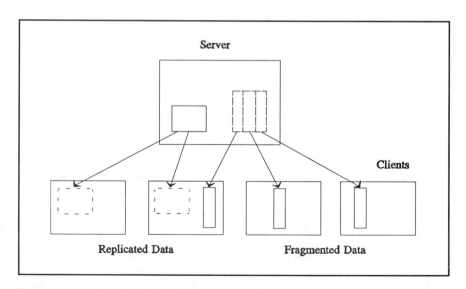

Figure 1.4 Replicated and fragmented data

application could be running on multiple nodes. Updates to the multiple copies would be handled by automated development products and version control utilities. The processing for individual applications could be split among multiple nodes, either by coding the processing destination node into the application itself or by allowing the enterprise system to assign the processing based on run-time resource utilization.

1.6 Overview of Language Evolution

Advances in software often lag behind advances in hardware. Language improvements lag behind both. As organizations build their strategies for using IT for competitive advantage and build applications for the new enterprise environment, languages cannot be overlooked. The languages used to build applications must fit the new environment, so that an organization can maximize its efforts.

Thankfully, the days of the first two generations of computer languages are gone for most of us. The first generation—machine code—was developed to program the first computers. The second generation—assembler code—was developed to make it easier for programmers to write code.

Machine code is a series of 1s and 0s. Assembler code uses an abbreviation to represent a function, such as SUB for subtract. With machine code and assembler code, there was nearly a one-to-one correspondence between the statement written by the programmer and an executable step by the computer.

1.6.1 Third-Generation Languages

Third-generation languages (3GLs) allowed programmers to step out of the one-to-one ratio of statement to executable step. These languages, such as COBOL, C, and ADA, are procedural. The programmer instructs the computer exactly how to perform a particular task. The programmer also defines all of the data needed for the task, where the data is located, how the data is physically organized on the storage medium, and how the data is presented to the user. It is important to remember that 3GLs were developed when data was primarily stored on tape. They have evolved into their current capabilities, which include specifications for screen outputs and calls to database schemas for data definitions.

3GLs continue to have a place in today's IS organizations. 3GLs are highly standardized, efficient, reliable, and compatible—the code for a 3GL from one vendor is almost identical to the code from another.

They have built-in audit trail capabilities. If structured techniques are used to generate the code, the code can be easily read and understood. Products are available that can generate 3GL code from application specifications and structured charts.

Over time, the third-generation languages have been extended to take advantage of newer technologies, such as database management systems, data dictionaries, and screen interfaces. The environment in which programmers work with 3GLs has also been enhanced by newer technologies, such as online development and an automated code-compile-test loop.

3GLs are often used for applications that are static. The data is known and the processes to be performed on that data are known. Since these are traits of transactional and operational applications, such applications are suitable for 3GL implementation.

However, the use of a 3GL as a production language for an application should not preclude the IS department from supporting report writers and query products that can be used against the data maintained by the application. Or preclude the department from using some of the newer user-oriented development methodologies for determining application requirements and design.

1.6.2 Fourth-Generation Languages

The attractiveness of fourth-generation languages (4GLs) is that a task requires fewer lines of code than would be required in a 3GL. 4GLs, such as FOCUS from Information Builders, Inc., Oracle from Oracle Corp., and PROGRESS from Progress Corp., are nonprocedural and are designed to be used both by business users and IS professionals. However, 4GLs are often used by the IS staff to develop sophisticated decision-support applications and to do prototyping.

Data is defined in a data dictionary which is accessed by the 4GL. The user describes the task (what is to be done). The 4GL determines how the task is done—determines the location of the data, accesses the data, and formats the results.

4GLs are proprietary and there are no standards. 4GLs are ideal for *ad hoc* applications where speed is more important than efficient use of resources. 4GLs increase productivity: one instruction in a 4GL may be equivalent to a page or more of 3GL code. Many 4GLs also contain specific functions, such as statistical and mathematical models. Most 4GLs contain a graphics component, which allows a user to review data in tabular form and then graph the same data by simply typing in the graph command.

The development methodology for an application that is being developed with a 4GL (a 4GL application) is very different than that of an application that is being developed with a 3GL (a 3GL application). The development of 3GL applications is very structured. Coding does not start until the user requirements are fully defined and the application is designed in detail. 3GL applications are, by their very nature, process-oriented.

Appropriate applications for 4GL development are data- and function-oriented. The development of 4GL applications is iterative and starts with the assumption that users will determine their requirements faster and more precisely in response to a working application (a prototype). The 4GL developer does some analysis to begin the process but then writes 4GL code to develop a prototype, which is used to determine the remaining requirements. By working with the prototype, users determine additional data needs as well as functional needs, such as generating reports, performing statistical analysis, drawing graphics, and issuing queries.

4GLs have a solid place in the IS organization today. They are ideal for decision-support applications and prototyping. The use of a 4GL increases user involvement in the design specifications and allows IS to react quickly to users' requests. In addition, 4GLs allow users to handle many of their own processing needs, eliminating those requests from a possible IS backlog.

Samples of 3GL and 4GL code are shown in Figure 1.5.

1.7 Overview of Development Product Evolution

IS organizations looked to code generators as a means of improving programmer productivity. But IS quickly realized that during a successful development project, more time and effort was spent on the requirements (analysis) and design phases than on the code. In addition, if the output from the requirements and design phases was of better quality—a clearer and cleaner representation of what was required for the application, less rework was required during coding.

Products that support this trend facilitate the requirements and design phases of application development. As these products found their way into IS toolkits, products that could generate code from the specifications were also developed.

These products fall into three categories, which are discussed below. Each category best supports a particular type of application and development methodology. When choosing a development product, the project team must ensure that the product fits the type of application and selected development methodology.

1.7.1 4GLs

As mentioned earlier, 4GLs can be appropriate development products for determining application specifications—for data, processes, and presentation. The iterative process requires heavy user involvement. Its prototyping nature allows the users to react to a working application. They can experience how it feels to use the screens and menus. They can "see" the application—an animated picture is worth more than a thousand words or hand-drawn charts.

The results of an application developed with a 4GL can be a working application—after it has been documented and enhanced for security and audit trails. If the 4GL was used to determine application working specifications, they would then be translated (coded) into a 3GL, which is unfortunately still a manual process.

```
                          3GL Code

OPEN-INVOICE-FILE.
     OPEN I-O INVOICE-FILE.
READ-INVOICE-PROCESS.
     PERFORM READ-NEXT-RECORD
          THROUGH READ-NEXT-RECORD-EXIT
               UNTIL END-OF-FILE
     STOP RUN.
READ-NEXT-RECORD.
     READ INVOICE-RECORD
          INVALID KEY
               DISPLAY 'ERROR READING INVOICE FILE'
               MOVE 'Y' TO EOF-FLAG
               GOTO READ-NEXT-RECORD-EXIT.
     IF INVOICE-AMOUNT > 1000
          INVOICE-AMOUNT = INVOICE-AMOUNT * .97
          REWRITE INVOICE-RECORD.
READ-NEXT-RECORD-EXIT.
     EXIT.


                          4GL Code

FOR ALL INVOICES WITH INVOICE-AMOUNT > 1000
INVOICE-AMOUNT = INVOICE-AMOUNT * .97;
```

Figure 1.5 Sample 3GL and 4GL code

1.7.2 Client/Server Development Products

This class of development products was designed specifically for the event-driven, client/server environment and focuses on the application's design. Such products facilitate developing the GUIs and Structured Query Language (SQL) processing required for an application. Many of these development products also include a 4GL that can be used to write the application's processes. These products are also referred to as GUI/4GLs. Other products require that the developer write the process code in a 3GL, such as C or SmallTalk.

Client/server development products can generate the code for the GUIs and the SQL statements necessary for data retrieval. Most of these products support a variety of server platforms—operating systems and relational DBMSs. Some of these products can generate the GUI P-code for more than one GUI platform. P-code—pseudocode—is interpreted into the native machine language of the particular platform when installed, thus supporting portability.

Ideally, a developer should be able to design and generate the application in one environment and then port it to other environments by simply recompiling the application in the new environment.

The recent growth in the number of client/server and distributed environments can be attributed in part to this new generation of client/server development products. Organizations can quickly put the environment in place, develop applications for the environment, and begin to show a return on their investment.

There is a range of automated development products for each element of an event-driven application. The elements are GUIs, events, responses, and data (see Figure 1.1). GUI painters can be object-based or object-oriented. A visual programming facility or 4GL can be used to provide scripts as responses to individual events. Data access can be handled via embedded SQL statements or be provided transparently.

However, client/server environments are not a panacea. There is a culture change, both to IS and to the business users, although the change is not quite as disruptive as the change resulting from the use of CASE products. Client/server development products do have a shorter learning curve than CASE products, but their learning curve is complicated by the requirement to understand the new environment and its limitations. Many of the products begin their development process from an existing database schema, which means developers must create a data model before even using the product. But the end result—the actual GUI P-code, the relationships between the GUI screens, the SQL code for data access, and in some cases, procedure logic—is worth the upfront work.

1.7.3 CASE Products

Computer-aided software engineering (CASE) products were developed to support the structured techniques introduced in the mid-1970s. These techniques (structured analysis and structured design) use diagrams and charts to depict the requirements (the end result of analysis) and the design of an application.

Data entity definitions and entity-relationship diagrams are used to represent data and its interrelationships. Process decomposition diagrams and data flow diagrams are used to represent processes and the flow of data among processes. Process decomposition and data flow diagrams can be decomposed into lower level diagrams which reveal greater detail. The decomposition process is continued until the elementary processes are defined. These manually-produced diagrams are difficult to keep current and consistent between levels of diagrams and across diagram types.

Early CASE products were introduced to automate the production and maintenance of these structured diagrams (this term will denote the diagrams *and* charts used in structured analysis and structured design). The products allowed developers to draw the structured diagrams using a micro as a workstation connected to a host and make modifications to them as more work was completed in the analysis and design phases. Once an application was designed using these early CASE products, the application was coded manually.

These CASE products were enhanced to incorporate automated techniques to verify the consistency and completeness of the structured diagrams. This type of CASE product is primarily a graphical design and analysis product.

Next in the evolution of CASE offerings was the introduction of integrated CASE (I-CASE) products. I-CASE products can generate the code for the entire application from the design specifications stored in the repository of the I-CASE product. However, even though this integration does represent an ideal situation, I-CASE products are not widely used. Only a few exist (they are expensive to develop) and they are expensive to purchase.

The current advanced state of CASE products incorporates newer development methodologies, such as rapid application development and prototyping. Designers build the prototype applications on a micro workstation in close communication with the users or during a Joint Application Development session. These products use GUIs to build the specifications and can generate GUIs as part of the prototype.

CASE products have been available since the mid-1980s. But they are still not used by many IS organizations. CASE products are expensive, require a great deal of machine resources, and have a long learning curve. Although recently introduced micro-based CASE products are affordable, they have limited capabilities.

The use of CASE products also requires a major cultural change within the IS organization and for the users. Many organizations have just recovered from the cultural change that resulted from adopting structured analysis and structured design techniques. Still other organizations are going through the cultural change brought on by 4GLs and are not ready to go through the upheaval again.

Figure 1.6 compares CASE and client/server development products.

1.8 Fitting the Development Product to the Application

One important tenet of this information technology evolution is that there are different types of applications and the development of each type is best handled by a particular category of development product. The term *mission-critical* is often used to differentiate applications, thereby reducing the number of categories appropriate for development.

1.8.1 Mission-Critical Applications

The term mission-critical conjures up different images in the minds of most business and IS professionals and in the media and vendor literature. There is only one point of agreement: a mission-critical application is an important application to the business. It operates at the heart of the business and provides significant value to the business.

	Client/Server	CASE
Model	Event/response	Data and process
Environment	GUI windows	Diagrams
Technique	Object-based	Structured
Methodology	Flexible	Rigorous
Training	Moderate	High
Cultural change	Minimal	High
Cost	Moderate	High

Figure 1.6 Comparison of CASE and client/server development tools

Some of the other characteristics attributed to mission-critical applications are:

- Require high availability
- Have high online transaction volume
- Require high integrity in the analysis and design phases
- Move money or update inventories
- Require high data integrity

However, a mission-critical application does not necessarily have all these additional characteristics. An order-entry application might have all these characteristics except high data integrity might not be cost-justified. A decision-supporting application might be critical to a retailer and have none of these characteristics except the requirement for high availability and data integrity.

Developers need to understand the characteristics of the application being developed in order to choose the right development approach. Critical applications must be developed using reliable products that provide development productivity. High-volume applications should be developed with products that can produce efficient execution times and work with other components of high-volume environments, such as transaction monitors. Applications that require high integrity in the analysis and design phase should be developed with CASE tools. Applications that require high data integrity should be built with products that provide backup, recovery, and transaction-tracking. High-availability applications should be built with redundancy in mind.

1.8.2 Choosing the Approach

Choosing the right approach and product among CASE, client/server development, and 4GL products requires that IS understand:

- Whether the application is transactional or informational
- Whether the application is mission-critical or DSS
- Whether the application is process-oriented or data-oriented
- Whether the requirements are well understood by the users
- Whether the application will be implemented in an end-user *ad hoc* environment or a controlled environment, where the users follow menus to initiate tasks
- Whether IS personnel have the skill set for the proposed approach

Some practitioners believe that CASE products should be used for mission-critical applications that run the organization and client/server development products and 4GLs should be used for DSS applications and less-critical (also referred to as *near mission-critical*) applications.

CASE products formalize communication between developers and users. Communication is facilitated through the use of structured analysis and design methodologies. CASE products should be used to develop applications which fit all of the characteristics discussed for mission-critical application in Section 1.8.1.

Client/server development products begin at the design phase of an application. Appropriate applications for client/server development products do not require high integrity in the analysis and design phases. Client/server development products differ in their support for data integrity (whether it is internal or it relies on the DBMS back-end), redundancy, and robustness.

CASE products are beginning to provide integration capabilities with client/server development products. Developers can use a CASE product to specify the data model and generate the database schema. The generated database schema can be used directly by the client/server development product to define the layout of the relational database tables and to develop GUI screens. The developer may use the product's SQL and 4GL capabilities to access the relational database and to code application-specific procedures. This integration allows organizations to leverage the existing skill set of their employees, speed up application development time (from analysis to cutover), and generate high-quality applications.

However, it is important to note that some applications may be very well suited to a combination of approaches. The development of an operational application that is not transaction-based might progress well with a 4GL prototyping approach. The final design might then be coded in a 3GL for efficiency.

1.9 Staffing

The skill set of the IS staff should include expertise in CASE and client/server products and their associated development methodologies. Because it is difficult to become proficient in multiple methodologies, each member of the IS staff should be proficient in one approach or the other. An organization has to develop a strategy for how its IS staff will get the training and experience required to become proficient. For some IS professionals, this may require a short learning curve; for others, very long learning curves. The IS organization has to build this diversity into its strategy for reaching its optimal mix of skills.

In most organizations today, typically only 20 percent of the development effort is on transaction-based operational applications. Ideally, these applications should be developed with I-CASE products within an Information Engineering methodology. The same percentage (20) of the IS staff should have expertise with these products and their accompanying methodologies, including structured analysis and structured design.

The remaining development effort is for informational or decision support applications. These applications are best developed with a client/server development product, such as PowerBuilder from Powersoft Corp., SQLWindows from Gupta Technologies, Inc., EASEL Workbench from Easel Corp., or UNIFACE from Uniface Corp.; or a fourth-generation language, such as Oracle from Oracle Corp., PROGRESS from Progress Corp., or FOCUS from Information Builders, Inc. Roughly 80 percent of the IS staff should have expertise with these products and their accompanying methodologies, such as rapid prototyping.

1.10 Going beyond Client/Server Environments

Organizations must not assume that they have taken full advantage of this current IT evolution simply by implementing client/server environments. The reduction of costs and increased profitability that are realized by such implementations are less important than the strategic benefits that can be realized with a distributed, enterprise-wide IT solution that allows an organization to retool their business processes, build products faster, respond quickly to changes in the market, and improve customer satisfaction.

2

Components of a
Distributed Environment

In distributed environments, both data and processes are distributed. This architecture is also referred to as distributed computing. In a cooperative processing architecture, data is generally distributed but the processing may or may not be distributed. In both cases, the user should be unaware of the location of data or of any execution.

The fundamental differences between distributed and client/server technologies is how the data is distributed and stored and how applications distribute tasks among nodes. The client/server model supports distributed processing through the use of stored procedures and triggers.

The user's view of the organization's computing infrastructure is the machine on the desk—the client. Each client is networked to a server, which may be networked to other servers. The enterprise network—the network, the applications, and data distributed across its nodes—must be as reliable as if it were running on a single computer. As far as users are concerned, the enterprise network is a single entity—"the computer."

The many layers of software required to support a distributed environment are shown in Figure 2.1. The client machines handle the presentation logic and most of the application logic, which could be a custom application, an application package, or a combination of the two.

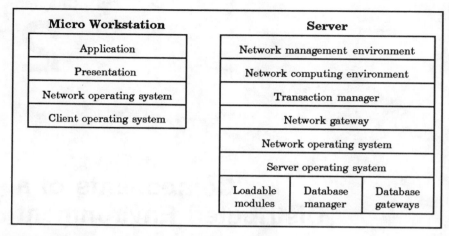

Figure 2.1 Layers of software in distributed environments

The server handles the data requests and the remaining application logic. However, since the data requests generated by applications may span multiple servers and multiple data sources, the environment must be able to manage the transactions.

The environment must be able to route requests along the fastest path to their appropriate node within the enterprise network. To accomplish this, the environment needs to be able to access and manage heterogenous networks.

2.1 What Is a Distributed Environment?

Traditionally, organizations have developed applications that reside on a central mainframe computer. Data for these applications was stored on the same machine. As the price/performance ratios of micros and micro/servers improved, centralized application processing was no longer the only cost-effective alternative as an environment for applications. Today, businesses are looking to distributed environments to meet the corporate goal of reducing costs while improving customer service.

A distributed environment is a structure that makes optimal use of network protocols and bandwidths, operating systems, hardware, and databases. It is comprised of secure subsystems with data flowing freely over a variety of networks. Interoperability is critical and usually achieved through adherence to standards.

Distributed environments can provide real benefits to organizations.

These benefits include:

- Ability to develop enterprise-wide solutions
- Increased responsiveness to customer requests using a decentralized operation
- Transparent access to data located at multiple sites
- More efficient use of computer-related resources
- Reduced operating costs

A distributed environment provides users with transparent access to computing resources within the network. Users are only aware of the computer on their desk.

In distributed environments, client applications request services. Server applications provide services. Messages are the sole means of communication between these applications.

When processes are distributed, they:

- Communicate via messages
- Request and receive services
- Are distributed among applications
- Reside across multiple, geographically distinct processes
- Cooperate to complete a business transaction

In the past (and, unfortunately for many, still), the steps needed to complete a job might be similar to those detailed in the left column of Figure 2.2. To a user in a distributed environment, the process would be more like the steps listed in the right column of Figure 2.2.

A distributed environment allows a user to access the data on the mainframe, do the analysis, upload it into a spreadsheet package, route the graphs to the graphics computer, access the CD-ROM "jukebox" (multidisk CD-ROM reader), and upload saved text into a word processing package. While there may not be fewer steps, each step is more straightforward from a user's point of view and the transition between each step is painless and often transparent.

This is just the first phase of distributed computing—transparent data access from all nodes and resources of the infrastructure. The second phase also distributes the applications and the databases. This book deals primarily with the second phase. Organizations see the productivity gains in the first phase as the primary benefit of this new environment. Once the intrastructure is in place, working reliably and readily accepted, organizations move on to the second phase: distributing the database and the application processing. Benefits from this move are more strategic, such as improved customer service, flexibility to react to changes in the market, and faster product introductions.

Nondistributed Environment	Distributed Environment
■ Use a mainframe to access and extract data. ■ Switch software to download the data to a micro. ■ Start up a spreadsheet package and load the data into the spreadsheet. ■ Perform some analysis, save some graphs, and save the spreadsheet. ■ Switch software to access a CD-ROM "jukebox" and extract text. ■ Start up word processing software and load the text files. ■ Edit the text files into a document format. ■ Import the spreadsheet into the document. ■ Print the document. ■ Switch to a graphics computer. ■ Print the saved graphics.	■ Click on the spreadsheet icon. ■ Pick the menu choice for nonlocal data. ■ Specify the data object and extract criteria. ■ After the data has populated the spreadsheet, perform the analysis. ■ When a graph format is finalized, click on the graphic computer icon to have it print. ■ Save the spreadsheet and exit the package. ■ Click on the word processing icon. ■ Click on the CD-ROM "jukebox" icon. ■ Specify the text to be retrieved and do a search. ■ Click on the return icon. ■ Perform any editing necessary. ■ Use DDE or OLE to implement transparent data sharing with the spreadsheet. ■ Click on the print icon.

Figure 2.2 Steps required to complete a task

2.2 Stages of Distributed Computing

The first generation of distributed computing connected workers in a department or group, as illustrated in Figure 2.3. The impetus for this move was to share files and peripherals, usually laser printers. The micro that runs the software that facilitates the sharing is called *the*

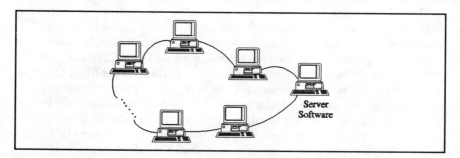

Figure 2.3 First generation of distributed computing

server. This micro might more appropriately be called *the coordinating workstation*.

The next generation connected the individual departments, as illustrated in Figure 2.4. E-mail facilities were often the justifying capability for this move. Most of the software ran on the coordinating workstation and the connected networks were homogeneous. Security and reliability were not major features of these architectures.

Client/server technology is used in the next generation of distributed computing, as shown in Figure 2.5. The machines at the users' desks do most of the business-specific application processing and the data is managed by the server. As the technology began to mature and client/server networks were interconnected, an application could make a request to its server for data that resided on another server. The idea of distributed access became commonplace.

As the hardware technology matured, so did the support for distributed processing: any node could perform a task for any other node, all transparent to the application and the user. The distinction between a server and a desktop client machine becomes blurred. Either

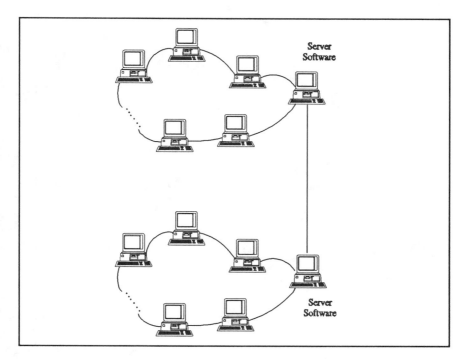

Figure 2.4 Second generation of distributed computing

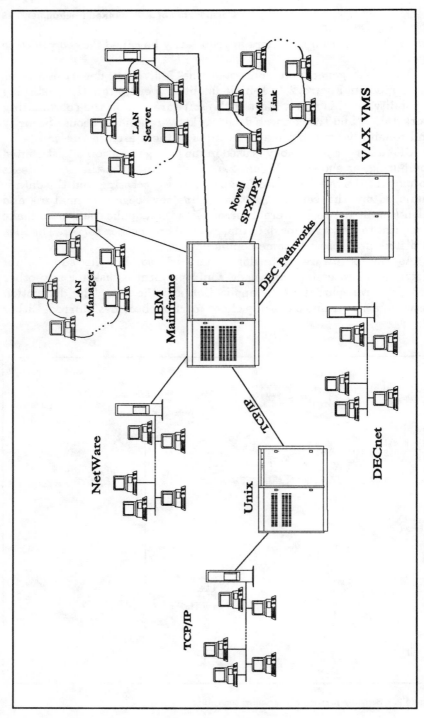

Figure 2.5 Third generation of distributed computing

computer can be a client or a server, depending on whether it is making a request or responding to a request. The entire enterprise network—the users' machines, the servers, the LANs, and the network connection devices—becomes the computer system.

2.3 Role of Open Systems and Standards

Distributed environments usually contain heterogeneous platforms and software. For the environment to be successful, there must be connectivity among the components. That connectivity is provided, in part, by adopting open systems and adhering to standards.

Standards specifications are developed by consensus and are publicly available. They are developed by standards groups, such as Open Software Foundation, Inc. and UNIX International, Inc., whose members are hardware and software vendors and, occasionally, organizations that are major users of the technology. These standards are known as *de jure* standards.

De facto standards are based on market share and market demand. These standards include relational database structures for data storage, SQL for data access, Microsoft for micro operating systems and GUIs, Intel for chips, Novell's NetWare for networking, and UNIX for midrange server operating systems.

By adhering to *de jure* and *de facto* standards, organizations maximize their software portability and extensibility. They can easily move applications to new platforms, adopt a new DBMS, and add new nodes to their enterprise network.

Open systems, a methodology for integrating divergent technologies, supports platforms from a variety of vendors. Open systems start with standard operating platforms and conform to a set of *de jure* and *de facto* standards for distributed computing, networking, and application development. All elements of the system communicate with each other.

Open systems provide a basis for portability and interoperability and allow future implementations of the technology to build on current implementations.

2.4 The Client

The client hardware is the desktop machine (micro or workstation) that runs client software. It is robust enough to support the presentation requirements and the client-based processing of the applications run by the user. Client software makes requests of server-based applications or formulates data requests for the server. These requests are passed on to the network software.

The network software forwards the requests to the server, accepts the responses from the server, and passes them on to the client-based software. The server receiving the request may in turn forward processing requests back to the network software to be routed to another node or nodes.

If processing logic is to be performed on the data, it is done before the data is passed to the presentation software for display. The user views and interacts with the interface produced by the presentation software.

The presentation software is usually a GUI, which provides a graphic-oriented window to applications and either simulates or provides true multitasking (the ability to run two or more applications at the same time). Each GUI is designed for one operating system, although newer versions can run applications designed for other selected environments. Most discussions treat the client operating system and the GUI software as a single entity—this book will as well.

The operating system running on the client may or may not be the same operating system that is running on the server. Client operating systems do not need the same robustness required for servers but must be robust enough to quickly perform the presentation and application requirements for the applications run from the client machine.

There are currently two GUI approaches. The X Window System runs on UNIX-based systems. The two major X Window environments are Motif from Open Software Foundation (OSF) and OpenLook from Sun Microsystems, Inc. The other approach is called, in this document, windowing. The popular environments for windowing (with their operating system) are Windows from Microsoft Corp. (with Microsoft DOS), Presentation Manager from IBM (with OS/2), and Macintosh from Apple Computers, Inc. (with System 7).

2.4.1 Windowing GUIs

The most popular windowing GUIs are designed for the DOS and OS/2 platforms. Each interface has its own look-and-feel and there is some commonality among the features of the major environments, primarily based on adherence to IBM's Common User Access (CUA) standards.

Windows 3.x

The native operating system for Windows 3.x from Microsoft is MS-DOS, a 16-bit operating system also from Microsoft. One of the major disadvantages of MS-DOS is a memory ceiling of 640 kbytes. Any memory over this limit is used for caching (intermediate memory storage). To minimize the effects of this memory ceiling, MS-DOS 5.x loads automatically into extended memory, has improved memory management and data protection, and allows device drivers, terminate-stay-resident software, and network software also to be loaded into extended memory.

Microsoft recently released, as an upgrade, MS-DOS 6.0, which does not overcome the 640-kbyte boundary either. The major features of this new version of DOS include:

- A memory management facility which automatically frees up conventional memory
- On-the-fly compression techniques which increase the available disk space on a hard or floppy disk (Microsoft claims the techniques nearly double the available space)
- Windows and DOS versions of backup, antivirus, and undelete facilities

Windows 3.x augments the capabilities of DOS with its own memory-management routines that simulate multitasking operations. It also supports event-driven interaction—the nature of client/server computing—with queued input messages.

Windows 3.x is most noted for three built-in technologies. They are:

- **Dynamic link libraries.** DLLs allow routines to be coded as modules and linked, as needed, by applications.
- **Dynamic Data Exchange.** DDE can be used to exchange data (objects) between Windows-supported applications.
- **Object Linking and Embedding.** OLE is an extension of DDE. The object and the software that created the object are linked between applications. If the data has been changed since the last link was executed, OLE automatically refreshes the replicated data (Windows 3.1 only). Recently released OLE 2.0 provides an object-oriented environment for Windows and consolidates Window's APIs into a collection of objects.

An important selection criterion for packages that operate in the Windows environment is that they support DDE and OLE interfaces. This support allows applications built with the package to share data with other Windows applications.

Microsoft is positioning Windows as the common interface to enterprise networks. To enable users to access information and services across heterogeneous platforms, including midrange and mainframe computers, Microsoft offers Windows Open Services Architecture (WOSA), a collection of published, proprietary APIs that can be used to integrate Windows and Windows-based applications with larger enterprise systems. WOSA incorporates Open Database Connectivity (ODBC) and Messaging Application Programming Interface (MAPI).

The ODBC interface provides a single database-access application programming interface for accessing a variety of SQL dialects. MAPI is a database API based on the work of the SQL Access Group that allows communications among messaging applications.

Presentation Manager

The native operating system for Presentation Manager is OS/2. As a 32-bit operating system, OS/2 2.x recognizes and uses all available memory. As a multitasking operating system, OS/2 2.x supports multiple threads of execution. DOS supports only one thread. Another advantage of OS/2 2.x is its use of named pipes, which allows processes to pass information to each other. Named pipes are not hardware or software dependent.

Presentation Manager has built-in support for OS/2's major features—multitasking, dynamic link libraries, and named pipes. The most effective Presentation Manager applications are built with the concept of multithreading in mind.

During the next few years, IBM expects to put its 32-bit WorkPlace Shell on top of DOS, OS/2, AIX, and its forthcoming Taligent object-oriented operating system. WorkPlace Shell is being positioned as a multiplatform alternative to a Windows interface. As this effort evolves, the OS/2 windowing environment will most likely be referred to as WorkPlace instead of Presentation Manager.

Macintosh

The Macintosh from Apple Computer introduced the mouse and the iconic interface to the general public. The interface was developed at the Xerox Palo Alto Research Center specifically as a way for children to use computers. Apple has spent the last decade trying to convince business it is not just an educational product.

The Macintosh interfaces uses a desktop metaphor. The desktop is made up of folders that can contain folders within folders or other types of objects, such as programs or data files. Objects are represented by icons.

Users select an object and then select some action to be taken on the object from a menu, specified by a command, or executed directly with the mouse by double-clicking or dragging.

Double-clicking "opens" the selected object. If the selected object is a folder, the contents are displayed on the screen. If it is an application, the program is brought into memory and given control. If it is a data file, the program that created the data file itself is brought into memory, and given control after opening the data file itself—the user can start work on the data file immediately.

Dragging an object moves the object from one folder to another, copies it from one disk to another, or deletes it (by dragging it to the trash can icon).

This direct manipulation interface relieves the user from having to remember what program created each data file. Current memory-jogging techniques include naming conventions and directory (and sub-directory) structuring.

2.4.2 X Window GUIs

The X Window System architecture is based on the client/server model: applications can transparently access displays on networked client stations. However, the terminology is used in reverse. The client acts as a presentation server and the server runs the client for that presentation server. The process is illustrated in Figure 2.6.

An X Server program provides an interface between itself and X

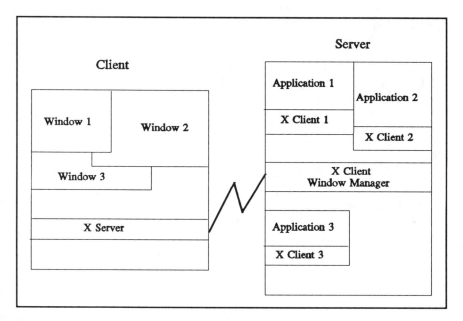

Figure 2.6 X Window System architecture

Clients, which are usually application programs. X Clients and X Servers, which may be running on the same or different network nodes, communicate by exchanging messages using the X protocol.

A Window Manager, acting as an X Client, is used to move, resize, and iconize windows. The Window Manager interacts with the applications through the X Server and determines the way input is directed to the client applications. It is the Window Manager that determines the look-and-feel of the GUI. The popular X Window GUIs, Motif and OpenLook, behave and look differently because they use different window managers.

Windowing GUIs, such as Windows and Presentation Manager, execute application logic as well as presentation logic. The server is a data repository and the data manager for the application. The server processes only integrity-related and resource-intensive tasks that have been assigned to it. In X Window Systems, the server handles all the processing—application and presentation—and the client merely displays the presentation screens.

In X Window Systems, the server is in control. In windowing systems, the client is in control.

Motif

The Motif GUI from Open Software Foundation is implemented using a single application programming interface (API) for all supported hardware platforms. It was enhanced to support Presentation Manager-style behavior and, therefore, has some CUA-compliance. Motif, based on OSF standards, is considered an open technology.

The resource definition is stored separately from the application code. Motif contains few operating system and network protocol dependencies. These two features simplify the enhancement process.

OpenLook

Developed by Sun Microsystems and AT&T, OpenLook also contains few operating system and network protocol dependencies. Developers have a choice among three APIs that can be used to develop OpenLook-compliant applications. The look-and-feel of OpenLook differs quite significantly from Motif, Windows, and Presentation Manager.

2.5 The Server

Servers store data and perform some application logic. Servers are also the path to data stored anywhere in the infrastructure. For data not located on their own storage devices, servers pass requests on with routing information—the node where the request is going (the data location) and the return node.

Relational databases have become the *de facto* standard structure and Structured Query Language (SQL) the *de facto* standard access language for distributed environments. Gateways to nonrelational data sources are offered by most major vendors of DBMS software, as well as third-party vendors.

The two classes of servers are:

- **Micro/server.** This class of server is a micro that has been optimized to support server functionality with expanded memory capacities and large hard-drive storage capacity. Some micro/servers also support disk arrays.
- **Superserver.** These machines were developed specifically to support client/server architectures. These micros have been further optimized by including multiple processors, parallel disk arrays, parallel I/O (input/output) buses, increased speed, memory, and disk capacity. The power of a superserver permits it to support scalable multiprocessing, provide high availability through the use of redundant components, boost disk I/O access rates, and improve network support.

2.5.1 Server Operating Systems

The server operating system manages the resources of the server, interacting with the network operating system and the data-handling software to receive and respond to user requests for services. Most organizations have found DOS to be inadequate for this task and have turned to OS/2 and UNIX-based operating systems. (OS/2 1.x is a 16-bit operating system which is widely used today. This book will focus on OS/2 2.x because it better supports the server environment.) Another player in the server operating system market is Microsoft's Windows New Technology (Windows NT), which was released in mid-1993. IBM has announced plans to release Portable OS/2 for RISC platforms by early 1994.

The major features of these four 32-bit operating systems (Windows NT, OS/2 2.x, UNIX, and Portable OS/2) are compared in Figure 2.7. The preemptive multitasking feature allows applications with time-critical tasks to get control of the processor when needed.

In early 1993, IBM, Intel, Microsoft, Borland, Lotus Development Corp., MetaWare Inc., Watcom International Corp., and The Santa Cruz Operation Inc. formed the Tools Interface Standards (TIS) group to promote the interoperability and portability of development tools across these 32-bit environments by developing standards—resolving the differences in interface formats used by compilers, debuggers, and linkers.

The consortium is currently publishing standards for three formats:

- Object Module Format
- Executable and Linkable (or Loadable) Format
- Debugging with Arbitrary Record Format

These standards are based on current specifications developed by consortium members and third parties.

OS/2 2.x

OS/2 2.x (Operating System 2) is a component of IBM's Systems Application Architecture (SAA). OS/2 recognizes and uses all available memory (unlike MS-DOS) and provides true concurrent multitasking support with data integrity protection. It has an icon-driven, object-based interface based on IBM's CUA '91 specifications for windowing applications. OS/2 is portable only within SAA and its lack of support for symmetric multiprocessing limits its use for scalable services.

OS/2 2.0 can run DOS, Windows (3.0 but not 3.1), and OS/2 applications in separate windows. OS/2 2.1, released in early 1993, has support for higher display resolutions, support for Windows 3.1 applications, and improved performance/speed rates.

	OS/2 2.x	Windows NT	UNIX	Portable OS/2*
Multithreading	Yes	Yes	Yes	Yes
Preemptive Multitasking	Yes	Yes	Yes	Yes
Multi-user Support	No	No	Yes	Yes
Symmetric Multiprocessing Support	No	Yes	Yes—in some versions	Yes
Portability	No	Yes	Yes	Yes

*Based on vendor's claims

Figure 2.7 Comparison of 32-bit operating systems

OS/2 uses demand loading to maximize memory utilization. Only the parts of a program that are needed at that moment are loaded into memory. OS/2's memory protection assigns each active application absolute boundaries, beyond which it cannot access. The memory protection increases system reliability to the point where users rarely have to reboot because the behavior of one application program cannot impact the performance of another.

IBM has announced plans to split OS/2 2.x into two versions. The client version will include elements of multimedia and pen-based support. The server version will include multiprocessing and distributed computing capabilities across OS/2 and UNIX platforms. Both versions will share system-management functions.

Windows NT

The microkernel architecture of Windows NT ensures its compatibility with applications not written specifically for Windows NT and other future supported operating systems. By writing an API (application programming interface), Microsoft can extend Windows NT to support other operating environments.

Windows NT supports multithreading and multiprocessing. It incorporates fault-tolerant features, such as exception handling routines that can impose quotas on each process in order to protect system resources and a built-in, fully-recoverable file system with features including disk mirroring, duplexing, and striping. Its file system, NT File System (NTFS), is a recoverable, transaction-based system which maintains a log of every change to the disk, allowing a disk to be reconstructed in a matter of seconds.

Windows NT includes basic networking services and APIs for messaging, security, and file and print management. Windows NT also has built-in support for local network protocols, such as Novell's IPX/SPX, and enterprise transports, such as TCP/IP, OSI, and Banyan VINES.

To facilitate application porting, Windows NT isolates its Executive Kernel from system hardware through its Hardware Abstraction Layer, which acts as an interface between the operating system and the specific hardware it runs on. Consequently, Windows NT applications are portable at the source code level.

Windows NT applications are POSIX compliant. The Portable Operating System Interface (POSIX) from the Institute of Electrical and Electronic Engineers (IEEE) is viewed as a standard for server operating systems. It defines a uniform method for a C language application to request services from an operating system regardless of the underlying hardware architecture or operating environment. Standard library functions and system header files are provided. Applications developed using these functions and files will work in any POSIX-compliant operating system.

UNIX-Based Operating Systems

UNIX is one of the oldest operating systems for servers. When originally developed in the 1970s, AT&T licensed it liberally, first to educational institutions and then to commercial computer vendors, because AT&T was forbidden by law to compete in the computer business. Once freed from its legal bonds, AT&T began to take actions to position UNIX as an industry standard.

In 1988, UNIX System Laboratories (USL), then a division of AT&T and now a subsidiary of Novell, teamed up with Sun Microsystems (Sun) to merge their two UNIX-based operating systems (UNIX System V and Berkeley Software Distribution, respectively) with Microsoft's XENIX, a 16-bit version of UNIX for micros. The new product, known as UNIX System V Release 4 (SVR4), incorporates the best technology from these popular versions of UNIX and offers interoperability, portability, and compatibility.

Two features of SVR4 that directly affect distributed environments are:

- **STREAMS.** This framework for character I/O eliminates the need for an interface between each device driver and the kernel. STREAMS hides the network protocol and media and permits a program to link transparently to resources anywhere in the infrastructure.
- **Transport Level Interface** (TLI). This interface provides media and protocol independence. Any network conforming to the Transport Provider Interface specification can be accessed by a program using TLI.

When USL and Sun began their joint project, a number of other UNIX-based product vendors such as IBM, Digital Equipment Corp., and Hewlett-Packard Co., uncomfortable with the idea of Sun playing such a central role in the development of SVR4 and anticipating that licensing conditions would become stricter, formed the Open Software Foundation (OSF). OSF developed its own version of UNIX called OSF/1, which now incorporates most of the features of SVR4.

Another derivative of SVR4 is UnixWare from Univel Inc., the result of a partnership formed by Novell and USL. The marriage was designed to address only the shortcomings in the Novell environment. The product is a blend of SVR4, Novell's NetWare, and other variants. It offers many of the same features as Windows NT, such as the server operating system capabilities and basic networking services. However, Windows NT is open; UnixWare supports only NetWare.

USL was recently purchased by Novell and Univel will be folded into the Novell/USL unit. Novell has indicated to UNIX licensees that it intends to keep UNIX as an open system and that its primary goal is to further broaden the UNIX marketplace. It is too early to predict the actual effects of the merger.

One of Novell/USL's early announcements concerning SVR4 was that it would be moved to a micro kernel architecture based on the technology from Chorus Systems, Inc. Its modular nature allows users to customize their operating environment and provides the foundation for an object-oriented version of UNIX by the late 1990s.

Also worth following is the early 1993 announcement made by IBM, Hewlett-Packard, Sun Microsystems, USL, Univel, and The Santa Cruz Operations. These vendors agreed to produce a common set of standards across their UNIX platforms by mid-1994. The Common Open Software Environment (COSE) would include a consistent set of desktop APIs and common networking products, and support a variety of existing and emerging standards in graphics, multimedia, and object technology. Among the technologies to be integrated into COSE are OSF's Motif, Sun's Tooltalk and DeskSet tools, and Hewlett-Packard's Visual User Environment (VUE).

All the interfaces and technologies adopted under this effort will be turned over to the X/Open Co., a standards body that will certify the products and publish the full specifications. A note of caution, however—the vendors are promising to support competing technologies such as OSF's Distributed Computing Environment and Sun's Open Network Computing, but not necessarily to make them interoperable.

Portable OS/2

To compete with Windows New Technology and versions of UNIX on RISC platforms, Portable OS/2 will layer the current file system used by Intel processors on top of the Mach micro kernel developed by Carnegie Mellon University. The Mach is also the basis of the next version of the OSF/1 operating system from Open Software Foundation (OSF). IBM is also working with OSF to develop a micro kernel that will support multiple file systems concurrently.

With OS/2 on the Mach micro kernel, IBM can support symmetrical multiprocessing, multiple users, and higher levels of security.

The initial version of Portable OS/2 will support PowerPC, the

RISC-based microprocessor from IBM, Apple, and Motorola. Support for other RISC platforms will be added based on customer demand.

Moving a 32-bit OS/2 application to Portable OS/2 is expected to be a straightforward process—recompile and run. IBM is expected to support Portable OS/2 and the Intel version of OS/2 concurrently.

2.5.2 Data Management

A key to a successful distributed environment is to optimally partition and locate the data and have the data accessible from any node in the infrastructure regardless of its source. The server data management software must be able to distribute data and maintain its integrity. Database gateway software must be available to access data sources other than those managed by the server data management software.

Topics relating to data management are covered in Chapter 6, Detailed Design Issues, and Chapter 9, Production.

2.6 The Network

The network is the least visible and least understood component of distributed architectures. The network consists of the cabling (usually behind walls), communication cards (inside the client machines), and communication devices (usually in locked closets) that link the server and the clients. The connections between client-and-server and server-and-server allow users to access data on any network nodes.

The network has to be designed so that it is never inoperable. If the network fails, applications don't run. The network must provide fault-tolerant capabilities to recognize broken cables or failed components and automatically reroute network traffic around them—all handled transparently to the users. The network must be able to easily adjust to changes in its environment, such as adding a new network to the infrastructure, moving people among departments, upgrading bandwidth capacity, or swapping servers.

The communication and data flow over the network is managed and maintained by network software. The network operating system manages the network-related input/output processes of the server. Each network operating system has its own protocol, the rules that define the formats and order of the data exchange and any actions that are to be taken on the transmission or receipt of data.

A network architecture defines the protocols, message formats, and standards used within that architecture. Products that support the architecture or were created within the architecture are compatible.

The most robust network architectures use a layered structure with each layer consisting of hardware components and/or software processes. The rules and formats for communication between adjacent layers are collectively called the interface.

Protocols are the rules and formats for communications within the same layer across different devices. Protocols include formats and order of data exchange and any actions to be taken on the transmission and receipt of data. The layered structure allows protocol changes to be made within a layer without affecting the functions (protocols) of the other layers. Each layer is only concerned with the services provided by the layer directly below it.

2.6.1 Network Standard Architectures

Network standards allow networks to communicate with each other in heterogeneous environments. The three most common network architectures in distributed environments today are:

- OSI model
- TCP/IP
- System Network Architecture (SNA)

OSI Model

The Reference Model of Open Systems Interconnection (OSI) is the standard for a common network model developed by the International Standards Organization (ISO). OSI is the standard network model for government agencies as stated in the Government Open Systems Interconnection Profile (GOSIP).

The seven-layered model, illustrated in Figure 2.8, covers all aspects of networking from the physical wiring to application support. Layer 1 protocols (functions) interact with Layer 1 protocols on the connecting machine. Layer 2 interacts with Layer 2 and so on.

The functions of the individual layers are (in reverse order):

- The **Physical** layer is concerned with the physical transmission of signals. Its functions are performed by the hardware components of the network.
- The **Data Link** layer is concerned with error-free transmissions and shields the upper layers from details of the physical transmission. The Data Link address, known as the local address, is used for send and receive identification. The functions of this layer are also performed by the hardware of the network.

- The functions of the **Network** layer and all those above it are handled by software. The Network layer establishes, maintains, and terminates the network connection between two users and transfers messages and data over connections.
- The **Transport** layer corrects failures that occur at the Network layer. It also takes the packets of data from the Network layer and assembles them into messages.
- The **Session** layer creates, manages, and terminates the dialogs between the users.
- The **Presentation** layer handles network security, character-code translations, and format translations.
- The **Application** layer provides utilities to support applications but does not actually include applications.

Unfortunately, the OSI standard has not lived up to early expectations. It has proved to be slow, difficult, and expensive to implement, and not exactly bug-free. In many cases, organizations have not needed the OSI model because networks already work well together using combinations of other protocols.

Some industry watchers attribute this lack of success to a flaw in the model—it does not recognize APIs (application programming interfaces). Applications are written for specific network protocols and specific platforms, often using APIs. Since the OSI application-layer interface is different from other protocol APIs, porting applications to OSI networks often require rewriting.

In addition, applications do not always use a single network protocol. Many networks are running combinations of SNA, TCP/IP,

	Layer	Function
7	Application	Support for application programs
6	Presentation	Code and format translations
5	Session	Dialogue management between users
4	Transport	Quality control of packet transmissions
3	Network	Internetwork routing
2	Data Link	Creation of frames
1	Physical	Transmission of signals

Figure 2.8 Open Systems Interconnection model

and various LAN protocols. Adding another protocol to the enterprise network does not necessarily make sense.

TCP/IP

Transmission Control Protocol/Internet Protocol (TCP/IP) specifies the rules for the transmission of datagrams (transmission units) across a network. It supports end-to-end acknowledgment between the source and destination of the datagrams, even if they reside on separate networks. Often used as the network protocol for connecting UNIX-based systems, TCP/IP's current popularity has been attributed to its low cost and high reliability.

As illustrated in Figure 2.9, TCP/IP is a four-layered architecture built on a network interface with conventions for traffic routing and communications and network interconnection. Unique addresses are assigned to each network in the infrastructure, but nodes in different networks can have common names. TCP/IP provides the same functionality as the bottom four layers of the OSI model: Physical, Data Link, Network, and Transport.

The transmission control protocol (TCP) handles data delivery, data concurrency, and sequencing. It uses connections between two points, rather than individual end points, as its fundamental tenet. TCP also deals with connections to applications on other systems, error checking, and retransmission.

The internet protocol (IP) handles the delivery of data packets. It specifies the packet processing rules, identifies conditions for discarding packets, and controls error detection and error message generation.

System Network Architecture

Systems Network Architecture (SNA) from IBM uses a seven-layered architecture which is similar to the OSI model. However, there is not

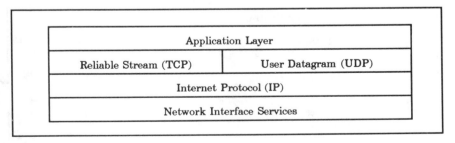

Application Layer	
Reliable Stream (TCP)	User Datagram (UDP)
Internet Protocol (IP)	
Network Interface Services	

Figure 2.9 TCP/IP architecture

a one-to-one correspondence between the layers of the architectures, as illustrated in Figure 2.10.

Users in one SNA network can transparently access programs and data in other SNA networks using SNA gateways. SNA provides resource sharing and includes reliability features such as backup host and alternate routing. Security is provided through login routines and encryption facilities.

SNA is designed to provide networking facilities for IBM platforms only. Recognizing that some organizations (most notably the United States government) have standardized on the OSI model, IBM recently released its MultiProtocol Transport Network (MPTN) protocol which enables TCP/IP Sockets applications to communicate over an SNA backbone (and vice versa) via an OS/2 server.

2.6.2 Network Hardware

Network hardware includes the cabling and the hardware connections. Figure 2.11 illustrates how the characteristics of the networks to be connected determine which device or method can be used.

Repeater

As a signal travels along a cable, it loses strength. Repeaters regenerate

SNA		OSI Model
End User		Application
Transaction Services		Presentation
Presentation Services		
Data Flow Control		Session
Transmission Control		
Path Control		Transport
Data Link Control		Network
		Data Link
Physical Control		Physical

Figure 2.10 Systems Network Architecture model

	Repeater	Bridge	Router	Network Gateway
Physical characteristics (OSI Layer 1)	Same	Different	Different	Different
Access and transmission control (OSI Layer 2)	Same	Same	Different	Different
Other functions (OSI Layers 3-7)	Same	Same	Same	Different

Figure 2.11 Comparison of LAN connecting hardware

the signal at its original strength. Networks on both sides of the repeater must be identical.

Bridge

Networks with different physical transmission characteristics and protocols can be connected with bridges. Bridges temporarily store messages forwarded to another network in case retransmission is required. They operate at the Data Link layer of the OSI model.

Router

Routers can be used to connect networks whose first two protocol layers (referring to the OSI model) are different. These hardware devices manage the route selection for data packets and allow linked networks to share traffic loads.

Routers use the Network layer (the OSI model's third layer) address to determine the best internetwork path between any two nodes. Because each individual router understands the entire enterprise network's topology, a router can automatically recognize a failed router and reroute traffic around it.

Network Gateways

To connect networks that are entirely different, network hardware gateways can be used. These hardware devices perform all the conversions necessary to go from one set of protocols to another, such as message format conversion, address translation, and protocol conversion.

In addition, network software gateways that run on the server can be used to send and receive data across networks. This type of software performs the same functions as the hardware devices and is ideal for supporting occasional cross-network traffic. Examples of these products are Database Gateway from Micro Decisionware, Inc. and SQLNetwork from Gupta Technologies, Inc.

Intelligent Hubs

Intelligent hubs, also called smart hubs, are designed to integrate heterogeneous networks and workstations from multiple vendors. The hub-based network service infrastructure is based on open and scalable platforms that are physically linked to the smart hubs. It centralizes the support and administrative functions for communication services and increases platform security, for example, sounding an alarm if a server is turned off or removed, and allows administrators to reset platforms after power failures.

For example, an alliance between Novell, Ungermann-Bass (U-B), and NetWorth Corp. has migrated Novell's NetWare application services into an open, intelligent hub with two application platforms created by U-B and NetWorth. Many value-added network service applications, such as host connectivity, messaging, internetworking, and network management, are moved to the managed and physically secure hub environment.

Backbone Networks

A backbone network is not a hardware device but a network to which the other networks are connected. A backbone network requires a high bandwidth and a higher quality and reliability than the networks it is connecting. It usually uses microwave-based links or FDDI (Fiber Distributed Data Interface).

2.6.3 Network Operating Systems

A network operating system manages the services of the server and exists at the Session and Presentation layers (referring to the OSI model) of the client machine's network management software. Network operating systems shield the application programs from direct communication with the hardware.

In a server-based system, the network operating system and files are stored on a dedicated machine that manages file traffic across the network. The popular network operating systems discussed below provide utilities for adding users, changing passwords, and maintaining system security. They support file and printer sharing, E-mail, remote access, and internetwork connections. These network operating systems offer their own global naming services, although some naming services are more advanced than others. Each network operating system includes some fault-tolerant features and more are promised in future releases.

NetWare

Novell's NetWare 3.11 supports TCP/IP and its native IPX/SPX protocol and can emulate NetBIOS. Support for additional protocols can be provided via NetWare Loadable Modules (NLMs). Netware has built-in network management functions and a name service that simplifies multiple server management. Novell currently offers disk mirroring, where two hard disks on the same controller replicate each other, and disk duplexing, where two hard disks are on separate controllers. The next major release of NetWare is expected to support mirrored servers.

However, NetWare was not designed to support multiple networks and runs in Ring 0, the execution mode associated with greater privileges and less protection. NLMs are written as APIs to NetWare. During the linking process, NLM code is linked to NetWare code and therefore also runs at Ring 0. Because NetWare lacks a preemptive scheduler, the NetWare kernel cannot get control of the CPU (central processing unit) back from an NLM until the NLM surrenders control. So if an NLM crashes, so does the server.

NetWare features are also bundled into UnixWare, the SVR4 UNIX-based operating system from Univel, which is a joint venture between Novell and USL. Since USL is now a subsidiary of Novell, Univel efforts will be merged into the Novell/USL unit.

LAN Manager

Microsoft's LAN Manager works with multiple protocols, supports NetBIOS and TCP/IP (but not both concurrently), and is compatible with IBM's OS/2 LAN Server. LAN Manager is tightly coupled with Windows. LAN Manager requires an OS/2 server but can be accessed by other client operating systems. Its fault-tolerance capability consists of disk mirroring and disk duplexing, as well as a "hot-fix" capability (the ability to replace parts, reroute traffic, and do other maintenance while the network is running).

But LAN Manager's continued success is dependent on Microsoft's commitment to OS/2 as a server platform. Although Microsoft recently released a new version of LAN Manager (2.2), it has announced plans to move much of LAN Manager's capabilities into Windows NT. Such a move could mean that Windows NT will be the platform of choice for enhancement developments for LAN Manager.

OS/2 LAN Server

IBM's OS/2 LAN Server 2.0's code is based on LAN Manager 2.0 from Microsoft. Applications written for LAN Manager can run on an OS/2 LAN Server network. IBM enhanced the product to facilitate the administration of large networks. These enhancements include:

- **Dynamic resource sharing.** A shared resource is not created until a user requests it. When the user unlinks from the resource, OS/2 LAN Server removes the share notation from the shared-resource table and frees up the slot.
- **Aliases.** A one-word alias can be given to any resource in the domain, including shared resources, regardless of where the resource resides. When the user references the alias, the controller completes the link to the resource.

IBM has already announced OS/2 LAN Server 3.0, a 32-bit network operating system that will be available in two versions—an entry version for departmental use and an advanced version for high-end servers.

VINES

Banyan's VINES integrates network management, security, and directory services on interconnected servers. It can also run over wide area networks. It provides easy-to-use configuration and monitoring facilities.

Its StreetTalk global directory facility provides a directory of all nodes on the network. It maintains the name, location, and attributes of every network user and resource. StreetTalk can direct local servers to connect automatically to remote servers and update the master directory of StreetTalk users.

VINES supports disk mirroring but does not currently support disk duplexing.

2.7 Linking Heterogeneous Components

If all components in a distributed environment are from the same vendor, have built-in integration, and/or conform to open systems, maintaining these environments would not be the headache it is. In reality, distributed environments link together hardware and software from many vendors, networks with competing protocols, data sources with a variety of formats, and GUIs with incompatible drivers.

There are two strategies IS organizations can follow to merge a heterogeneous array of components into a framework that supports all the components as if they were part of a single system. These two strategies are:

- Bottom-up
- Top-down

2.7.1 Bottom-Up Strategy

The bottom-up approach is to write remote procedure calls (RPCs) and application programming interfaces (APIs) to pass the necessary messages (links) between each component.

RPCs provide a vendor-neutral method of communicating requests for service from a node acting as a client to a node acting as a server. Requests for information are automatically translated into a RPC, which is transmitted over the network to the serving node. The requested information is translated into a RPC for transmission back to the requesting (client) node. RPCs are discussed in more detail in Section 6.2.2.

APIs define how data should be presented to another component of the system: another computer, network, database, packaged application, or even an E-mail application. APIs are discussed in more detail in Section 6.2.1.

In addition to the code needed to perform the links, developers would also have to write the code required to react to a failure in the link. This bottom-up approach puts the success—or failure—of the distributed environment squarely in the hands of IS.

2.7.2 Top-Down Strategy

A top-down approach is vendor-neutral. It uses software that operates above the components to provide the links and all the associated code. Organizations are looking to middleware and automated development software to provide this layer.

For example, applications written with Ellipse from Cooperative Solutions or PowerBuilder from Powersoft generate ANSI-compliant SQL so that the resulting commands can run against any relational database. Distributed Computing Environment (DCE), a middleware product from OSF, can support multiple network protocols, which allows a TCP/IP network to communicate with a NetBIOS network. Object Management Group's Object Management Architecture (OMA) integrates distributed processing and object-oriented computing by providing a standard method for creating, preserving, locating, and communicating with objects, which can be an entire application or a portion of an application. Its major component, Object Request Broker, specifies the information required by an object to communicate with another object.

2.7.3 Request Methods

There are two major methods used by client processes to make requests of servers in a client/server or distributed environment. These two methods are:

- **Message-based.** The client sends the server a message but does not wait for a reply. Message-based products can navigate diverse network protocols and are better for peer-to-peer communications but require more communication expertise.
- **Call-based.** The client sends an RPC to initiate processing on the server or an SQL call to obtain data from the server database. This is similar to traditional 3GL subroutine calls except the call goes out over the network. The requesting application waits for a reply. This request method is easy to use and is very appropriate for most client/server applications, where the application needs to wait for a response before additional processing can be executed.

Both methods reduce the amount of communication traffic required to facilitate processing. Another benefit is that new clients and servers can easily be swapped into the enterprise network, if vendors use common APIs.

Features of
Distributed Environments

Distributed environments have often been referred to as decentralized operations with centralized control because this new architecture blends the advantages of both. The data and processing are localized as much as possible, resulting in speed and promoting the feeling of ownership. The centralization of control ensures that the mission-critical applications continue to support the organization as a whole.

3.1 Distributed Architecture

In a distributed environment, the architecture—the equipment and the user—is geographically dispersed.

3.1.1 Distributed Equipment

The idea of distributed equipment is not new. Satellite systems that used midrange machines to support a department or a division have become commonplace. These groups usually employed their own IS staff to maintain the system and (often but not always) create and modify applications. For the most part they were autonomous from the central office staff, although occasionally, standards were dictated by corporate headquarters to facilitate such tasks as the consolidation of divisional data for accounting and human resource information.

The new technology interconnects the distributed equipment, allowing each node to process standalone or in tandem with other nodes. Processing at one node could rely on data from another node, thus reliability of all nodes becomes a critical issue for distributed environments. At first glance, it is the processing power of each node that is being shared. However, the greatest benefits from distributed architectures are derived from the fact that data is being shared.

3.1.2 Distributed Users

Having users spread throughout an organization is not new, either. The evolution began with terminals showing up in offices. Soon micro computers replaced the terminals. Now the computer industry is talking about a micro on every desk and a notebook computer in most briefcases.

The older technologies (centralized and decentralized) forced users to work in a vacuum. Each application and its data were managed separately and treated as separate entities. Responsibilities were assigned along application lines. Companies were organized according to what was possible from a processing point of view.

This view is changing. Users work with each other and share data. The same data may be used for different purposes by different users. To improve productivity, users must have data at their fingertips; they must be able to access data quickly and easily. Companies should be organized in such a manner as to optimize their businesses and fit technology into that structure. It is distributed technology that is allowing this to happen.

3.2 Distributed Data and Applications

As organizations recognized the reasons for distributing users and equipment, and derived the benefits from such distribution, they looked at applying the same rationale to data and applications.

3.2.1 Distributed Data

Enterprise data can be spread over multiple systems by distributing the data and the DBMS. Access across the network to the data should be transparent to application end users. Distributed data management keeps data local to the site that uses it the most (usually the site that updates it) while still providing transparent access to that data from other nodes in the environment. A portion of the database management system resides on each node as well.

Data can be replicated (copied) or fragmented (broken into pieces along row or column boundaries). Procedures must be followed to ensure that replicated data stays in synchronization. The integrity of fragmented data should be handled by a distributed DBMS.

3.2.2 Distributed Applications

A very early definition of distributed applications appeared in the issue of *IBM Systems Journal* (Vol. 27, No. 3, 1988) that defined Systems Application Architecture (SAA). Earl Wheeler and Alan Ganek wrote:

> Distributed applications are those written to exploit multiple system configurations to satisfy a variety of requirements, including specialized processing needs and those motivated by geography, security, capacity, availability, and organizational considerations.

When an application is distributed, the application's processes are split into logical components, which execute cooperatively and transparently on the clients and servers in the infrastructure. The processing can be distributed in two ways. The first method would specify in the application code the node assignments for specific application tasks. For example, an application that gathered a great deal of data and performed statistical analysis on that data might assign the I/O to the node where the data resides and the analysis to a little-used server or a compute server (a server that is optimized to do computations but little I/O).

The second method would not be coded into the application itself. The assignment of tasks would be made by the CPU itself, in multi-processing machines, or assigned based on resource availability within the infrastructure—determined by either the application software or distributed management software.

For example, if the user's connection node is too busy to perform a process, the execution of the process could be assigned to another node (server or client) for processing. An organization with a WAN (wide area network) that connects LANs on the east coast and on the west coast could take advantage of the time zone difference. The east coast LANs take advantage of the west coast LANs' resources in the morning, east coast time, when the west coast LANs are underutilized. The west coast LANs take advantage of the east coast LANs' resources late in the afternoon, west coast time, when the east coast LANs are underutilized.

If there are multiple tasks within a program that can be handled simultaneously, where no one task depends on the results of another task, the program can dispatch these tasks simultaneously into the processing queue to be processed by idle nodes. As the results of each task are returned to the program, another task may be dispatched to the queue or the program may need to wait for the results of all the tasks before the processing can continue. This type of distribution requires retraining the IS professional staff, which is used to working with sequential events. This new focus also becomes more natural as a by-product of the implementation of object-oriented technologies, which are more data-oriented than process-oriented.

For this type of distribution to be successful, there must be a great deal of coordination among the nodes in the enterprise network. This is usually a function of middleware software and is also a feature of some client/server products, such as Ellipse from Cooperative Solutions.

Triggers are another method for distributed processing and are used in client/server configurations. Triggers, discussed in detail in Section 6.1.3, are procedures coded with the DBMS and invoked by the server database when attempts are made to access or modify the data in the table associated with the trigger. Triggers have full access to SQL functionality and can perform searches, update data in other tables, and access other databases over a network via remote procedure calls (RPCs), which are discussed in Section 6.2.2.

3.3 Heterogeneous Equipment and Software

Today's corporate IS structure includes DOS, Windows, OS/2, and Macintosh desktop machines, as well as workstations running UNIX. These desktop machines are connected to servers, superservers, midrange machines, and mainframes, each with its own operating system. The network itself is managed by a network operating system.

The chances of all the hardware being from one vendor or all the software being from one vendor is remote. The days of one vendor IS shops are gone. IS is faced with the responsibility of tying all this heterogeneous equipment and software together into a workable infrastructure that can support enterprise-wide computing.

In a truly distributed environment, there is no such thing as a *foreign source*—data stored in another DBMS format that cannot be accessed. All data should be accessible, regardless of its storage format, to all software and applications. Users should not be concerned with such things as EBCDIC or ASCII coding schemes, or relational or hierarchical database structures.

3.4 Role of Data Dictionaries and Repositories

In order for distributed environments to be effective, users must be able to easily determine the existence of data elements and processes (procedures) using a friendly interface.

Data dictionaries provide the meaning of tables (and files) and columns (attributes and fields). The centralization and imposed naming conventions required for data dictionaries allow a company to identify, organize, and maintain the integrity of enterprise-wide data.

One requirement for a successful data dictionary is the use of naming standards. Naming standards are a set of standard words and abbreviations for naming data objects that limits the number of synonyms used and controls redundancy.

A dictionary also provides the links between the data and the processing models. Business decisions must be based on consistent and shared data. Consequently, changing a data structure can impact multiple applications. Data dictionaries can be used to analyze that impact.

As organizations began to manage their enterprise-wide data, it quickly became apparent that data was only the tip of the iceberg. There were processes and their code, report formats, and screen formats (to name a few), which could also be shared. Repository technology, a key component in the successful integration of enterprise-wide information environments, expands the concepts of a data dictionary to include the management of data and process models, definitions, rules, and addresses. A repository is a metadatabase application.

But repositories and repository-based application development have not been readily accepted by IS communities. Some feel that the benefits are still unproven and the change required to adopt repository methodologies is not worth the effort. Others point to the fact that there are few standards for repositories and their facilities are not integrated. Many of the implementations are proprietary and not extensible. Interfaces for uploading and downloading repository data to third-party products must be written and maintained. Updates to uploaded/downloaded (redundant) data must be synchronized.

But standards do exist for repositories. The ANSI Information Resource Dictionary System (IRDS) standard includes extensibility, an API (application programming interface), and specifications for how multiple, heterogenous repository facilities can be used to integrate logical services. However, the products that adhere to this standard are primarily the database servers which support front-end products such as integrated-CASE. Until repository-based products are built on effective, open IRDS standards, their acceptance will continue to be an uphill battle.

Data dictionaries are discussed in more detail in Section 5.2.1. Repositories are discussed in more detail in Section 5.2.2.

3.5 Major Trends in Supporting Technologies

A mid-1992 study by Gartner Group (Stamford, Connecticut) reported that approximately 9.3 million micros and workstations were on networks running distributed processing applications. The research firm also predicted that as many as 31 million machines could be on networks by 1996.

Better, faster, and cheaper solutions and a client machine on every desk, however, will not magically result in higher productivity and shorter payoff periods. A distributed environment with distributed data and distributed applications has many potential obstacles. If one component fails, in effect, they all fail. Implementors of this new technology must take very methodical steps, deal with multivendor integration problems, proceed slowly, test and then test some more at each step of the way, and plan, plan, plan.

3.5.1 Acceptance of Open Systems and Standards

The trend towards open systems is a necessity for the success of distributed processing. Vendors that have long rested on their proprietary ties to customers have to be able to access other hardware and other software or they will find their proprietary ties remaining on existing legacy systems and their new business nonexistent.

By adhering to standards, organizations are looking for protection— an insurance policy. However, it is difficult to decide on competing standards (*de jure* or *de facto*) for the many pieces of a distributed environment. Many organizations standardized on OS/2 over Windows early in the OS/2 battle for GUI supremacy—only to watch Windows pull ahead.

Some of the *de jure* standards are:

- **POSIX**, Portable Operating System Interface, from IEEE is a C-based standard for server operating systems. (See the Windows NT discussion in Section 2.5.1, Server Operating Systems)
- **OSI** (Open Systems Interconnection) **model** from International Standards Organization outlines communications system standards. (See Section 2.6.1, Network Standard Architectures)
- **GOSIP**, Government Open Systems Interconnection Profile,

requires that network products purchased by governmental agencies must be compliant with or show long-term migration to the OSI model.

- **DCE,** Distributed Computer Environment, from Open Software Foundation, provides services in heterogeneous environments. (See Section 8.4.1)
- **DME,** Distributed Management Environment, from Open Software Foundation, provides a consistent user interface to network management applications. (See Section 8.3.1)

Some of the *de facto* standards are:

- **Windows** from Microsoft as the GUI platform
- **Intel** processors for the components
- **OS/2** from IBM and **UNIX** as server operating systems
- **NetWare** from Novell as the network operating system
- **Relational** as the database structure
- **SQL** as the data access language

The safety factor in this new environment is that much of the software for distributed environments, especially middleware, supports multiple standards. Organizations can actually have different standards for different groups, such as Windows for business users and Motif for engineers, and still be able to achieve the benefits of distributed environments, such as flexibility and accessibility.

3.5.2 Server Technology

The popularity of micros and workstations is due to their relatively low processing costs as compared to compatible central processors. The server technology has made distributed computing a reality. Many of the advances discussed below were developed specifically for servers. The servers themselves are becoming more powerful, more reliable, and more flexible. Organizations are replacing their mainframes and their infrastructure with low-cost networks of micros and servers.

Intel 486 microprocessors currently provide 20 to 30 MIPS (millions of instructions per second) at a cost of about $75 per MIPS and can support up to 500 Mbytes of memory. The newly released Intel Pentium 5 chip, a fifth-generation microprocessor, is five times faster than the 486, increasing the processing power to 100 MIPS per processor, and at half the cost per MIPS. Initial pricing is about $1,000 per Pentium chip, compared to about $600 per 486DX2/66 chip.

Systems that use the Pentium chip will compete with midrange RISC (reduced instruction set computing) systems. Competing with the

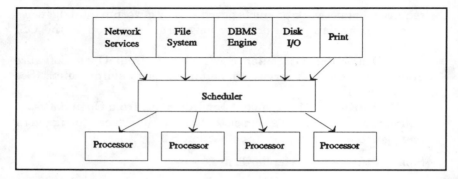

Figure 3.1 Symmetric multiprocessing

Pentium chip is the Alpha chip from Digital and PowerPC chip from Apple, IBM, and Motorola.

Pentium 6 is expected by the end of 1994 and Pentium 7 is already under development. Intel's stated goal is to bring a 2 billion instruction per second chip to market by the year 2000.

3.5.3 Multiprocessing

Vendors are including multiple processors in their hardware to increase processing speed. Servers perform either symmetric or functional multiprocessing.

Symmetric multiprocessing allows a task to be dynamically assigned to any processor, as illustrated in Figure 3.1. The hardware as well as the application software must be able to support multiprocessing. Multiprocessing allows a server to ensure that each task in an application is processed as quickly as possible. Consequently, resources do not sit idle if there is work to be done. However, this capability has to be supported by either the network operating system or the server operating system.

Among the major LAN operating systems, Banyan VINES SMP, Sun Microsystems' Solaris, and the Santa Cruz Operation's SCO MPX currently support symmetric multiprocessing. Among the major server operating systems, UNIX System V Release 4.2 and Windows New Technology support symmetric multiprocessing. IBM's Portable OS/2 will also support symmetric multiprocessing.

Functional multiprocessing assigns a fixed set of tasks to a processor, as illustrated in Figure 3.2. Consequently, one processor (usually the I/O processor) may sit idle while another is overloaded. Using LAN Manager as an example, one processor is dedicated to the OS/2 API set, which includes APIs for login and client/server APIs such as named pipes. The other processor is dedicated to network I/O, including the Network Interface Card drivers, printing subsystem, OS/2's High Performance File System, and other file-related code.

Multiprocessing supports multithreading, the concurrent execution of multiple tasks (discussed below). However, operating systems and network operating systems must be written to support multithreading in order for portions of the application to run on different processors.

3.5.4 Multithreading

A thread is the smallest unit of execution that the system can schedule to run. Each thread contains:

- A stack
- An instruction pointer
- A priority
- The CPU state
- An entry in the system's scheduler list

A thread may be blocked, be scheduled to execute, or be executing.

Threads communicate by sending messages to each other. Threads compete for ownership of various *semaphores*, which govern the allocation of computing resources between the individual threads. The threads ask the system for an instruction to execute. If there are no instructions waiting, the thread is suspended until there is something to do. If an instruction is ready, the thread performs the task and then makes another request of the system for more work.

Older operating systems achieve multitasking by creating multiple processes, which involves a great deal of overhead. In a multithreaded environment, a process is broken into independent executable tasks (threads). These threads then collectively perform all the work that a single program could execute, allowing applications to perform many

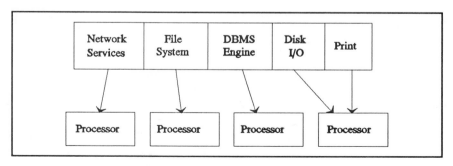

Figure 3.2 Functional multiprocessing

tasks simultaneously. The separate threads complete their tasks in the background and allow continued operation of the primary assignment. The challenge is to break the application up into discrete tasks which can become threads.

3.5.5 Disk Arrays

Fault-tolerant disk arrays, also referred to as redundant arrays of inexpensive disks (RAID), are available on superservers and micro/ servers. The multiple RAID drivers are treated as a single logical drive by the operating system. RAID can transparently recover from the failure of a single drive and allow the failed drive to be replaced while the server remains online.

As illustrated in Figure 3.3, data is actually broken into chunks and simultaneously written to multiple disks, a process called striping. If a disk fails, the data is reconstructed by reviewing the remaining pieces of data. While the data is being reconstructed, server performance is degraded but the process is otherwise transparent to the user.

To keep the penalty for reliability to a minimum with little or no impact on performance, RAID levels use the following techniques:

- **Parity checking** to improve reliability. An extra bit is added to ensure that data is transmitted accurately. The extra bit is used to restore data in the event that a hard disk crashes.
- **Data striping** to improve I/O performance.

There are five RAID levels of data protection and error correction. The level currently provided by most systems is RAID-5, also referred to as distributed data guarding. RAID-5 protection does not require a dedicated ECC (error-correction code) drive. Data and ECC information is striped across all available drives. RAID level 5 supports multiple simultaneous reads and writes, which can be performed in parallel.

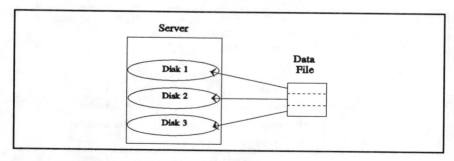

Figure 3.3 Redundant arrays of inexpensive disks (RAID)

3.5.6   Memory Subsystems

Memory and its reliability are critical components in distributed environments. ECC memory and parity checking (often with automatic recovery) are used to prevent corruption of data traveling within the server. ECC memory is a memory subsystem that automatically corrects single-bit errors and detects multiple-bit errors. It is used primarily with disk arrays.

Each time data is written, an ECC is written to an extra disk in the array or to an area on the storage disk(s). The ECC is calculated by applying an error-correction formula to the data written to the other drives. If one drive fails, the lost data is reconstructed from the ECC, the intact data on the remaining drives, and the formula.

Many physical faults can be tolerated by system memory designed with ECCs. However, the faults must be within the error-correcting capability of the ECC. The method uses the conventional one-bit-per-chip design with each bit of a codeword stored in a different chip. Failure can thus only corrupt one bit of codeword.

3.5.7   Redundant Components

Redundant server components, such as disk drives, processors, I/O buses, power supplies, fans, and automatic recovery features, are used to ensure that the nodes in the infrastructure continue to operate. Replacing a failed disk or even recovering from a disk failure should not require the machine be brought down. Some servers offer mirrored processors (the backup processor automatically goes on if the primary processor fails) and include remote alarms, which immediately warn of network trouble.

As users request data that could reside on any node of the infrastructure, every effort must be made to ensure the accessibility of each and every node.

3.5.8   Distribution of Processing Logic

The driving force for the distribution of processing logic off the host and onto the micro workstation is the power of GUIs (graphical user interfaces)—a power that has revolutionized the computer software industry. The original GUIs, as implemented by software such as EASEL from Easel Corp., converted host-generated, character-based screens into graphical representations of the screens, including features like radio buttons and pull-down menus.

Today's GUIs are the workhorses in distributed environments. GUIs handle all the processing logic for the displays and handle most, if not all, of the processing for the application logic. The GUI formulates requests for data, usually as SQL commands, and passes those requests to the server. The GUI then accepts the results of the request from the server, performs presentation logic and possibly application logic on the data, formats it for presentation, and presents it to the user in graphical format. Most of the resources necessary for application processing are handled on this lower-cost platform rather than the host.

The host (server) becomes the keeper of the data. It accepts requests for data and returns results to the requesting node—client or another server. The server manages the data and ensures its integrity.

3.5.9 Distributed Relational DBMSs

Before data could be distributed with guaranteed integrity, the relational DBMSs had to be enhanced to provide that environment. Distributed DBMSs (DDBMSs) can manage data that is distributed as copies of existing data tables or as portions of existing data tables. The DDBMS also works in tandem with the copies of the DDBMS that exist on every node that contains distributed data.

In addition, the DDBMS supplies transparent access to the data within the enterprise network and is able to manage the integrity of that data.

3.5.10 Development Products

Windows-based application development products provide shorter development times, system transparency, and skills portability. Development products for distributed environments are easy to use, generally use a GUI front end, and support the event/response model. These products allow developers to build GUI screens and specify processes for the events in the application. The code for the screens and processes can then be generated for the target platform.

Object-oriented techniques permit the encapsulation and reuse of common business processes. Using object-oriented techniques, business processes are organized as classes of objects, with inheritance of attributes and methods. Subclasses of objects may be created that inherit properties from the parent object, but also incorporate attributes and methods specific to the application. Applications send messages to encapsulated objects in response to user-activated events. Object-oriented techniques reduce the cost of application development through the reuse of business processes.

These newer development products are discussed in more detail in Chapter 5, Top-Level Design Phase, and in Part 5, Application Development Products.

Analysis and
Top-Level Design

The development of an application has four phases: Analysis, Design, Construction, and Cutover. For distributed environments, the end product of these phases is no different than those for mainframe-based environments. What is different are the products and the methodologies that support the application development process for distributed environments.

The analysis phase of application development studies the business area. This phase does not attempt to design the application. The purpose of the analysis phase is to understand and model the processes and data required for the application. The resulting document is referred to as the application's user requirements.

The design phase of application development produces a technology-independent high-level design of the application based on the user requirements. These design specifications include the designs for input and output screens and reports. Processes are specified using structured techniques, such as decision trees, decision tables, and structured English.

The design phase may include a prototyping phase during which a prototype is designed and developed and demonstrated to the users. The users react to the working application prototype and the design specifications for the prototype are fine-tuned until the prototype meets with the users' approval.

Users should be heavily involved in the analysis and design phases of distributed applications. The requirements and designs could be determined in Joint Application Development workshops or by using prototyping techniques. The information about the application could be represented using structured techniques, object-based prototyping techniques, or an object-oriented approach.

Automated development products could be used to facilitate the analysis and design phases. CASE products, client/server development products, and 4GLs are designed to involve the users in the specification process. In some cases, these products can also be used to generate the code for the designed application.

Analysis
Phase

A textbook definition of systems analysis is the phase of application development during which the development team gains a clearer understanding of the reasons for developing the new application. IS professionals and the users work together to define the application's requirements. At the conclusion of the analysis, a document is generated that contains the findings and recommendations of the IS team. If management and the users agree with the contents of the document, the development team proceeds to the top-level design stage, which is the focus of Chapter 5.

4.1 Pilot Project

Picking the right first application for a new technology has always been tricky. As one would expect, distributed environments are no different.

On the one hand, it does seem best to start small, maybe with a departmental application. The costs would be lower. Requirements would be more focused and easier to define. The work would be done quickly. And the impact of failure would be primarily confined to a single area rather than the organization as a whole.

On the other hand, by starting small, the organization might lose the global view of the technology and its benefits. Decisions made for a small, focused project might not be suitable at the global level and could lead to complications if the technology is adopted by other parts of the organization.

Some consultants recommend starting with a retrieval-only, decision-support application (DSS) using a snapshot of a central database. This eliminates the problem of concurrent updating across servers, but the problem of synchronization still must be addressed.

Organizations that have cut their IS budgets by half (or more), have eliminated their mainframes, and/or built applications in record time have not started small or started with retrieval-only applications. They have started with mission-critical applications. Organizations are not as willing to fund "learning-curve" applications as they are those applications that can favorably impact the bottom line. In addition, success with a mission-critical application will attract and hold top-level management support, which is critical for continued success.

4.2 Analyze the Process

There are no magic tools for analyzing the processes that are being considered for automation. There are the tried-and-true methods of interviewing, reviewing documentation, and observing. Some of the newer techniques, such as rapid prototyping and Joint Application Development workshops, are discussed in Section 4.3, Determine the Development Methodology.

Whichever process is used, this stage produces the user requirements for the application. However, in many cases, as the process is reviewed, it becomes apparent that the process itself is fine—its implementation just needs updating. Although this book focuses on developing new applications, it would be remiss not to present alternatives for updating an application's implementation.

4.2.1 Update Implementation

If it is determined that the implementation needs to be brought up-to-date, an organization has two choices: translate the code, as is, or reengineer the application.

Translate the Code, As Is

Many organizations are finding that minimal effort is required to translate their mainframe COBOL applications into Micro Focus COBOL applications to be run on smaller platforms. The resulting applications need only minor modifications to run in a distributed environment.

Micro Focus also offers Dialog System, which allows developers to create GUIs for COBOL programs running under DOS, OS/2, Windows, and UNIX. Dialog System isolates screen and keyboard logic from COBOL applications, replacing lines of screen definition code with a simple CALL statement to generate the screen. User interfaces can be prototyped, developed, and updated without impacting the application logic.

Software Redevelopment

Software redevelopment (sometimes referred to as software reengineering) examines and converts the existing code into a new form. The resulting application has its original features but with a simpler code structure. Software reengineering can be used to convert an application to another hardware platform, operating system, source-code language, or DBMS.

The two steps in software redevelopment are:

- Software reengineering: program understanding and reverse engineering
- Forward engineering

Program understanding involves analyzing the code to determine the physical design of the application—its components and their interactions. Ideally, the information about each component should be stored in a repository. The output is an application that contains its original features and platform support but with an easier-to-follow code structure for maintenance. The program-understanding process is illustrated in Figure 4.1.

The program-understanding process is also useful to document what an application is currently doing. The output depicts the technology design. However, the results must be reviewed manually to determine what business rules are being enforced by the application and whether these are the business rules the organization currently wishes to be enforced. The program-understanding process is not a substitute for enterprise modeling which depicts the business rules independent of technology.

Program understanding leaves the source-level code at the same level of abstraction. Reverse engineering converts it to a higher level of abstraction. However, it is currently only possible to reverse engineer data, not processes. This creates the gap between reengineering and forward engineering as illustrated in Figure 4.2. A great deal of manual effort is required to bridge this gap.

CASE products are generally used to forward engineer an application, although some organizations are also using 4GLs and client/server

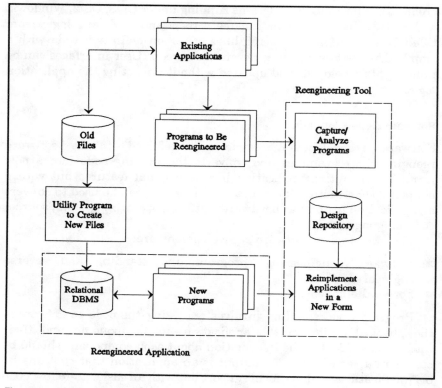

Figure 4.1 The program understanding process

development tools to forward engineer applications. The CASE products also allow developers to add functionality to the specifications for the application and clean up data relationships before the application is regenerated.

Ideally, the reverse engineering process should produce the specification information required by CASE products to generate the application code, such as data flow diagrams, entity-relationship diagrams, and functional decomposition diagrams. However, most

Reengineering				
Inventory Analysis	Restructuring	Program Understanding	Reverse Engineering	Forward Engineering

Figure 4.2 Software redevelopment

software reengineering products only provide some of the required specification information.

- **Analyzers** evaluate the complexity of a program and look for redundant data definitions.
- **Diagrammers** produce charts of the physical structure of the application code and the physical layout of the data.
- **Documenters** generate low-level information about the organization of the code, including cross-reference lists.
- **Restructurers** replace "spaghetti code" with structured code.
- **Reverse engineering** tools extract from the code a high-level data model that is independent of the target environment.

Most reengineering products simply produce reports and only a few use a repository to store results. To pass information from one reengineering step to another requires some manual transformation of the information. In addition, extracting data flow, process flow, and high-level process specifications from existing application code does not lend itself to automation and continues to be a manual, labor-intensive process.

4.2.2 Reengineer the Business

The idea of reengineering is now being applied to the entire business system—organizational structures, management systems, processes, values, beliefs, and jobs. Instead of simply automating existing procedures and processes with newer technology, organizations are rethinking and redesigning the business process itself.

The business requirements should be determined before the enabling technology is selected. Applications developed with this approach can respond faster to business changes because the application architecture does not focus on technology but rather on the business needs.

To effectively reengineer a process within an organization, there must be visible commitment from upper management, a willingness to see the reengineering process through to completion, and excellent interpersonal communications—to reengineer the process, manage change, and control rumors. Although an outside consultant familiar with new information technologies may be required, the organization's staff is the best source for the critical information required to support reengineering.

Agreeing that business reengineering is not an easy task, people who have reengineered their businesses feel that the dramatic benefits made the effort worthwhile. These benefits include greater flexibility in business operations, increased access to data, a dramatic reduction in the cost of computer systems, and increased competitive capabilities.

4.3 Determine the Development Methodology

Some of the methodologies for generating application requirements and designs for distributed environments are based on automated products, such as prototyping tools. Other methodologies are traditional ones that have been enhanced by automated products. The separate stages of development for a rapid prototyping methodology are sometimes referred to as Joint Requirements Planning, Joint Application Design, Construction, and Cutover.

4.3.1 Development Teams

Applications are usually developed by self-directed teams that consist of users and IS professionals. The IS members of these teams are sometimes referred to as SWAT (specialists with advanced tools) teams if they are skilled in modern methodologies, modeling tools, and techniques. The users are as heavily involved in the development process as the IS professionals are.

In the traditional development process, IS professionals interview users and then develop the user requirements. There is little communication between the users being interviewed. The IS team typically communicates using telephones, memos, E-mail, and overhead displays in conference rooms.

This process is changing quickly. Interteam communication methods are now augmented by groupware software, repositories, and team-oriented CASE and client/server products. Groupware software, such as Notes from Lotus Development Corp., facilitates group communication rather than the one-to-one E-mail approach. It allows team members to communicate thoughts and questions as they occur and promotes feedback from many instead of few.

Repositories encourage the sharing of procedures, ensure consistency among the data structures used in the application, and eliminate redundancy. They provide a common foundation for the analysis and design efforts.

Tools that support multiprogrammer construction require features such as:

- Standard tools, including compilers and editors
- A repository that supports concurrent access and consistency

- Versioning support
- Configuration management
- Source code control

4.3.2 Rapid Prototyping

A prototype is a working model of the application. It allows users to take part in defining the requirements and deciding how the application will meet those requirements. Working with the users, a series of prototypes can be viewed and revised interactively (hence the name rapid prototyping). The automated products are usually installed on a micro. The number of prototypes could range from several to hundreds. The prototype process is illustrated in Figure 4.3.

Prototypes can be:

- Hand-drawn
- Created with programs such as Apple's MacDraw, Microsoft's PowerPoint, and IBM's PC Storyboard
- Developed using CASE products
- Developed using client/server development products
- Developed using 4GLs

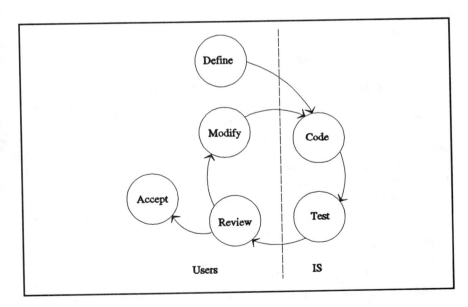

Figure 4.3 The prototype process

The prototype methodology could be used in many ways, such as:

- Development of a more refined prototype
- Development of user requirements that are difficult to define
- As a pilot application and later discarded
- As a working version that evolves directly into the final production application

A prototype is usually in constant evolution. Prototyping is best used to develop applications which have components that are not completely understood. It addresses the situation that occurs when what users ask for is not exactly what they want, and what they want is not exactly what they need. But, unfortunately, the users don't always recognize this disparity until they begin to work with the finished application. Prototyping allows users to see and react to a working model of the application. The model is rebuilt or refined until users are satisfied with the results.

In many cases, a prototype becomes the working application while developers work on the remainder of the application. Studies have shown that 80 percent of user requirements can be identified with 20 percent of the systems analysis and design effort. Rapid prototyping can quickly identify the remaining 20 percent. While users work with the resulting prototype, they identify the missing requirements, which can then be addressed by the development team.

4.3.3 JAD Workshops

Joint Application Development (JAD) workshops use a top-down approach to application development. JAD workshops can be in used in all phases of development but are especially useful in system analysis and top-level design. IS professionals often misinterpret the users' requirements and users often view presentations by IS as too technical. The traditional methods used by IS—interviewing users and then returning some time later with specifications in text form—are inadequate. However, users cannot design complex procedures without the help of IS professionals.

JAD workshops require heavy involvement by users in the development of the application. JAD workshops typically have more business end users in attendance than IS professionals.

JAD workshops are usually full-day, consecutive workshops lasting from three to five days, depending on the dynamics of the group and the scope of the problem. By getting away from their day-to-day business operations, the participants can focus on the application being developed during the JAD workshop.

All participants have equal rank. Direct communication among participants is encouraged. Differing points of view are discussed. Users are informed of their options regarding technical issues. Users and IS come to a joint decision that is a strategic and business-supporting resolution.

The key players in a JAD workshop are:

- **End users.** They should be easy to work with, well respected, and articulate; understand the business area; and have decision-making authority.
- **JAD leader.** This team member prepares for the workshop and directs it, encourages the members to participate, and keeps the workshop on track toward achieving its goals.
- **Scribe.** This participant records the findings of the workshop using tools to build diagrams, create screen and report designs, extract repository information, and create prototypes.
- **Project manager.** The manager responsible for the project should attend and participate in the JAD workshops but should not be the JAD leader.
- **IS professionals.** There should be one or more IS professionals attending a JAD workshop to ensure that the developed design is good technically.

In addition, there may be visiting specialists who attend on a part-time basis to give advice in their areas of expertise.

A JAD room is usually a separate room configured specifically for JAD workshops. There are no phones or beepers in a JAD room. The workshop is highly visual, as illustrated in the layout of a typical JAD room shown in Figure 4.4. White boards are used to display designs and dialogues. Flip charts are used and flip chart pages can be hung on the walls. A workstation with CASE or client/server software is used by the scribe to record user specifications and build prototypes. The designs and prototypes generated by the software and displayed on the micro's screen are projected on a screen using an LCD display device. The participants take copies of the design with them in the evening and mark them up, ready for the next day's discussion.

The success of the JAD methodology is due to the strong user involvement in the development of the application that will ultimately be theirs. The feeling of ownership provides a motivation to work with the process and the application and a strong commitment to support the inevitable change the application will create. User-oriented development results in better solutions and requires less training since the users gain a great deal of knowledge during the development process.

An important by-product of JAD workshops is that IS professionals

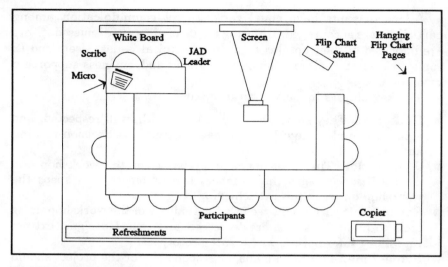

Figure 4.4 Layout of a typical JAD room

develop an awareness of what users need to be more productive in their jobs and users get a feeling for what it takes to develop a multiuser application in today's technology. Users can begin to understand the constraints involved in developing applications, whether those constraints are technological, strategic, or financial.

4.3.4 Information Engineering

Software engineering applies structured techniques to a project. Information engineering applies structured techniques to an enterprise as a whole or to a large sector of the enterprise. It is not one rigid methodology but, rather, a generic class of methodologies, whose characteristics include:

■ An enterprise focus
■ A top-down development methodology
■ Strong end user involvement
■ A long-term IT (information technology) evolution focus
■ Support of the organization's strategic goals

Information Engineering (IE) was first proposed by James Martin and Clive Finkelstein. Information Engineering uses a layered approach to application development, as illustrated in Figure 4.5. Information Engineering is generally more successful if an integrated-CASE (I-CASE) product and a repository are used to support the process. The repository holds the detailed information about the enterprise strategy and the business area analyses.

The top layer is information technology planning. Efforts at this level focus on the strategic IT planning for the entire organization. There must be an awareness of existing strategic opportunities that would make the enterprise more competitive. There must also be a strategy relating to future technologies and their impact on the organization—its products, services, and goals. The top-level planning is necessary to prioritize computing expenditures.

The next layer relates to a business area. A separate analysis is done for each business area. The results are integrated into the overall repository, which contains information about the information strategy plan and the analysis done for other business areas. The focus of this stage of IE is to understand and model the processes and data required to run the business area—what processes are needed, how do the processes interrelate, and what data is required.

The next layer focuses on creating applications within the framework of the information gathered in the top two layers and which is stored in the repository. If a good business model exists, a model for an application can be quickly extracted from it.

The bottom layer contains the actual construction and cutover phases of the application development process.

Information Engineering formalizes the information technology planning done in an organization. It facilitates the development of a comprehensive systems architecture and enterprise model for the

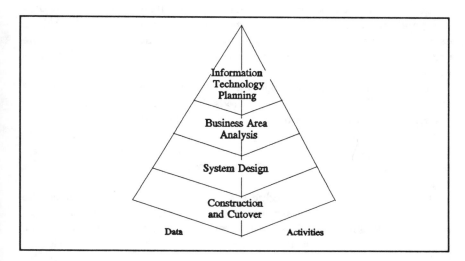

Figure 4.5 Information Engineering layered approach

business applications of the organization. IE provides a top-down approach to application development.

Rapid application development (RAD) is a subset of Information Engineering. It implements primarily the lower two levels of the pyramid. RAD provides a bottom-up approach to application development.

4.4 Decide on an Automated Tool

After the development methodology has been determined, a review of available automated analysis products that support the chosen methodology should be conducted. With today's technology, the actual information gathering process may not be automated but how that information can be stored, revised, and illustrated can be automated. The use of an automated product to support the analysis effort should not be overlooked.

4.5 Define the Application Requirements

Some of the major outputs in the analysis process are the application requirements—the users' needs for the application. Modeling products, such as CASE products, may be helpful in specifying user requirements graphically.

Requirements should be independent of a target technology, which is chosen in the detailed design phase. The requirements should also be independent of the current organizational structure, especially in the case of business reengineering. Very often the structure of the organization has to change, for the better, to reflect the new business processes.

There are no automated tools for pulling requirement specifications out of users. The products and methods discussed earlier in Section 4.3 promote user participation, which will usually generate better user requirements, and facilitate rapid definition of those requirements. CASE products automate the use of modeling techniques to illustrate user requirements and allow them to react to a visual image of the requirements.

But the use of these products does not change the focus of the analysis phase. For transactional and operational applications, all requirements should be determined before design begins. But for other types of applications, the line between when analysis ends and design begins becomes very fuzzy.

4.6 Object-Oriented Analysis

Using object technology, objects communicate by sending and responding to messages. At one point in time an object could be making requests as a client, at another point, as a server. An object has its own data and the ability to perform certain actions on that data. To use an object, a message is sent to perform a particular task. That object may in turn send messages to other objects, requesting that they perform services using their own data. This process is illustrated in Figure 4.6.

4.6.1 Object-Oriented Characteristics

The major characteristics of the object-oriented paradigm are:

- **Encapsulation** combines the data attributes and the methods (behaviors) of the object, treating them as one.
- **Classification** is the organization of objects into classes and subclasses. All objects in a class share characteristics, such as attributes and methods.
- **Inheritance** states that subclasses have the same attributes and methods as the class they belong to by default. Each subclass can exclude inherited attributes or methods and include additional attributes and methods.
- **Polymorphism** allows the same message to be sent to different objects and have each object implement the message appropriately (which could actually be different implementations).

By combining data and procedures in an object (encapsulation), all accesses to the data are controlled by the object. A change to one area of the application can be dealt with inside the object directly affected by the change. Inheritance links concepts into a related whole: when

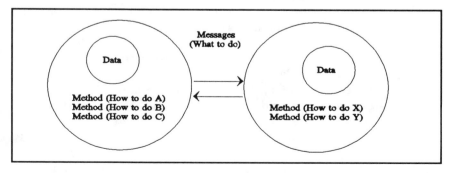

Figure 4.6 Objects communicate via messages

a change is made to a higher-level concept, the change is automatically applied throughout the subclasses.

4.6.2 Object-Oriented Development

The term object-based refers to development software which has an object orientation for generating design specifications but does not require that the developer use object-oriented techniques for specifying the design specifications.

One advantage of object orientation is that an application can be designed before it is decided whether it will be localized or distributed first. The functionality of the application is defined by the actions (methods) of the objects and the communications facilities of the environment. One of the benefits of the orientation is reuse, which speeds up application development time.

Object-oriented application development differs from traditional development in several areas. Some of these differences are:

- An object-oriented application simulates the activity.
- The code and data is bundled together into objects, not maintained separately.
- The data is active, not passive: the object (the data) knows how to perform work on itself.
- The characteristics of object-oriented languages promote the reuse of existing components.

4.6.3 Object-Oriented Analysis Stages

Object-oriented analysis models the application using the following steps:

- **Identify objects and classes.** This step is similar to the process of identifying entities. An object is something about which the application maintains data. As objects are identified, the initial definition of their attributes and behaviors is documented. Classes are collections of objects that can be described with the same attributes and methods.
- **Identify structures.** Objects tend to have a natural classification structure. Attributes and behaviors should be assigned to the highest class possible, so that they can be inherited by subclasses. Objects are also composed of parts, which create an assembly structure.
- **Define subjects.** Subjects are groups of objects related by classifi-

cation and assembly structures. Subjects provide a means of abstracting objects into larger units. There should be a subject for each structure. Tightly coupled subjects can be combined into a higher-level, composite subject.

- **Define attributes.** Attributes describe the information that is manipulated by the methods. They clarify the class/object's meaning. Whenever possible, inheritance should be used to assign attributes. Entity-relationship diagrams are used to identify attributes and their relationships.

- **Define methods.** Methods are activities that are under the control of each object, are performed upon the receipt of a message, and are independent of the object that requests the method or initiates the activity. This step identifies which events each object can react to and the responses that the object will generate. The emphasis is on the message and the response, not on how the behavior is actually implemented.

5

Top-Level
Design Phase

Top-level design, also referred to as user design or conceptual systems design, translates the user requirements produced in the analysis phase (the *what*) into design specifications (the *how*). Inputs and outputs are designed. Processes are specified with structured techniques, such as structured English and decision tables. In RAD-based methodologies, the design specification is determined through prototyping the application.

The design should not be technology-based or developed with a particular technology in mind, if at all possible. If a network is to be designed as part of the application, only its characteristics, such as speed, number of supported users, and estimated traffic, should be determined at this stage and further specifications of the network topology deferred until the construction phase.

5.1 Available Design Products

As development languages evolved from machine language to assembler to COBOL, analysts who determined the users' requirements and programmers who designed and coded the programs had few tools or methodologies available to increase their productivity in the analysis and design stages of application development. Organizations developed their own coding standards to facilitate the maintenance process.

Before long, there was a standard coding practice—structured code. The evolution continued and structured analysis and structured design (SA/SD) methodologies began taking hold in organizations.

The evolution of analysis and design techniques then started going off in tangents. The use of 4GLs does not fit nicely with SA/SD techniques. The effective use of 4GLs is based on the concept of prototyping, which does not have the rigid beginning and end points that SA/SD dictates. Due to the features of 4GLs (such as dynamic data dictionaries and nonprocedural specifications), making a change to a prototype while determining user requirements is not usually a monumental task. Some organizations use 4GLs to fine tune the user requirements, and then translate the 4GL code for the prototype into a more production-oriented language.

Another tangent is CASE (computer-aided software engineering) products. These products build structured diagrams—data flow diagrams, entity-relationship diagrams, decomposition diagrams, and action diagrams, to name a few—diagrams that were familiar to those schooled in SA/SD. CASE products insure consistency and completeness within the diagrams. Most CASE products do not generate code or program-specific designs. They are used primarily to fine-tune data requirements and to facilitate data administration.

A subset of CASE products allows organizations to take existing applications and generate high-level data specifications and data definitions, a process called reverse engineering of data. These data models can then be forward-engineered to the same or a different environment. These products allow organizations to extract data models from their existing legacy applications and port them to a new environment. Unfortunately, there are no comparable tools to reverse-engineer processes embedded in 3GL source code to a higher-level model. Reverse engineering and forward engineering are discussed in Section 4.2.1, Update Implementation.

Another tangent has been client/server development products. They focus on the end product—the completed application. These products allow developers to concentrate on the application rather than the GUI APIs (application programming interfaces), access code for relational databases, network protocols, and detailed coding. Client/server development products start with a database schema which is accessible from the development platform. Developers design the graphical presentations and the events that occur in the application.

The output of the analysis stage of application development produces user requirements. The communication media can be either oral, such as user interviews, or written, such as user specifications. The users respond to the specification document, either orally or in writing, the analysts change the specifications and return the entire document to the user for review—and the cycle begins again.

Under the System Development Life Cycle methodology, the design stage does not begin until all analysis is complete. Many IS organizations are finding that today's environment requires a merging of the various methodologies. They begin the process with structured analysis until most of the application has been specified, say 70 percent. Then they turn to 4GLs and CASE products to prototype and define the data, thereby fine tuning the requirements as they go along. The end result might be a structured design with database schema or an operational version of the application.

5.1.1 CASE Products

CASE products formalize communication between developers and users in the early stages of development—analysis. These products have been used by IS professionals to improve the quality of their applications and facilitate the maintenance function. Conventional CASE products assume that the application and its data are on one machine. CASE products are evolving from character-based screens to GUI-based screens, although not all CASE products have made the transition.

Structured diagrams that support structured design methodologies are used as a means of communication. High-end CASE products rely on data models, data flow diagrams, entity-relationship diagrams, and functional decomposition diagrams. Low-end CASE products, such as application generators and screen editors, support rapid prototyping and automatic code generation. Many high-end CASE products can also generate skeletons (fragments) of the procedural code (usually COBOL) for processes specified as decomposition diagrams.

A rigorous methodology is required to implement the structured development process used by CASE products. The learning curve for proficient use of a CASE product and the development methodology is usually quite long. Converting to structured techniques and a disciplined methodology generally results in a high degree of cultural change within IS. In addition to the training costs, the high cost of the CASE product itself makes the transition to CASE technology expensive.

Although CASE products can be used to develop decision-support applications, their reliance on structured diagrams and complex development methodologies are overkill for such applications. CASE products are well suited for enterprise-wide applications that require a high degree of integrity.

Support for distributed environments varies among CASE products.

While many allow developers to design GUI screens, not all CASE products generate the code for the screen or support multiple GUI-platforms. For example, even though it has a Windows-based development platform, a CASE product might not be able to generate the code for any designed GUI screens. If the product can generate code for the screens, it may not be able to generate GUI code for multiple platforms, such as Motif, OpenLook, and OS/2.

Developers are also looking to CASE products to assist in the determination of the allocation of processing between the client platform and the server platform. Most of the CASE products that do support client/server computing place all the processing on the client platform. The ability to split the processing between client and server is promised for future releases.

Examples of CASE products are discussed in Chapter 12.

5.1.2 Client/Server Development Products

Client/server development products have no self-contained analysis capability. They start at the design phase after a database schema has been prepared and installed on the server and business transactions have been defined.

Client/server applications are event-driven. The processes in the application are executed based on user responses, such as entering data and pressing Enter, or clicking on an icon or menu choice. To generate client/server applications, developers specify the events that can occur within the application and represent these events in the GUI.

Processes that cannot be handled with the features of the client/server development product may be included in the application during the detailed design phase. Processes are coded in the 4GL provided with the development product. Those processes that cannot be completely handled by the 4GL are usually coded in C, the *de facto* processing language for client/server environments.

Client/server development products do not have an analysis capability and are, therefore, not well suited for the development of transactional mission-critical applications. These products are ideally suited for developing graphical informational and decision-support applications which require transparent access to distributed data.

The transition to client/server development products can be done at low cost and with little cultural change. The products themselves are relatively inexpensive (compared to CASE products). The basic skill required for such products is familiarity with the functionality of a GUI such as Windows.

The more successful client/server development products are object-based. An object—a set of transactions (activities) sharing a common user interface—consists of the definitions of data types, variables, and constants used by the transactions, as well as the definitions for reports and procedures for calculations and data manipulation which can be performed on the object's data. Objects can be organized into class hierarchies and can be reused in multiple applications.

Examples of client/server development products are discussed in Chapter 11.

5.1.3 4GLs

When 4GLs were first introduced, they were not viewed as design tools. But as IS used 4GLs to build end-user applications quickly and iteratively, their appropriateness for prototyping became apparent. During the top-level design phase, the data is determined ("designed") and how that data will appear to the users is specified. Among the output from the structured design phase are report layouts (which used to be done on 132-column report-layout sheets but are now usually done on a word processor), screen layouts, and input forms.

4GLs support all of these processes. Data definitions are stored in a data dictionary. If the users need to add a new element of data, it can easily be added to the dictionary and immediately retrievable in the prototype. Reports can be generated using the nonprocedure statements for the 4GL. Columns can be easily moved, added, and removed. Some 4GLs have GUI front ends to facilitate using the 4GL itself and may or may not have the capability of generating code for designed GUI screens for the application being prototyped.

Very often 4GLs are used to refine the user requirements. In these instances, the focus of the iterative prototyping process is on defining the requirements, not developing the design, although most of the design effort may be accomplished during the same process.

4GLs have no analysis or design capabilities. They should be used to prototype or develop a production application. Some 4GLs, such as Focus from Information Builders, Oracle, and Ingres, are suitable for transaction processing, others 4GLs are not.

Examples of 4GLs are discussed in Chapter 10.

5.1.4 Integration between Tools

The traditional CASE vendors are beginning to recognize that their products need to be able to integrate and interact with client/server development products. The client/server development product vendors are building alliances with traditional CASE vendors to support integration of the analysis and development tools. This integration is illustrated in Figure 5.1.

CASE products focus on analysis issues, such as refining the data requirements and identifying the structure of the application. Client/server products focus on design issues, such as the users' view of the application and breaking the application into events (rather than tasks or process-decomposition diagrams). Since CASE products generate database schemas and client/server products build from a database schema, integrating these two techniques at the database level will shorten the development cycle and manage the database definitions.

The CASE product is used to create a high-level model of the database in the form of entity-relationship diagrams and to generate the physical database for a client/server application. The client/server product is used in a prototyping environment to build the GUI for the application and identify all clickable events. The client/server product is then used to specify the response to each event using the product's high-level procedural language or C.

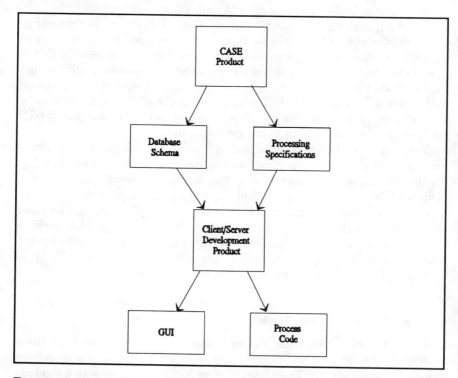

Figure 5.1 Integration of CASE and client/server development tools

CASE products can also generate code for processes. Some can generate the code in C, the production language for many client/server environments. CASE vendors are also evaluating the feasibility of generating the process code in the 4GL of some of the more popular client/server development products, such as PowerBuilder from PowerSoft.

The ideal marriage of the two development tools would move the CASE work down to the client without requiring a great deal of reengineering to be done on the client. The perfect scenario would support entity-relationship modeling using CASE, generation of SQL statements by the client tool, and automatic incorporation of the SQL into a client application. Currently, no product or set of products can do all three seamlessly.

Alliances between CASE vendors and client/server development tool vendors are slowly being built and should result in commercial products by the end of 1993. KnowledgeWare's newly acquired ObjectView is being integrated with ADW, KnowledgeWare's CASE tool. Powersoft has announced alliances with Bachman Information Systems, Inc.; LBMS, Inc.; INTERSOLV, Inc.; and Popkin Software & Systems Corp.

5.2 Evaluating Design Tools

It is important to recognize the strengths and weaknesses of the design products discussed above and determine which functionality is best for the application at hand and the IS development staff. Once the organization has determined which type of design product is appropriate for the application being developed, it can review the available products in that category. Each of these categories is covered in its own chapter in Part 5, Application Development Products. Critical functionality for each type of product is discussed in those chapters.

Application design and development products generally fall into two categories:

- **Bottom-up.** These products are designed for homogeneous LAN environments and favor quick development over data modeling.
- **Top-down.** These products are designed for larger systems and multiple hardware environments, begin with an analysis of application requirements, and develop a logical data model.

An important feature in any design product is the use of a data dictionary or a repository. The data dictionary and repository facilities should be integrated with the planning, analysis, design, and construction components of the development tool.

5.2.1 Top-Down or Bottom-Up Design

The strength of the bottom-up products lies in designing and developing client applications that can be quickly designed and built and maximize the use of windowing operating environments. They feature capabilities for creating windows and managing objects and support Windows interfaces (DDE and OLE). These tools include Microsoft's Visual Basic, Powersoft's PowerBuilder, Easel's EASEL Workbench, KnowledgeWare's ObjectView, and Gupta's SQLWindows.

The strength of the top-down products is support for cross-platform development. Users can mix and match hardware platforms, GUIs, DBMSs, and networks without redeveloping the applications. These products are suitable for designing and developing complex, distributed applications for heterogeneous environments. Products that are integrated with CASE tools to populate a repository from the CASE-defined data model include Ingres's INGRES/Windows4GL, Oracle's Cooperative Development Environment, and Uniface's UNIFACE.

The bottom-up products vary in their ability to design and develop complex SQL applications in heterogeneous environments and to build applications from an enterprise data model. Most bottom-up products automate the creation of the GUI but require the developer to write the code for database transactions. The products also differ in their implementation of SQL. Some use a translator to convert queries into SQL, others have no knowledge of the back-end server activities. While most of these products provide access to SQL databases, they do not necessarily support SQL processing as part of the application.

In contrast, the top-down products use SQL as the foundation for all design and development activities from data modeling to reporting. This allows the product to access multiple, heterogeneous database tables within a single transaction, without requiring code by the developer. However, the products do not provide the same level of GUI support as the bottom-up products nor do they necessarily take advantage of the micro operating environment.

Even with all their differences, there is a place for both types of design and development tools in an organization. For simple applications, the top-down products are overkill. For applications that need to get out the door fast, bottom-up products are the answer. For applications requiring heterogeneous database access with data integrity, top-down products fit the bill.

5.2.2 Use of Data Dictionaries

As the design phase proceeds, it is important that all designers have access to a list of existing (previously defined) data elements and processes (procedures). They must be able to get at this information using a friendly interface. They should not need to know how to spell the data element name in order to look it up in the dictionary.

It is not productive to provide developers with a long list of all the data elements and processes and expect them to look up items. It would take too much time to look through such a listing. The look-up process needs to be real-time, interactive, and user-intuitive. Hypertext, which provides links between data elements, is very useful for these searches.

Graphical displays that show the layout of relational table simplify the selection of data elements. These same displays often permit the user to specify relational operatives, such as Select, Join, and Project, without learning a relational database language.

Data dictionaries focus on managing the data about data—metadata. Repositories also manage processes. While reusable code is not a consideration during the top-level design phase, it certainly is during the construction phase.

Data dictionaries provide the meanings of tables (and files) and columns (attributes and fields). A data dictionary can help identify data redundancy—when the same data, often with a different name, appears in more than one place.

Data dictionaries impose naming conventions. Adherence to these conventions and the centralization of the dictionary itself permit an organization to identify and organize their enterprise-wide data and maintain its integrity.

Naming conventions are a set of standard words and abbreviations for naming data objects. The conventions would specify:

- How words are to be selected for the name of an object
- How those words should be ordered
- How aliases (abbreviations) can be created

The use of naming standards will improve communication (by the use of a consistent vocabulary), eliminate redundancy, and avoid inventing a new entity when one already exists in a very similar form in the data dictionary. For example, if naming conventions are followed when naming a "new" data element, the data dictionary would indicate that the name already existed—that the data element was not "new."

In addition, naming standards also allow users to search using a standard name. If existing names are developed using the standards and the data element exists, the user should be able to find it.

A dictionary records the links between the data and the processing models. Data dictionaries can be used to analyze the impact of changes to a data structure, which is likely to impact multiple applications.

A data dictionary that is used only by users (developers) is said to be a *passive* dictionary. Typically, its original use is to facilitate the development of the data structures. Any changes to these structures must be made manually to the data dictionary. If the data described in the data dictionary is to be used by an application, the developer must know of its existence and name, then search (usually a sequential text string search) the dictionary and make a copy of the definition.

In contrast, an *active* data dictionary is one that is used by programs (applications). For example, a COBOL program could name a file or view of a file, and a precompiler would automatically generate the code for the I/O area of the program from the dictionary. A file change would require a recompilation of the program but would not require changing the program.

A *dynamic* data dictionary is one that is accessed at execution. The repository is accessed directly by the operating system or DBMS for information needed to complete the processing. This type of data dictionary is especially useful for prototyping applications and generating queries with 4GLs.

5.2.3 Use of Repositories

Repository technology extends the concepts of a data dictionary to include the management of data and process models, addresses, rules, and definitions. A repository stores the diagrams, the meaning represented in the diagrams, and enforces consistency within the diagrams. A repository is an intelligent facility that "understands" the design; a data dictionary does not.

All the design information is entered into the repository of the development product. The information is accumulated first at a high level and then at progressively more detailed levels. The specification process continues until sufficient detail about the design for the application has been accumulated so that the program code can be generated automatically. As illustrated in Figure 5.2, the repository integrates the front-end planning, analyis, and design components of the product with the back-end code, database, and documentation-generation facilities.

A repository does the following tasks:

■ Manages information about repositories
■ Allows the data resource manager to create object views that reflect conceptual schemas
■ Defines the underlying knowledge bases, objectbases, databases and files: knows where they are, how they are accessed, and how they

are modified; and handles interfaces, data transfer formats, and APIs

- Supports queries of multiple systems for objects and packages the requested data as a single response
- Runs on any node or combination of nodes and knows which repository facilities are running on the network
- Runs passively, actively, or dynamically

Repositories also provide naming services, repository management facilities, such as time services and object management services, and repository administration facilities to install and manage information repositories.

To an application programmer, a repository is a collection of standard and custom objects. For example, processing in an organization might be segmented along primary users: Manufacturing, Finance, Sales, and Human Resources.

At first glance, there is very little overlap of data and processing needs. First, let's look at data and consider the concept of a customer. To the Sales staff, the term *customer* might mean a potential customer, one in the selling cycle, one who has agreed to buy the product, *and* one who has bought the product. To Finance, a customer is most likely

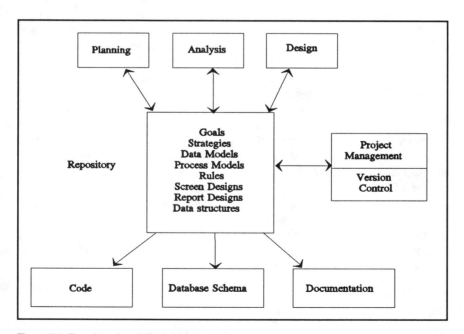

Figure 5.2 Repository-based development

the latter only—one who has already bought the product.

Now consider processing. Some sharable elements of processing are fairly obvious, such as screens that ensure applications look and feel the same (although adherence may be dictated by IS). Another less obvious element might be preparing mailing labels. Sales most likely has written and implemented such a process. But unless the other departments know of its existence, they might develop their own instead of using the existing procedure.

Repositories are implemented as database applications and, as such, provide standard services such as data access, data sharing, and data management. In addition, they can also manage:

- Data and process models generated by data modeling products
- Processes required for referential integrity
- Reference facilities, such as dictionaries and concordances
- Directories of data addresses and attributes

But the acceptance by IS communities of repositories and repository-based application development has been slow in coming. Reasons for this lack of acceptance include the following:

- There is little integration between repository software. Repositories use custom file systems, either provided by a development product or by repository vendors such as Manger Software Products, Reltech Products, Inc., and Brownstone Solutions, Inc. Third-party software can interface to a repository via import/export facilities, usually provided with the repository software. This redundant information must be kept in synchronization with the repository.
- Very few repository-based development products provide APIs to support an online session with its repository encyclopedia and a third-party product. Bridge technology is used to upload and download repository data to a third-party DBMS, which also results in redundant information which must be kept synchronized.
- Repository software is expensive and requires a long learning curve for efficient use.
- Migrating existing applications to a repository-based environment can be a major undertaking unless the applications were designed using structured techniques in which the data was carefully modeled, processes well structured, and naming conventions and shared-copy books were used.

Repository Standards

The ANSI Information Resource Dictionary System (IRDS) standard for repositories specifies how heterogenous repository facilities can be integrated to provide logical services. It includes extensibility and an application programming interface (API).

The acceptance of IRDS has been hampered by its inability to deal with existing repository applications and to separate the conceptual model from the logical database design, which should be independent of the conceptual model.

ANSI is currently rethinking its approach to IRDS. The standards group is now viewing repositories as an outgrowth of traditional DBMS technology and its enhancements, namely in the areas of object orientation and knowledge management.

There are also standard specifications in a trial stage of acceptance. These include:

- **CASE Data Interchange Format** (CDIF) from the Electronic Industries Association is defined as a CASE tool and repository communications standard.
- **IEEE 175-Semantic Transfer Language** specifies nongraphical communications among CASE products.
- **Portable Common Tool Environment** (PCTE), a UNIX-based standard from the European Computer Manufacturers Association, is supported by Object DBMS from Versant Object Technology Corp., which is embedded in the HP Softbench CASE engine.

Until developers can easily combine information residing in heterogeneous repositories, the wide acceptance of repository technology will continue to be nonexistent.

5.3 Define the Data Structure

There are two approaches for identifying data needs. They are:

- The **process-oriented** approach examines all existing input, output, and processing for a given application. This approach does not require heavy user involvement. Data flow diagrams are frequently used for this approach.
- The **data-oriented** approach examines the decisions made in the application and works backward to identify the data required for those decisions. This approach, which requires heavy user involvement, is appropriate when the input, output, and processes are relatively undefined. Entity-relationship diagrams support this approach.

If an application has a component that is well defined and a component that is not fully defined, both of these approaches could be used.

Once the elements of data have been identified, their characteristics must be determined. These characteristics include:

- Size
- Type
- Description
- Validation criteria
- Valid ranges
- Security levels
- Access privileges
- Where used

The actual database structure is not designed at this stage; it is done in the detailed design stage.

5.4 Define the Interfaces

Once the data has been determined, designers should begin to focus on the human interfaces, such as GUIs, character-based screens, input forms, and printed or displayed reports.

Designing character-based screens, input forms, and report formats involves creating a mockup. The process has not changed over the years. How the mockups are generated has. Today designers can use word processing packages, graphic packages, or client/server products to generate the mockups. Users' changes can be easily incorporated.

GUI screens are best designed with GUI-builder software, ideally a program that can generate precompiled P-code, which can be executed immediately. P-code is pseudocode that is interpreted into the native machine language at runtime. The GUI-builder software allows the designer to develop the screen using any of the GUI-available features, such as icons, radio buttons, pull-down menus, and multiple window placement. Many designers find that the process is more productive if the first layout of the GUI-screen is developed (with the users) as a rough sketch by hand. After a screen is built, users and designers can interactively make modifications to the screen.

Another feature of GUI-builder software is its ability to provide linkages between GUI screens and processes, as well as support for a menu structure.

A development product that integrates a GUI builder with the power of a 4GL (called a GUI/4GL) allows the prototype to be expanded to a production version using the same product.

When defining screens (even in prototype mode), developers should:

- Make screens as user intuitive as possible
- Adhere to organization-wide GUI standards
- Ensure that GUIs are consistent across the application

5.5 Define the Events/Processes

If a CASE product is used to develop the user requirements and the top-level design, the application's processes and data model will have been specified in decomposition, data flow, and entity-relationship diagrams.

If the application is a client/server application and executed from a GUI screen, the designers must identify the events that are to occur from within each GUI screen. For example, what happens when the user clicks on the Open icon or clicks on the Update button? These specifications can be provided using the capabilities of the GUI-builder software.

If the event triggers the execution of a process, the code for that process should be specified, at a minimum in structured English and at a maximum in the GUI-builder's 4GL. A notation should also be made if the process cannot be completely handled by the 4GL and will, therefore, require coding in a 3GL.

5.6 Object-Oriented Design

Just as structured analysis and design methods were developed to support structured programming techniques, object-oriented techniques were developed to support object-oriented programming languages. In these languages, the building block is a logical collection of classes and objects. The physical structure appears as a graph, not a tree. Data and operations (methods) are united. It is this view of the application that is the outcome of object-oriented analysis. But the identified subjects, class/objects, structures, attributes, and methods do not specify the users' view of the application, only its contents.

Structured methods are used to design an application around processes or data; object-oriented methods are used to design around objects. The object-oriented model shows object classes and the relationships between the objects and classes. In object-oriented design, a change in an object is made by adding or changing the operations and supporting methods of that object only, leaving the rest of the application's structure untouched.

At the heart of object-oriented design is the idea of reusability—a class library which contains all the objects and is documented, publicized, and easy to use.

During the object-oriented, top-level design phase, the human interface is specified. The formats for the screens and reports are generated. Classes may be specified for the types of interfaces, such as a Window class with subclasses of graphic and field.

Most of the rest of the design effort is detailed design. Changes might be made to the analysis specification for the following reasons:

- The application can use existing classes.
- Inheritance hierarchies may be modified for performance reasons.
- The tasks would be identified.
- The actual data structure designed.

Proponents of object technology maintain that this approach is more flexible than structured design techniques and more easily understood by users. Objects represent concepts familiar to users. To comprehend the design, users simply have to understand the object's behavior and what messages are sent to invoke the required behavior.

Construction

*After the requirements for an application have been determined and a
technology-independent top-level design generated, the development
team generates a detailed design for the application. It is during the
detailed design phase that the developers introduce technology-specific
considerations into the application's design.*

*Developing detailed designs for distributed applications differs
from traditional structured methods. Detailed designs resulting from
structured methods deal with program specifications. The technology
issues have usually been dealt with in the requirements proposal or
are nonexistent in the case of the organization's guidelines ("All new
applications will be built using Product X").*

*The detailed design phase for distributed applications focuses on
technology issues such as determining the DBMS and which features
of the DBMS will be used, such as triggers and stored procedures;
determining how access to data anywhere in the enterprise network
will be provided; and designing the data structure. The detailed
design also addresses how the components will exchange messages,
how the data will be distributed, and where data and where processes
will be located.*

*The development team must select technologies that support the
detailed design, choose development products and development
methodologies that will facilitate the construction phase (as well as
the implementation and operations phases), and select a methodology
for managing the project and testing the results of the construction
phase.*

During the construction phase of the application development for distributed environments, the application is built using the selected development methodologies and products. For some applications, rapid prototyping might be used. For other applications, rapid application development methodology and a CASE tool might be used. Regardless of how the application is built, the end result should be a fully tested, quickly developed, easily maintainable application that meets the requirements laid out during the analysis phase.

6

Detailed
Design Issues

The methods used to generate the detailed design for an application in a distributed environment are fundamentally different from the methods used for a mainframe-based or macro-driven application. In a distributed environment, the programmers must be isolated from network intricacies but still be given easy access to network functions. Databases must be designed to provide maximum support for each user, maintain the integrity of the data, and provide transparent access to data anywhere in the infrastructure.

Designers are accustomed to developing layouts for screens, windows, reports, and forms. Distributed applications require another level of detail as well—the specifications for how all the pieces will tie together and where the pieces will be located.

6.1 Database Design Issues

The power of distributed environments is in the implementation of the database. Data can be spread among the nodes to provide optimal response times for individual users while it is controlled centrally to maintain integrity.

6.1.1 Distribution Method

As discussed in Section 3.2.1, Distributed Data, data can be replicated (copied) or fragmented. Entire tables or a subset of a table (usually segmented along row boundaries) can be replicated.

Procedures must be in place to ensure that replicated data stays in synchronization—that one copy of the data is not updated without also updating all other copies of the data. One less-than-desirable procedure is a manual one. Once a table has been updated, all users known to have copied the table are informed of the update and are responsible for downloading the new table. A more automated version would use a batch job that automatically downloads the table to users' machines. The most desirable option is to leave the process under the control of the DDBMS (distributed DBMS).

Fragmentation is a more complex procedure which involves splitting a table horizontally, vertically, or both, and storing the resulting table at the appropriate node. Maintaining the integrity of fragmented data is a function of the DDBMS. The DDBMS recognizes that the table is fragmented and how it is fragmented. The local DDBMS treats the subtable as a complete table at that node but also recognizes that it is a subtable—i.e., there is more to the table. The central DDBMS that has control over the entire table can also "reconstruct" the table by accessing all the subtables as needed. Physically the table exists in pieces. There is no complete copy of a fragmented table.

Replication and fragmentation are discussed in more detail in Section 6.6, Methods for Distributing Data.

6.1.2 Stored Procedures

Stored procedures are SQL (Structured Query Language) statements which are compiled and stored on the server database. The procedure is executed via a call (with parameters) by a user or an application. In comparison, as illustrated in Figure 6.1, when an SQL query is sent to the server database, the server performs a variety of steps before executing the process.

Stored procedures allow developers to code common queries and groups of statements once, then compile and store them on the server, and have them invoked directly from applications. The first time the procedure is called in a session, the procedure is compiled and the compiled version is stored in cache memory where it is retrieved by subsequent calls to the same procedure.

Stored procedures can be used to enforce data integrity and business rules. They execute quickly because they are compiled code and are automatically recompiled when changes are made to objects they affect. Stored procedures can be nested and remote calls can be made to stored procedures on other systems.

Because they accept parameters, stored procedures can be used with a variety of data by multiple applications, as illustrated by the following example. The concept of debit and credit is used throughout an organization, although not always referenced by the same name. In each case, the debited side of the equation must have a value equal to or greater than the amount in question. The most obvious use is in accounting, where funds are routinely debited and credited. Another area is inventory when new goods arrive and goods are shipped out. Another use is in order entry when the term back-ordered applies to items that could not be shipped when the order was placed.

A stored procedure called *transfer* could accept three parameters: a debit object, a credit object, and an amount. The stored procedure would verify that the debit object could cover the amount specified, then deduct the amount from the object, and add it to the credit object. Two examples of such calls are:

- Transfer(Saving-balance, check-balance, 50)
- Transfer(Inventory-balance:Item 345, Order 391:Order Item 3, 4)

The stored procedure could be further modified to check the

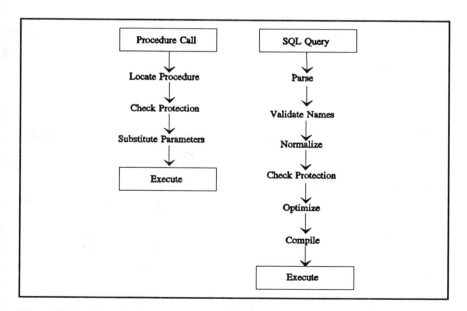

Figure 6.1 Stored procedures compared to interactive queries

application and make partial transfers, if appropriate. In the case of an order entry application, if the debit object does not have enough to cover the full amount, the amount that could be transferred would be computed and a record generated to track the back-order of the item in another part of the order entry application.

When designing an application, stored procedures should be used for shared business rules or common procedures, even though at first glance they might not appear to be common. This top-down, object orientation can reduce development times, reduce maintenance efforts, and produce faster execution times (stored procedures are compiled once only, when first referenced, and the compiled version is stored for subsequent references) and programs of higher quality.

However, not all relational DBMSs support stored procedures and triggers (discussed below). The database products from Oracle Corp., Sybase, and Ingres do support stored procedures. PowerBuilder from Powersoft and Ellipse from Cooperative Solutions allow developers to write stored procedures that are independent of a particular RDBMS.

6.1.3 Triggers

Triggers are stored procedures that are invoked by the server database rather than explicitly called by a user or an application. Triggers and validation rules are both associated with a particular table. Rules can perform simple checks on the data. Triggers are executed when attempts are made to access or modify the data in the table. Triggers can use all of SQL's functionality and, therefore, can perform complex checks on data, perform searches, update data in other tables, and access other databases over a network via RPCs (remote procedure calls).

Some examples of trigger uses are:

- A *delete-customer* trigger would be invoked when a customer number was flagged for deletion. It could check all account tables for open accounts with that customer number and, if one existed, refuse the delete request.
- A *change-customer* trigger would be invoked when a customer number was changed. It could check all account tables for the old customer number and replace it with the new customer number.
- A *bad-risk* trigger would be called when an order was placed. It could refuse to accept the order if the customer had an outstanding balance.
- A *too-risky* trigger would be invoked when a request to increase a credit limit was received. It could refuse all those requests over a set

amount, send an E-mail message to a supervisor for those requests within a specified range, or call a stored procedure to analyze the customer's payment history and authorize a higher than normal increase.

■ A *YTD-add* trigger would be invoked when an order was placed. It could add the amount of the order to a YTD (year-to-date) sales object for the salesperson, a YTD sales object for the branch, and a YTD sales object for the region.

6.1.4 Database Gateways

Database gateways can be used to link application requests from one database to another, as illustrated in Figure 6.2. They can connect clients and servers running on dissimilar networks. The client, gateway, and server can reside on the same platform or different ones.

Database gateways know the details of the products to be accessed, such as data format, data types, and catalog naming conventions. The trade-off for this accessibility is speed, as translation is usually required at each step. The database gateway must be able to handle all conversions and translations transparently to the user.

Database gateways have the following functions:

■ Accept statements from a client application
■ Translate the statements into the format of the target database
■ Transmit the statements to the target node
■ Receive and translate, if necessary, the results into the appropriate format for the client application
■ Return the results to the client application

A database gateway allows developers to provide access to data that exists in sources other than the one used by a particular application. It is an important alternative when data from legacy applications must be

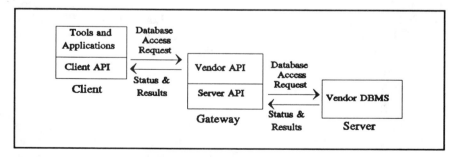

Figure 6.2 Database gateways

linked with newer applications. Database gateways can also be used to tie together data sources used in individual departments (or branches) as the infrastructure is first being built and these departments are tied together for the first time. Some popular database gateway products are discussed below.

EDA/SQL

Enterprise Data Access/SQL (EDA/SQL), from Information Builders, Inc. (IBI), is a family of client/server products which provides SQL-based access to enterprise-wide heterogeneous datas residing in over 50 relational and nonrelational data sources on 35 platforms. It provides a uniform, relational view of data, regardless of its storage structure. The operating environment and file location is transparent to the user.

Using a variety of end-user products that support EDA/SQL, the user develops SQL requests, which EDA/SQL distributes and processes against local or remote data, returning the results to the end-user product. Users can join relational databases and nonrelational data sources. EDA/SQL can directly update relational databases and uses RPCs to update nonrelational databases. It can also be used by 3GL applications to send and receive SQL requests within the network.

The EDA/SQL family of products also includes EDA/SQL Gateways. Currently, only access to IBM's DB2 and SQL/DS is available. The Gateways use EDA/SQL Data Drivers to read and support respective tables and catalogs. Gateway users can also issue RPCs to incorporate custom written 3GL procedures which read and update the databases. The Gateways offer access from remote client environments, including the DOS, Windows, and OS/2 operating systems along with Macintosh, UNIX-based computers, and MVS, VM, VAX/VMS, AS/400, and MPE/iX. They support communication protocols such as LU6.2, TCP/IP, and Interlink.

These Gateways can be used from over 100 EDA/SQL front-end tools such as IBI's PC/FOCUS, EDA/EIS for Windows, EDA/Compose, PM/FOCUS, and Visual Planner along with Lotus 1-2-3, Microsoft's ACCESS, EASEL, DataEase, and others. The gateways can also be accessed from 3GL application programs.

Database Gateway

Database Gateway from Micro Decisionware, Inc., runs on OS/2 servers. SQL transactions accepted from client machines can be redirected to DB2, SQL/DS, or Teradata DBC/1012. The client machines can be running DOS, Windows, or OS/2. Database Gateway supports a remote unit of work and automatic rollback-commit or user-controlled integrity. A connection manager balances the traffic between two or more gateways, provides security levels for access to data, and can halt client transactions when a CICS mainframe application crashes.

SQL Bridge

SQL Bridge, from Microsoft Corp. is a protocol gateway that allows applications to access SQL Server data through one protocol, rather than several. It supports Windows, DOS, OS/2, UNIX, Macintosh, and VMS environments. Using SQL Bridge, clients can access DB2 data using Database Gateway from Micro Decisionware.

SYBASE Open Client/Server

SYBASE Open Client interface, a client-based API (application programming interface) for non-SYBASE tools and programs, provides communication with SQL Server and Open Server applications. SYBASE Open Server is an API for access to non-SYBASE data sources (relational and nonrelational) and services.

SYBASE Open Client and Open Server do not require the use of SYBASE SQL Server.

6.2 Program Design Issues

For mainframe-based applications, designing programs is very straightforward. Outputs and inputs are defined and the sequential processing for that program is coded. Programs cannot be designed that easily in distributed environments.

Consider the inputs and outputs. If the program interfaces with the user, the interface is most likely a GUI and the inputs will come from that environment. The data might be edited for completeness, validity, and authorization even before it is passed to the program.

Outputs from a program could consist of a screen display, a paper report, an E-mail message, and/or an event trigger.

Data retrieved and stored by the program could be anywhere in the enterprise network. Its location and accessibility should be transparent to the application. I/O specifications for data are returned as a result of calls to a data dictionary or repository.

Mainframe programs are written to perform a task. This is sometimes difficult to keep in mind when most 3GL-coded programs require more lines of code to specify the input and output requirements than to specify the task itself.

Programs written for distributed environments are also written to perform a task. They differ from centralized environments in the following ways:

- The GUIs in distributed environments do much of the data housekeeping tasks. Data is checked before it is passed to a processing task. The GUI also eliminates much of the code required for the user interface itself.
- Processing tasks can be split between the client and the server. Programs must therefore be designed in a different manner than with centralized systems. The tasks in an application must be thoroughly understood so that designers can determine which tasks are best performed on the clients and which on the server.
- Processing tasks can be executed simultaneously, under control of the same program. If three steps need to occur before the fourth can execute and all three steps are independent of each other, all three steps can be executed at the same time in distributed environments. This simultaneity must be coded into the program itself.
- Repositories should be reviewed to determine if there is any reusable code that could be included in the processing task being programmed, thus minimizing the amount of code that would have to be written from scratch.

In addition, programs should be designed independently of a GUI and data source. Programs should focus on the task at hand—the process. This independence ensures that any changes to the GUI or data source will not require any modification to the program itself. It also ensures that the program is portable to other platforms, thereby supporting scalability and flexibility.

6.2.1 Application Program Interfaces

An application program interface (API) is a set of programming routines that are used to provide services and link different types of software. APIs have been written to access data sources, network services, and pass control and data back and forth between software. APIs can be used to access resources and software that are not directly supported by the language used for development.

APIs define how data is presented to other components of a system, such as a computer, a database, or E-mail application. APIs are receiving a great deal of attention as organizations use them to provide the connections between their existing heterogeneous equipment and software, thus creating an open system.

However, there are very few standards for APIs. For example, there are two competing API standards for E-mail applications: Messaging Application Programming Interface (MAPI) from Microsoft and Vendor Independent Messaging (VIM) from Lotus, Novell, IBM, Apple Computer, and Borland International. An E-mail API provides the interface between the application and the messaging service, specifying how to send messages, access mail directories, and store mail.

6.2.2 Remote Procedure Calls

Remote procedure calls (RPCs) provide client-to-server and server-to-server communication allowing individual tasks of an application to be run on multiple nodes in a network. Server access control and directory services are common needs met through the use of RPCs. Security, system management, application programming, and distributed file systems also depend on the capabilities of RPCs. A simplified version of how RPCs work is illustrated in Figure 6.3.

RPCs are APIs that are layered on top of a network interprocess communication mechanism. A remote procedure call should look and act like a local procedure call to the programmer. Although RPC implementations are approximately the same, RPCs from different vendors are not always compatible.

RPCs have one major limitation—they typically require synchronous connections. If an RPC link is used to link to a server that is busy or otherwise unavailable, the application will wait for the server to respond rather than move on to other tasks.

RPCs are used by the transaction managers and the enterprise network managers as discussed in Chapter 8, Integration. RPCs are also available from third-party vendors.

RPC products usually include:

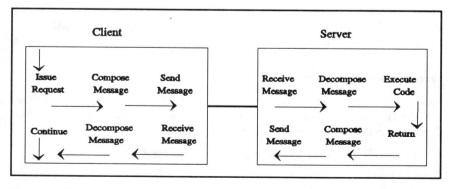

Figure 6.3 How remote procedure calls work

- A language and a compiler for producing portable code
- A run-time facility that keeps the system architecture and network protocols transparent to the application procedures

OSF and many client/server tools have chosen the Hewlett-Packard implementation of RPC technology, which is evolving into a *de facto* standard. HP's RPCs are easy to use, support multiple threads of execution, and are designed to be transparent to various network architectures.

Netwise Inc., which only sells RPC software, offers RPC Tool, which supports a large number of operating systems and network protocols, as diverse as AppleTalk, DECnet, LU6.2, Novell's NetWare, and TCP/IP.

SunSoft offers a general-purpose toolkit, Transport-Independent Remote Procedure Call (TI-RPC), which is based on technology from Netwise. The toolkit allows developers to use a single version of a client/server application across a range of operating systems, hardware, databases, and networks.

6.3 "True" Distributed Databases

There are currently two sets of definitions being used to define what constitutes a "true" distributed database. Both of these definitions are based on the premise that the underlying databases are relational.

6.3.1 Date's Rules

In 1987, Chris J. Date of Codd and Date Consulting Group proposed 12 rules that a fully distributed database management system should follow. These rules were proposed to bring clarity to the debates on DDBMSs and are not absolute requirements. The rules, which are summarized below, are now accepted as a working definition of distributed databases.

Rule 1: Local Autonomy

In a truly distributed database environment, the DBMS locations (sites) should be independent of each other. Each site where a distributed database resides is characterized by the following:

- A local database is processed by its own DBMS.
- The DBMS at every site handles the security, data integrity, locking, and recovery for its own database.

- Local data access operations use only local resources, such as a local DBMS.
- Although independent, all sites cooperate in accessing distributed data from multiple sites to meet the needs of a transaction.

Rule 2: No Reliance on a Central Site

A fully distributed database system should not rely on a central site. No one site should be more important or necessary than any other. While there usually is a central site for coordination, no individual site should be dependent on that site. In addition, the DBMS at any site could act as the two-phase commit coordinator.

Rule 3: Continuous Operations

In a distributed database system, there should be no planned database activity that requires a distributed system shutdown. These activities include backing up or recovering a database. Continuous operations should be implemented through such DBMS features as:

- Full and incremental online backup and archiving
- Quick online database recovery, often using disk mirroring
- Fault-tolerant hardware

Rule 4: Data Location Independence

Also known as the rule of data transparency, the rule of data location independence maintains that even though data is distributed among multiple sites, the data should appear and behave to users and applications as if it were local.

Rule 5: Data Fragmentation Independence

If a table has been fragmented and distributed, it must appear as a single table to users and applications. This rule is a corollary to the data transparency rule.

Rule 6: Data Replication Independence

This rule expands the previous two rules to include data distributed by replication. The main point for this rule is that the synchronization of the original data and the replicated data must be transparent to users and applications.

Rule 7: Distributed Query Processing

The performance of a given query should be independent of the site which issued the query. In addition, a query optimizer should take into account local and global factors, such as network characteristics and load.

Rule 8: Distributed Transaction Management

This rule addresses the data consistency, integrity, concurrency, and recovery (the ACID test for transactions, discussed in Section 8.1, Transaction Management) requirements in a distributed database environment. If an update at a local node fails and the remaining updates do take place, the database is not synchronized. Two-phase commit protocol addresses the consistency and integrity characteristics of distributed databases.

Rule 9: Hardware Independence

A distributed database system should be able to cross hardware vendor boundaries and run on different platforms. It should not be constrained by one vendor.

Rule 10: Operating System Independence

In addition to hardware independence, a truly distributed database system should not be limited to a single operating system.

Rule 11: Network Independence

A distributed database should not be limited to a particular network topology or communications protocols.

Rule 12: DBMS Independence

A distributed database system should support heterogeneous data access. It should be able to interoperate between DBMSs from different vendors.

6.3.2 Stonebraker's Transparency Rules

Date's principles describe a transparent system—a distributed database that looks exactly like a nondistributed database to applications and users. To further define a transparent system, Michael Stonebraker of the University of California, Berkeley, formulated seven types of transparency.

Stonebraker's transparency rules are:

- **Location Transparency.** A user can submit a query that accesses distributed objects without requiring the user to know where the objects are.
- **Performance Transparency.** A distributed query optimizer finds the best plan for executing a distributed command. The query can be submitted from any node in a distributed database and will run with comparable performance from any node.
- **Copy Transparency.** The system supports the optional existence of multiple copies of database objects.
- **Transaction Transparency.** When a user runs a transaction that updates data at multiple nodes, the transaction behaves exactly like a local transaction. The transaction either commits or aborts; no intermediate states of the affected databases are possible.
- **Fragment Transparency.** The distributed DBMS supports the segmentation of a relational table into multiple pieces and their placement at multiple sites.
- **Schema Change Transparency.** When changes are made to a distributed database, the change is made once to the distributed dictionary. Changes are not required at all sites that participate in the distributed database.
- **Local DBMS Transparency.** The distributed DBMS provides its services without affecting the local DBMSs that actually manage the local data.

6.4 Distributed Data Access

When data is distributed, all or part of the data management logic accompanies the data. The services should be provided in such a way that users and applications do not even know the data is distributed. The four types of distributed data access are:

- Remote request
- Remote transaction
- Distributed transaction
- Distributed request

The process will be illustrated using the terminology of client/server computing. For example, a client (micro or server) requests data from a server.

6.4.1 Remote Request

In a remote request, an application issues a single data request that can be processed from a single remote site. This is also referred to as a logical unit of work or a processing transaction. The application must know the physical location of the data. Remote requests can be used to perform the manual extract method of data distribution.

6.4.2 Remote Transaction

A remote transaction contains multiple data requests, but all the requested data resides on the same node. This is also referred to as a remote unit of work. For example, using the relational model, a remote transaction could contain two or more SQL statements that refer to data on a single node. The application must know the physical location of the data. For the transaction to be successful, *all* statements in the transaction would have to be successful.

6.4.3 Distributed Transaction

A distributed transaction contains multiple data requests that refer to data residing on multiple nodes. In the client/server model, a client can request data from multiple servers in a single processing transaction. The application must know the physical location of the data. For the transaction to be successful, *all* statements in the transaction would have to be successful.

6.4.4 Distributed Request

A distributed request is a transaction consisting of multiple requests that can be processed at multiple sites. Each request can reference data residing on multiple sites. All actions performed by a distributed request are considered one logical unit of work—one processing transaction. An application does not need to know where the data is physically located.

6.5 Distributed Database Standards

There are emerging industry standards for distributed data. Those receiving the most attention are IBM's Distributed Relational Database Architecture (DRDA) and Remote Data Access (RDA) from ISO. Figure 6.4 illustrates the differences between the two standards.

6.5.1 Distributed Relational Database Architecture

DRDA is a proprietary architecture for client/server database inter-operability within IBM environments and non-IBM environments that conform to DRDA. DRDA relies on other IBM technologies, such as SNA, LU6.2 and Distributed Data Management Architecture. DRDA provides the necessary connectivity between relational DBMSs and can operate in homogeneous (IBM only) and heterogeneous system environments. DRDA uses SQL as the common access language.

Currently, DRDA supports only remote units of work, which include remote requests and remote transaction types of distributed processing. A remote request occurs when an application issues a single data request to be processed at a single remote site. A remote transaction allows a transaction to contain multiple data requests but all the data must reside at a single remote location.

6.5.2 Remote Data Access

In contrast, ISO's RDA protocol is not an architecture. RDA is a communications protocol that fits into the OSI seven-layer model at the application layer (top layer) and has been optimized for heterogeneous data access. The RDA standard is divided into the Generic Model, which defines a common transfer syntax and database access protocol, and specializations, which customize the Generic Model for use with specific data models or languages.

In the DRDA environment, an application is connected to one database at a time. In the RDA model, an application can be connected

IBM's DRDA	ISO's RDA
Performance-centered	Portability-centered
Based on SNA	Based on OSI
Each server uses its native SQL	Only a common subset of SQL is supported
Maximizes support for existing applications	Minimizes the effort to port tools to different servers
Focus is on IBM interoperability	Focus is on multivendor, heterogeneous database interoperability
IBM, plus nine other vendors	Every major DBMS vendor except IBM

Figure 6.4 DRDA compared to RDA

to more than one database at a time. However, RDA does not currently address the problems relating to updating multiple databases.

6.6 Methods for Distributing Data

How an organization distributes data affects how the data is accessed. By simulating the interactions (read and update) and the resulting network traffic, designers can determine the optimal distribution method and the location of subsets of data.

6.6.1 Replication

The reason for intentionally placing copies of data at multiple sites, as illustrated in Figure 6.5, is to improve performance. When two groups of users at different nodes of the infrastructure both routinely access the same data, it may be beneficial to replicate it at both nodes.

One of the simplest approaches to replication is to allow users to make their own copies of a dataset from a central location. When the users require more recent copies of the dataset, they copy the new data to their nodes. An alternative to user intervention would be an IS-initiated process. The weakness in this approach to replication is its reliance on human intervention.

A more reliable alternative would be to use a DDBMS's capability to generate snapshots (copies) of the data and distribute those snapshots. The timing of the snapshots could be specified by the user. The DDBMS automatically builds the snapshot copy of the original

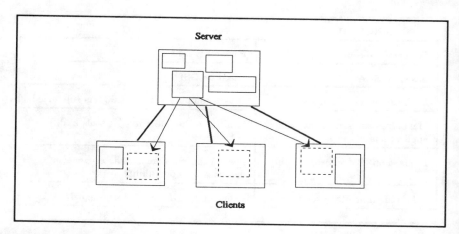

Figure 6.5 Data replication

data at the times specified. The DDBMS handles synchronization of the multiple copies of the data. Snapshots are usually restricted to read-only access because typically no provisions are made for transferring updates made to snapshot data back to the original source.

Another DDBMS-managed alternative is its capability to replicate data and handle updates at multiple locations. A relational database might use row or table replication. When a request is made for the data, a query optimizer takes into account all locations of the data and accesses the node that minimizes communication costs and response time.

The trade-off is the overhead required to keep all copies of the data consistent and to maintain the consistency transparently to the user.

6.6.2 Fragmentation

Distributing parts of the data (fragmentation) is a more complex method of data distribution. Relational tables can be fragmented horizontally along row boundaries, vertically along column boundaries, or both.

For example, a human resource application has a table of employees for a company with three divisions which are all in separate locations. Each division is responsible for maintaining the information for its own employees. The company must generate a variety of reports that summarize information about all its employees.

As illustrated in Figure 6.6, the actual table would be in four segments: headquarters plus one for each division. To the human resource applications running at headquarters, the four segments

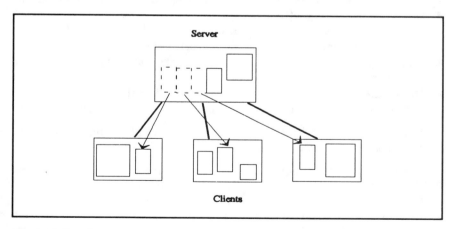

Figure 6.6 Data fragmentation

would be treated as one entity. The application at each node would treat the segment of the table at that node as a complete entity.

The main drawbacks of fragmentation are the complexity of its implementation and its lack of transparent access by other nodes. Somehow the fragmented data must be viewed as a single table at a single site. Fragmented data distribution is best handled by a DDBMS.

In our example, when applications must treat the four segments as a whole, processing time increases. The access would be transparent to the user and the application because it is handled by the DDBMS but response time would be impacted. If the user at one division wished to query the information at a company-wide level—perhaps looking for an employee with a particular skill set—the entire table (all four segments) would have to be "reconstructed" before the query could be executed. Another disadvantage is the overhead required to provide reliability. If the segments are to be treated as one and one node is down, alternative procedures must be in place to ensure that the application would handle the situation correctly.

6.7 Data Distribution Issues

When data is distributed, a portion of the distributed DBMS (DDBMS) as well as the data itself reside on the node. Data is usually kept local to the site that uses it the most (usually the site that updates it) while still providing transparent access to that data from other nodes in the environment.

Distributing data among multiple sites offers the following benefits:

- Data is closer to access locations resulting in quick response times.
- Data access is more efficient.
- Data traffic on the network can be minimized.
- Resource balancing occurs at its most critical resource—data access.
- Multiple copies of critical data can be stored at different locations to eliminate a single point of failure.
- Distributed applications are easier to expand as the user community grows and application complexity increases.

But data cannot be distributed without careful planning. Some rules of thumb for distributing data are:

- Every item of data should have a single point of update.
- Distributed updates should be kept to a minimum.
- Applications should use location-independent code.
- Distributed data should be as close as possible to the processors that use the data the most.

6.7.1 Technical Issues for Distributing Data

Among the many technical challenges designers of distributed data applications face, two stand out. These challenges are:

- **Synchronizing distributed databases.** Maintaining the integrity of the data is perhaps the most challenging technical issue designers face. Databases containing the same data must be changed in tandem, ideally using a two-phase commit protocol. (See Section 8.1.1) This capability should be a feature of the DBMS and not be coded into the applications themselves.
- **Optimizing queries.** A query optimizer needs to be able to determine the fastest and most efficient steps to handle a query, even if it may require moving data from one node to another to perform a join. The query optimizer needs to know the sizes of the databases, the speeds of the networks, the capabilities of the computers, and the workloads of the nodes.

6.8 Alternatives to "True" Distributed Databases

Even though the technology push might be towards distributed databases, there are alternatives that are not as complex and may be just as effective, depending on the application.

6.8.1 Downloaded Data

Downloading data from a central source to a micro is becoming commonplace. The downloaded data is extracted from production files via an IS-initiated process or by the user via a query product. The downloaded files may or may not be uploaded back to the central source as updated files.

6.8.2 Copies of Data

A working copy of the data file stored at individual nodes supports faster response to queries. These files are refreshed after hours when the central copy has been updated, usually at night. This process is under the control of IS rather than under the control of the distributed DBMS as in the case of replication discussed in Section 6.6.1.

6.8.3 Client/Server Databases

Most client/server databases do not support location transparency.

Since only a few nodes run the DBMS, applications must know where the data is located.

In a true distributed database, each node has a copy of the DBMS and the dictionary. Because each node can determine the access strategy, applications do not need to know the location of the data.

6.8.4 Federated Databases

Some industry analysts feel that organizations will ultimately have "federated databases" rather than distributed databases. Existing databases will retain their autonomy, their data will be defined independently of other databases, and the local DBMS will take care of itself. Rules will be provided for how their data can be accessed by users and applications.

This approach is used now when data from incompatible databases is required in a single application. The data is pulled together at the requesting node, often into a new format, without altering the original databases. As the capabilities of the micro workstations and LAN-based servers continue to expand, on-the-fly, merged databases containing data from a variety of sources will become a reality.

6.9 Determine Data Location

After it has been determined how data will be distributed, designers must decide on the location of the data—on which node(s) will the data reside. For data with only one group of users who are connected to the same server, this is an easy decision. But since most data is shared across LAN-imposed boundaries, it is harder to decide which node to place shared data on. A rule-of-thumb has been to put data on the node that updates it, the rationale being that updating creates most of the network traffic and is more open to possible failures (a server or network goes down). However, data updated at one node and often accessed by another node might be better placed at the accessing node if it is accessed often enough.

Designers must try to simulate the impact each placement decision will have on the entire enterprise environment. This can be done manually by determining the number of calls that will be made, the size of the data traveling on the network, and the number of hops the data would need to take. The other network activity would also have to be factored in.

There are some software products beginning to appear on the market that can simulate this process.

Either way, an effort must be made to determine the effects of data placement *before* the application is placed into production. Fine tuning data placement once an application is in production is expected; a major overhaul is not.

6.10 Determine Process Location

After the data has been attended to, designers must decide on the location of processes—on which node(s) will the process reside. Determining process location is very similar in nature to determining data location.

A process might be accessed by many users across multiple nodes and use data from multiple nodes, as well. Designers need to determine a location for the process that optimizes its access time—both by the user and for needed data—and minimizes network bottlenecks and server overload. The impact of each placement decision must be analyzed.

As is the case with data placement, the effects of process placement must be examined before the application goes live. Doing a major overhaul of process locations after an application is in production is the result of poor planning.

Software products intended to support processing distribution placement have been slowly appearing on the market. Ellipse from Cooperative Solutions assigns processing location at execution time. This dynamic allocation can be overridden by the developer within the application code.

7

Construction
Issues

The construction phase of application development includes generating the application's logic code, the database schema, the code for the screens, the test data, and the application and user documentation. The technologies that will support the designed environments are selected and installed.

As is true for all the development phases, the project is managed to ensure a timely and successful completion. Programs are individually tested and the application is tested as a whole. Existing data that is to be included in the application's data files is converted to the new format. A cutover strategy is outlined. Users are trained.

The fact that the environment is distributed does not change this process a great deal. The project must still be managed. Testing, training, and conversions must still be done. The documentation and code must still be generated. What is different is the multitude of choices available to the IS staff.

7.1 Selection of Enabling Technologies

The development team must determine what technologies are available that will support the decisions made in the detail design phase.

7.1.1 Select the DBMS

One important technology-related decision is the choice of the database management system. If data is to be distributed, the DBMS must support distribution of data and be able to handle accessing distributed data efficiently and transparently to the users and applications. Some DBMSs support all types of distributed data access—remote request, remote transaction, distributed transaction, and distributed request— while others support only remote request and remote transaction. Distributed data access methods are discussed in detail in Section 6.3.2.

If an application contains many common queries and shared business rules, the development team could use stored procedures to handle them. If many of the procedures are data-oriented, the development team could design triggers for the data in the database. However, the DBMS selected must be able to support stored procedures and triggers, and not all relational DBMSs do.

7.1.2 Select the Inter-Communication Methods

The development team must select technologies that will support communication between the nodes of the enterprise network. Database gateways can interface application requests from one database on one node to another database on a different node. They can operate over dissimilar networks. Database gateways are discussed in Section 6.1.4.

Communication between applications is also desirable. Developers can select:

- **Application program interfaces** (APIs) provide services and can link different types of software, such as DBMSs, network services, and application software. APIs are discussed in Section 6.2.1.
- **Remote procedure calls** (RPCs) provide communication between clients, servers, and other servers. RPCs are APIs layered on top of the network interprocess mechanism. RPCs are discussed in Section 6.2.2.

7.1.3 Select the Middleware

Developers also have to look at middleware (discussed in Section 1.1.6), which sits between the application and the operating system and ensures the integrity of the data and the processes across the multiple networks and environments.

Transaction managers, discussed in Section 8.2, manage the flow of transactions that impact multiple databases and require a high degree of database access integrity. They also send and receive the messages between nodes in the network.

Middleware software can also be used to manage the hardware, software, and networks in the distributed environment. Enterprise network management software handles communication between networks and operating systems, and translation of data access calls and data formats. These products are discussed in Section 8.3.

Developers also need to review technologies that will provide services to applications that are distributed among heterogeneous platforms. Network computing environment software provides an architecture that includes:

- **Distributed services** to support building applications
- **Data-sharing services** to support distributed data access

Network computing environment software is discussed in Section 8.4.

7.2 Project Management

Application development projects are managed to ascertain the status of the project in regard to time and budget. Project management involves:

- Knowing where the development process is at all times
- Providing products to automate as much of the management process as possible
- Providing products to automate the development process itself as much as possible
- Providing an environment that supports the sharing of information among project team members.

Some CASE products offer project management capabilities, either as a built-in feature or as an add-on integrated option. These products support traditional planning methodologies by providing for the generation of critical path diagrams and PERT charts. The project is broken down into individual tasks with completion times assigned to each task. A hierarchy is developed to identify any sequencing required for the completion of the tasks. The time required to complete each task is also established, as well as the skills required for each task.

The automated products accept as input the individual tasks, the hierarchy (sequence), and completion times. The products then generate a critical path for the development and estimated start and stop dates for the individual tasks.

As tasks are assigned to individual team members, the assignments are entered into the project management facility. Actual start and completion dates are also entered into the project management facility. As each task is completed, it is reviewed for adherence to project standards and for conformity with previously completed tasks.

After the actual times are entered into the project management facility, reports can be generated to give management the status of the project, both from a time perspective and a budget perspective. The project manager can review the accuracy of time and cost estimates. If the project is behind schedule, the project management facility can be used to evaluate alternatives for getting the project back on schedule, such as overtime for existing team members, reassigning tasks based on an individual member's adaptation to the new technologies, or adding members to the team, perhaps individuals who possess a different skill set.

With interactive and prototyping development products, project management techniques very often get less attention than they should. However, with these highly-automated development products, project management and control procedures are often more important to have in place to ensure an on-schedule and within budget project than is required by structured methodologies.

7.2.1 Metrics for Software Development

When interactive and prototyping products are used to develop applications, it is very often more difficult to break a project into small, manageable, self-contained tasks. It is also difficult to estimate how much effort will be required to complete the tasks. There are very few metrics (measurements) for the development effort when using client/server development products or 4GLs.

Metrics for software development are used to measure:

- Speed of development
- Development costs
- Development productivity
- Quality of delivered applications
- Maintenance costs

IS has become very comfortable with traditional metrics such as the number of production-quality lines of COBOL per programmer per day. But such metrics are not appropriate for rating the development effort of applications built with automated products.

Using these products, it is very easy to spend a great deal of time on a small portion of the overall application. It is also very easy to base the development on a structure that is later determined inefficient or otherwise unworkable.

Most of the automated development products can be used to produce screen, report, and application logic code, as well as both user and application documentation. If these products are used, most of the construction effort focuses on the environment itself and testing the generated application.

Metrics for distributed environments should be independent of the computer language or development product used. IBM developed a metric based on function points which is technology independent. This technique was further refined by GUIDE, the IBM user organization, and continues to be refined by the International Function Point Users Group (IFPUG) based in Columbus, Ohio, which in 1993 had a membership of 500 companies. IFPUG provides a "Counting Practices Manual" for determining the number of elements (explained below) used in an application and a set of conversion factors for converting lines-of-code measurements to function-point measurements.

Using the function-point method, the elements of an application (referred to as functions) are listed and counted. These elements include:

- Inputs, such as screens, messages, and batch transactions
- Outputs, such as screens, reports, messages, and batch transactions
- Queries
- Internal, application-specific data files
- External, shared data files

Each of the elements is classified based on its complexity—low, medium, or high—and a complexity factor assigned to the individual elements. The actual number of function points for an application is the aggregate of the number of functions times their complexity factor. A sample function-point analysis matrix is illustrated in Figure 7.1.

Function Points	Degree of Complexity			Total
	Low	Average	High	
Input	10 (2)	4 (5)	12 (8)	136
Output	8 (3)	15 (5)	22 (8)	275
Query	14 (3)	19 (6)	26 (8)	394
File	8 (4)	14 (7)	4 (10)	170
Interface	16 (4)	20 (6)	9 (10)	274
		Total Function Points		1,249

Figure 7.1 Function-point analysis matrix

The function-point metric measures what will be delivered to the end user and encompasses designing, coding, and testing. The function-point metric also measures efficiency and effectiveness. The actual measurement becomes the number of function points per person-month.

For applications of average complexity with simple user interfaces, one function point per person-month is roughly equivalent to five lines-of-COBOL per person-day or about 110 lines per person-month. The use of integrated-CASE products will generate a higher ratio because the code is generated from the specifications. For applications with more complex user interfaces (notably GUIs), this ratio should be higher because the code for the interfaces should be generated by the product used to specify the GUI.

7.3 Selection of Development Products

When the project team reviews available development products to determine which one will be used for the analysis and design of an application, they should not overlook how the products will impact on the construction phase. The goal of the IS organization should be overall productivity gain for application development, not only the gains on the analysis and design phases.

One of the major advantages of integrated CASE products is their ability to generate complete applications from high-level data and process specifications. Any modifications that must be made to the application design are made in the specifications maintained by the CASE product. The code is then regenerated automatically.

The specifications for the application are always up-to-date and the application code is clean and structured. Maintenance becomes an easier task: by modifying the specifications, the CASE product will handle any changes to the application structure and to the code as a result of the modifications.

Most client/server development products generate application logic code in the 4GL provided with the product and allow the developer to enhance that code with routines written in the C language. They also generate the P-code (pseudocode) for the screens. The P-code and logic are either distributed as a compiled version of the application or distributed with a runtime version of the development product.

With applications developed with 4GLs, the final product (the prototype) from the design phase very often becomes the production version of the application. Some 4GLs now support compilation of procedures, thus overcoming their earlier limitation of time-consuming, interpretive execution.

A substantial productivity gain may be achieved by converting a working prototype into a production application. However, the IS organization must be careful to monitor what types of applications are developed as a working prototype. An application that is developed quickly for reasonable cost but that does not represent reasonable trade-offs between resources and responsiveness or reliability and auditability is not a quality application.

Organizations that use 4GLs to prototype an application and then code that application in a 3GL run similar risks. The manner in which data structures are handled in a 4GL is very different from the methods used in 3GLs. Data can be dynamically created and then discarded within a 4GL procedure.

If the 4GL is being used to fine-tune the design of input and output, organizations should begin to consider some of the new prototyping products on the market whose only function is to aid developers in designing screens and reports. Some of these products can actually generate the COBOL of C code required for the designed screens and reports.

7.4 Selection of Database Products

If the organization wishes to take advantage of the productivity gains associated with stored procedures and triggers, the DBMS chosen must support them. Stored procedures are groups of statements (usually SQL statements since most implementations are on relational DBMSs) that are coded and validated once, stored on a server, and invoked directly by applications. The first time a stored procedure is called, it is compiled and stored in cache memory. Subsequent calls to the procedure will execute the compiled version. Stored procedures are used to enforce business rules and data integrity.

Triggers are stored procedures that are invoked by the database rather than called by applications. Triggers are invoked when attempts are made to access or modify the data in the table. Triggers have more functionality than the validity rules that can be specified in the DBMS. Triggers, having full access to SQL's functionality, can perform searches, update data in other tables, and access other databases. Triggers are also used to enforce business rules and data integrity but their focus is data-related, whereas stored procedures are process-related.

Database management systems that support distributed data should also support transparent backup and recovery of distributed databases.

A database should be backed up and restored while the database is online. If a new disk is required, it should be swapped into the server and the data restored onto it, all with little or no disruption of the users of the database.

A DBMS chosen for a distributed environment should support heterogeneous data access and adhere to one of the emerging standards for distributed data. These standards, which are discussed in Section 6.5, are:

- **Distributed Relational Database Architecture** (DRDA) from IBM supports distribution among IBM platforms and non-IBM environments that conform to DRDA.
- **Remote Data Access** (RDA) from ISO is a protocol that fits into the OSI model and was designed for heterogeneous data access.

In addition to features that support the distributed environment and development of distributed applications, developers should consider the end-user products that the DBMS provides or supports. Many future application modifications could be satisfied via a query product used by the user as productively as a report program written by IS.

Whether the DBMS is supported by the uploading and downloading facilities of the organization's popular micro-based, end-user products should also be a consideration. IS cannot lose sight of the fact that productivity gains for the users are just as critical to the success of the organization as IS's internal productivity gains are.

7.5 Testing the Application

Testing applications developed using traditional structured methods is straightforward. Each program is tested to ensure that it handles the specified logic correctly and generates the correct output. Interfaces to these applications are usually character-based screens, which are also easily tested. The developer can look at the generated screen and compare it to the specification in the design. The developer can also test each menu option displayed on the screen to ensure that the links are correct and that the user always returns to the menu screen.

Testing distributed applications is much more complicated. The developer must test that each piece of data requested by the application is accessible and that routines are in place to handle those situations when it is not accessible. The same holds true for processes that are distributed.

Most of the interfaces to distributed applications are GUI-based. If users only worked in one window at a time and that window was the application being tested, developers could easily test interfaces by comparing the screen to the design specifications and testing each of the menu or icon choices. However, users often get to the point where they are comfortable working with multiple windows and multiple applications. Developers must test the robustness of the application in such an environment. Does the application get "lost" if the users use it and Application B together? Does the application pick up key strokes left over from other applications? Will the application recover if running in background when the user's machine malfunctions?

In their haste to release an application on time or early, developers often fail to give an application a full "what if" test. For applications designed and developed with traditional methods, such a complete test might not be as critical due to the controlled nature of the environment and the development procedures.

However, for distributed applications, it is extremely critical. Moreover, the testing should be performed by IS professionals and potential end users of the application—members of the development team as well as other users. A test plan is critical. Project management during the test phase is essential. Version control procedures (see Section 7.7) facilitate the modification process as errors and omissions are uncovered.

7.6 Team Support

Most IS projects today are built by a team of developers, which includes system analysts and programmers. The team members must be able to work in concert with each other. While each individual program, screen, or report is most likely generated by one person, the team members must be able to review work done by others and share thoughts, questions, and information.

As they write programs, programmers must be able to search through the work done by others to look for procedures that can be re-used. The programs should also follow internal guidelines that should be available online.

Screens and reports should have a consistent appearance. This consistency could be checked at the detailed design phase or enforced at the generation stage. At the generation stage, common screen items would be stored in the repository along with a template screen layout. The template and common items would be used to develop the individual screens. Instead of being developed from scratch, a screen would be developed by editing and adding to the template, using common items and screen-specific items.

As is discussed in Section 5.2.1, the use of data dictionaries and repositories should be considered a requirement to support application development in distributed environments. Data dictionaries and repositories facilitate standardization and reuse of procedures and code, as well as providing a basis for communication among team members. Data dictionaries and repositories also promote the feeling of a team effort rather than a collection of many individual efforts.

The products in this emerging team engineering market include E-mail, groupware, project management, repositories, and CASE products that have a team orientation. The team orientation allows the team members to see the whole picture (of the project) and where their contribution fits. The supporting products help the team work together better and more productively.

7.7 Version Control

Version control is a procedure that is followed to ensure that versions of a program or shared procedures are kept in synchronization and that audit trails that identify who makes changes to individual procedures and programs are maintained. Most development environments today maintain libraries of programs and procedures that may be global or specific for an application. The libraries have a check-out/check-in facility, which is used by programmers wishing to review or update a program or procedure.

The library is used during development, as well as after the application is in production, for maintenance of the programs and procedures. Once the application is in production, version control is used to check-out/check-in programs and procedures that need modifications. Configuration control, which is discussed in Section 9.1, is used to ensure that the application software which resides on the various nodes is the most current version of the application software.

Operations

Once the application is tested and in production, the IS organization needs to turn its attention to providing and maintaining the integration of the components in the distributed environment and ensuring the reliability and integrity of the components.

In the past, once an application was in production, Information Systems focused on how the application ran and whether its results remained correct. If the application needed any modifications, the maintenance cycle began.

In distributed environments, IS needs to focus as much attention, if not more, on the environment itself. Applications are designed to operate across networks on multiple heterogeneous platforms. The reliability of the network and the network nodes is critical. Reliability includes speed of transmissions, reliable transmissions, uptime of resources, the management of transactions that span multiple platforms and network architectures, and the management of distributed data.

Systems management, network management, resource utilization, and application maintenance don't go away: they just take on a whole new meaning.

8

Integration

Client/server environments address the data and processing needs of their clients. As organizations begin their evolution into this new technology, they usually start with self-contained or straightforward applications. A client may need data from another server, but data for transactions are not usually split between servers. The processing for the application may be split between the client and the server, but is not distributed to other servers.

Distributed environments do distribute the data and processes for an application. When applications and data are distributed throughout the enterprise network, the environment of heterogeneous equipment from multiple vendors must be managed to maximize uptime, minimize network bottlenecks, and provide recovery procedures.

8.1 Transaction Management

Data location and distribution method (replicated or fragmented) should be transparent to the applications and the end users. One of the most important functions is data integrity and consistency, especially since transactions can update distributed databases on individual nodes.

A transaction is a sequence of statements that form a logical unit of work. All statements must execute successfully and completely or none should execute. A transaction is complete (committed) when all statements have been successfully executed.

A database transaction possesses the following traits, known as the ACID test:

- **Atomicity.** The entire transaction must be either completed or aborted. It cannot be partially completed.
- **Consistency.** The system and its resources go from one steady (consistent) state to another steady state.
- **Isolation.** The effect of a transaction is not evident to other transactions until the transaction is committed. However, any information needed by a transaction in process is locked to prevent other transactions from changing it.
- **Durability.** The effects of a transaction are permanent and should not be affected by system failures.

If any data manipulation statements fail, the entire database transaction fails and all partial changes to the database made before the failure must be rolled back. The database must be restored to the consistent state it was in before the transaction was attempted.

For example, consider a seemingly simple banking transaction where a customer transfers $300 from a checking account to a savings account. Both operations—debiting the checking account and crediting the savings account—must occur for this transaction to be considered complete.

If the debit is handled first and the credit doesn't occur, the checking account will reflect the withdrawal but the savings account will not reflect the deposit. After the debit portion of the transaction is handled, its table must be locked until the credit portion is handled so that some other transaction does not change the table while the credit portion is executing. If the credit portion does not execute, the effects of the debit portion must be reversed.

In a distributed environment, these database tables/files could be on separate nodes. The processes themselves could be on separate nodes. Network traffic is required to manage the process—the requests for updates, the "ready" messages, the "commit" message, and the "done" messages. Through all these steps, the process must be completed accurately and quickly.

8.1.1 Two-Phase Commit

A two-phase commit protocol is a set of rules used by a distributed DBMS or a separate transaction processing manager (TPM) which then becomes a participant in the transactions it manages. The TPM decides whether to make changes to the distributed databases permanent or to roll them back. The DBMS at each individual node is responsible for the local commit/rollback processing. The transaction services of the DDBMS (distributed DBMS) or TPM handle the coordination between the activities of the multiple participants—the local and remote DBMS resource managers.

The two-phase commit process is illustrated in Figure 8.1. In the first phase, called the *prepare* stage, each participant (a participant is the resource manager at a node that contains data to be updated or provides other services required for the transaction) performs its portion of the transaction and informs the coordinating participant that it is ready to commit its work. In the second phase, called the *commit* phase, the coordinating participant broadcasts a commit message to the other participants and records the transaction. If any participant fails to complete its portion, the coordinating participant cancels the entire transaction and broadcasts a rollback message.

The implementation of two-phase commit protocols has been the responsibility of data management products. This capability is beginning to show up in client/server products, such as Ellipse from Cooperative Solutions and transaction managers such as Encina from Transarc. These products internally handle the integrity of transactions that span multiple data sources as well as multiple machines. Products such as Encina from Transarc and TOP END from NCR provide two-phase commit protocols for transactions that affect multiple tables on a single node. Novell's NetWare 3.11 offers Transaction Tracking System, which provides two-phase commit processing for transactions affecting a single database.

8.1.2 Locking Schemes

In order to maintain the integrity of the data, when a multistep transaction uses more than one database, the database locks the affected records as each step is committed to ensure that the records are not updated while the rest of the transaction is being processed. Figure 8.2 summarizes the locking rules used by most DBMS products. A shared lock allows multiple transactions to read the same data. An exclusive lock is used when a transaction expects to update the data. When an exclusive lock is in effect, other transactions cannot access the data or be given any type of lock on the data. Exclusive locks can only be granted if no other transaction has any (shared or exclusive) lock on the data.

An alternative to locking is optimistic concurrency control or optimistic locking. Based on the premise that records are usually updated by a single application at a time, optimistic locking checks for update collisions at commit time. If the record has been read by other

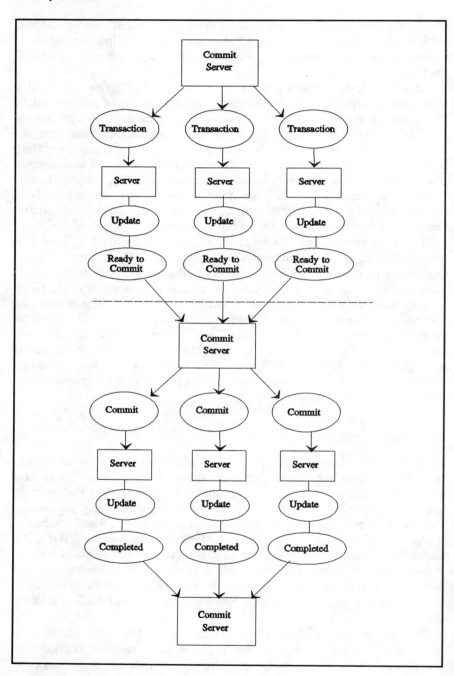

Figure 8.1 Two-phase commit

applications, those applications are notified of the impending update. The applications then react accordingly, usually by sending the user a screen message and refreshing the screen or by initiating a calculation by rereading the now-updated record.

Using client/server products, the locking mechanism is controlled by the product, not by the database manager. This allows a client/server application to handle transactions that span multiple data sources and to ensure the integrity of those transactions.

8.2 Transaction Managers

When designing applications that access data on multiple nodes of the infrastructure, developers have to provide procedures that will preserve the integrity of the data, something that is taken for granted in mainframe-based environments. These procedures can be written by the developer or provided by middleware.

As discussed in Section 1.1.6, the new class of software called middleware sits between the application and the operating system. A type of middleware called transaction manager is used to ensure the integrity of the data sources. As discussed earlier, updating data in distributed environments is more complex because the data required for a transaction might span many nodes and be in many formats. Transaction managers oversee the process to ensure that the database is always in a consistent state. If one portion of the transaction cannot be completed, then no portion should be completed. Transaction managers for open systems are currently UNIX-based.

Transaction managers must:

- Support transactions that impact on multiple distributed databases
- Manage the flow of transactions and distribute the workload
- Send and receive messages between nodes in the network

Asking for	Current Lock		
	Unlocked	Shared Lock	Exclusive Lock
Unlocked	OK	OK	OK
Shared Lock	OK	OK	NO
Exclusive Lock	OK	NO	NO

Figure 8.2 Locking rules

- Deal with resource managers, such as DBMSs, using standard interfaces
- Provide a flexible and powerful system administration facility

Several transaction managers are described below.

8.2.1 Tuxedo

Tuxedo, from UNIX System Laboratories (USL), formerly a division of AT&T and currently a subsidiary of Novell, provides interface specifications for applications and resource managers. The Application Transaction Manager Interface (ATMI) supports:

- Location transparency
- Load balancing
- Transparent data format conversion
- Context-sensitive routing
- Priority processing
- Network independence

In addition, Tuxedo uses UNIX System V Transport Layer Interface to provide access to underlying network technologies, such as TCP/IP, NetBIOS, OSI protocols, and APPC/LU6.2.

As illustrated in Figure 8.3, the Tuxedo transaction manager and resource manager components use standard interfaces to communicate with the systems' resource managers. The Tuxedo ATMI treats transactions that involve more than one resource manager and more than one physical location (also called global transactions) as one logical unit of work. For a global transaction to be successful, all local transactions must be successful.

USL recently announced Tuxedo Enterprise Transaction Processing, which consists of Tuxedo/WS and Tuxedo/Host. Tuxedo/WS supplies APIs that allow Windows, DOS, OS/2, and UNIX stations to be Tuxedo clients. Tuxedo/Host provides a framework for building gateway servers between legacy mainframe applications and UNIX products.

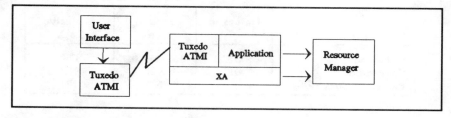

Figure 8.3 Tuxedo architecture

8.2.2 TOP END

A fairly new product from NCR Corp., TOP END is based on X/Open's Distributed Transaction Processing environment and uses XA (the X/Open Resource Manager) interfaces to UNIX-based DBMSs. As illustrated in Figure 8.4, TOP END divides the transaction processing into modules that can be distributed across the network for efficiency and flexibility. TOP END keeps track of their distribution and uses the information to do dynamic load balancing. A two-phase commit protocol, which is transparent to the user, ensures global transaction integrity.

TOP END is similar in architecture and functionality to the older Tuxedo. The major differences are in the following areas:

- **Administration.** In TOP END, resource definitions can be created interactively and stored in a repository. Tuxedo uses the UNIX editor to create definitions and the UNIX file system to store them.
- **Communications.** TOP END has direct support for major UNIX network protocols. Tuxedo uses UNIX Transport Level Interface only.
- **Security.** TOP END supports MIT's Kerberos security system. Tuxedo offers little authorization security.

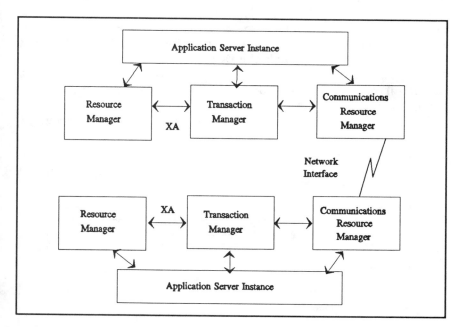

Figure 8.4 TOP END modules

■ **Workload balancing.** The workload balancing performed by TOP END is dynamic and network-sensitive. In Tuxedo, it is predefined.

As the dust settles from the AT&T and NCR merger, one of these competing products is likely to be phased out. TOP END is considered by most industry analysts to be the more robust product, but Tuxedo has a larger installed base. Only time will tell which product will be the survivor.

8.2.3 Encina

Based on the technologies of X/Open Consortium and Open Software Foundation's Distributed Computing Environment (DCE), the Encina product line from Transarc Corp. provides a highly reliable and easy-to-use transaction management software for distributed environments. Encina, released commercially in the first quarter of 1993, combines DCE's strengths, such as communication and management tools, resource location transparency, and security, with application development tools. Encina has its own multithreaded environment and supports nested transactions. Encina uses a two-phase commit for distributed transactions and a local two-phase commit for non-distributed transactions.

As illustrated in Figure 8.5, Encina is based on a two-tiered strategy, which is designed to support full-featured transaction processing (TP) managers, resource managers, or other distributed systems. The first tier expands the DCE foundation to include services that support distributed transaction processing (the Encina Toolkit Executive) and the management of recoverable data (the Encina Toolkit Server Core).

The second tier consists of TP services based on facilities provided

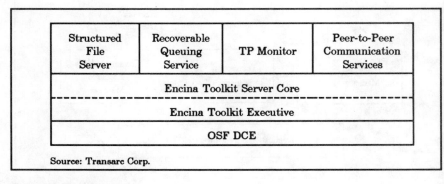

Source: Transarc Corp.

Figure 8.5 Encina components

by the first tier. These tools, developed by Transarc, include:

- The **Encina Monitor,** a full-feature TP monitor, provides an easy-to-use development environment, a reliable execution environment, and an administrative environment.
- The **Encina Structured File Server** is a record-oriented file system, which provides high performance and full transactional integrity, and can participate in two-phase commit protocols across multiple servers.
- The **Encina Peer-to-Peer Communication Services** supports transactional CPI-C peer-to-peer communications over TCP/IP and LU6.2 (for IBM's SNA) transports.
- The **Encina Recoverable Queuing Service** provides queuing of transactional data. It provides multiple levels of priority and can support large numbers of users and high volumes of data.

Transarc, which is 49 percent owned by IBM, has announced implementations of Encina for HP 9000s, Sun SPARC, and IBM RS/6000 systems.

8.3 Enterprise Network Management

As interconnected networks become critical in meeting the business needs of an organization, they define the way the organization operates and mirror the organization itself. These interconnected networks, sometimes referred to as the internetwork or internet, are beginning to be defined as the enterprise network. When viewed as an enterprise network, the pieces—the individual networks—and the links between the pieces are seen as a single entity and managed as such. This approach is essential for organizations that have distributed application processing and data throughout the enterprise network.

Enterprise network management deals with the hardware, software, and networks in the environment. Enterprise network management addresses:

- How networks communicate and how networks can be managed
- How data calls to a variety of databases are translated to a native call and converted to the receiving format
- How hardware with different data formats and operating systems can communicate

This process can be written into applications using RPCs; in-house applications can be developed; or the task can be accomplished using a variety of available software tools, such as those discussed below.

8.3.1 Distributed Management Environment

Open Software Foundation (OSF) offers a vendor-neutral platform that promotes network manageability within multivendor environments. Distributed Management Environment (DME) contains standard APIs that can be used to provide a consistent user interface to network management applications from multiple vendors. DME services (DME-compliant software) are expected to be available by the end of 1993 from contributing vendors.

The complete DME framework is expected to be released in mid-1994. The framework will define how vendors can fit the various DME components together. These components are:

- Data engine
- Data collection platform
- Graphical user interface
- Object-based management architecture

DME is designed to provide systems management as well as network management. By integrating systems and networks, IS can handle the management of its interconnected information technologies as a single process, not multiple processes.

OSF is implementing DME using an object-based approach to manage systems and networks. The DME manager, which is a network management application, interfaces with objects, which are network elements. Objects that share common traits are grouped into classes and all objects in a class inherit traits common to that class. For example, all routers have interprocess tables and emit alarms. When a new router is added to the enterprise network, it inherits these traits as well as the code created for the "router" class.

The following information about a managed object is stored in a software library:

- **Operations** that are performed on the object, such as stop and start
- **Events**, such as error messages
- **Associated data**, such as tracked statistics and configuration parameters

The network management application and the network administrator use the stored information to supervise the network and its nodes.

DME will incorporate Object Management Group's Common Object Request Broker Architecture—CORBA (see Section 8.3.2, Object Management Architecture). The CORBA standard defines a common set of APIs for handling tasks, pieces of data, functions, and devices required by an application. In addition, OSF is working with the Object Management Group to build management-specific features into CORBA. IBM is doing the actual integration of CORBA into DME.

The components of the DME architecture are shown in Figure 8.6 and discussed below.

User Interface

The use of resource management applications from different vendors is simplified by providing a consistent user interface. DME provides a toolkit for creating screens that access vendors' applications. It supports map, dialogue, and command-line interfaces.

Application Services and Management Applications

DME includes a defined set of utilities called application services and a management application for each service. These services include:

- **Distributed print services** track down printing problems.
- **Distributed license services** track software licenses and their users.
- **Software distribution and installation services** include utilities to package, install, and distribute software on heterogeneous systems.
- **Distributed host services** include utilities for determining internet addresses and starting up files.

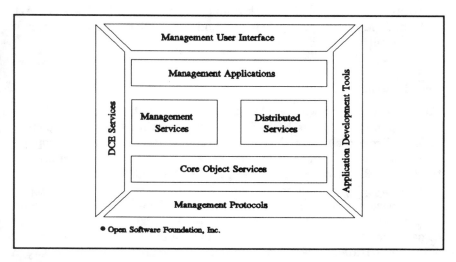

Figure 8.6 Distributed Management Environment architecture

- **PC integration** addresses the architectural limitations of DOS-based systems to ensure downward scalability and to permit micros to participate in host management activities.

Management Services

Management services are used by developers to write applications and to provide consistency between applications produced by different vendors. These services are presented as guidelines and include facilities for:

- Grouping managed objects together to be treated as an entity
- Specifying rules that govern individual objects
- Partitioning views of the network into manageable pieces
- Maintaining a class dictionary to serve as a repository

Development Tools

DME includes tools to simplify application development and support applications written in the C language or object-oriented C++ language. These tools include:

- Event language and compiler
- Dialogue language and compiler
- APIs: two object-oriented APIs and a low-level API to provide direct access to OSF's RPCs, Common Management Information Protocol (CMIP), and Simple Network Management Protocol (SNMP) (CMIP and SNMP are discussed in Section 9.4.2, Network Management Information Standards)

Object Services

To integrate the network and system management services, DME uses a management request broker and object servers. The management request broker ensures that tasks are routed and handled properly using standard APIs that allow objects to communicate. It is similar to the Object Request Broker proposed by OMG and X/Open.

One object server supports short-duration tasks, such as changing a user password or a printer configuration. The other object server, IBM's Data Engine, is internal and supports long-duration tasks, such as network monitoring. The Data Engine is a multithreaded server that supports parallel execution and efficient communication between objects. The Data Engine maintains historical data about an object that is used by network management systems to isolate and solve problems.

Summary

Some caveats concerning DME must be considered. Although DME does not require DCE, it is more effective if used in tandem with DCE. DME addresses the complexities of UNIX-based systems but can also be used to manage non-UNIX based systems. OSF is not expecting to release the complete DME specifications until mid-1994. Products that are completely DME-compliant are not expected until late 1994.

However, if network device manufacturers are willing to let OSF create and maintain network management systems and OSF can stick to its delivery dates, DME could provide the vendor-neutral framework organizations need to manage distributed environments.

8.3.2 Object Management Architecture

To support heterogeneous, distributed, networked environments, Object Management Group's Object Management Architecture (OMA) combines distributed processing with object-oriented computing. It provides a standard method for creating, preserving, locating, and communicating with objects, which can be anything from entire applications to pieces of applications such as graphical screens or complex number-crunching algorithms.

The OMA performs as a layer above existing operating systems and communication transports that support standard remote procedure calls (RPCs). As illustrated in Figure 8.7, the OMA consists of four main components:

■ **Object Request Broker** (ORB), which specifies the interface and information required for the object to communicate with another object.

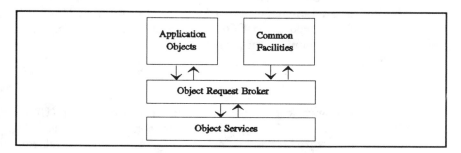

Figure 8.7 Object Management Architecture components

- **Object services,** which are objects that perform basic object-oriented housekeeping chores and provide for integrity, consistency, and security of objects and the messages that pass between objects.
- **Common facilities,** which are used by applications such as printing and spooling or error reporting.
- **Application objects,** which are created by independent software vendors or in-house software developers.

To link the OMA components, the Object Request Broker uses its Interface Definition Language (IDL). Object Management Group (OMG) provides mappings between the IDL and common programming languages such as C (currently the only mapping specified) or COBOL. Developers use the mappings to write to the ORB interfaces.

The ORB features for managing the interobject messages include name services (similar to an object directory) and exception handling. ORB allows objects to communicate dynamically or via a set of faster, preprogrammed static facilities.

OMG maintains that object management provides flexibility for cooperative applications. Rather than creating one-to-one RPC connections between applications, developers can access any application on the network as an object without knowing its physical location. The concept is to allow any object to communicate with any other object simply by sending a message to the common RPC interface.

The Object Request Broker is the foundation for OMG's Common Object Request Broker Architecture (CORBA), a mechanism that allows objects (applications) to call each other over a heterogeneous network. Within CORBA, objects are identifiable entities which provide one or more services to other objects. CORBA, based on the service technology found in Digital's Application Control Architecture, manages the identity and location of the objects, transports the request to the target object, and confirms that the request is carried out. CORBA-compliance provides a high degree of portability.

OSF has specified its own Management Request Broker and Interface Definition Language, as part of the OSF's DME. However, OSF is currently incorporating CORBA into DME and working with OMG to add management-specific services to CORBA.

8.3.3 UI-Atlas

UI-Atlas, the framework for open systems proposed by UI (UNIX International Inc.), specifies an open systems architecture can be created using hardware, software, networking, and other standards-based components.

UI-Atlas includes the OSI seven-layer network services model (see Section 2.6, The Network, for more details), a GUI that uses one API to support both Motif and OpenLook GUIs, and an expanded version of Sun's Network File System that operates over wide area networks and supports file replications. It also includes a global naming support system, a system management framework, and a distributed object management model that complies with OMG specifications. The UI-Atlas architecture is illustrated in Figure 8.8.

UI-Atlas can manage DCE environments as well as existing environments such as Sun's ONC (Open Network Computing) and micro-based LANs. Using a definition language based on the Class-Definition Language from the OMG, programmers can execute any supported RPC to provide interoperability between LAN environments. UI-Atlas can handle multiple RPCs; DME addresses only one RPC.

Some of the notable differences between DME and UI-Atlas are:

- For transaction management services, UI-Atlas uses Tuxedo, which is a mature product that has been retrofitted for distributed environments. DME uses Transarc's DCE-based OLTP Toolkit, which was designed for distributed environments.
- UI-Atlas supports the OSI model networking standard. DME plans to migrate to it.
- UI-Atlas uses Sun's Network File System. DME/DCE uses the Andrews File System.

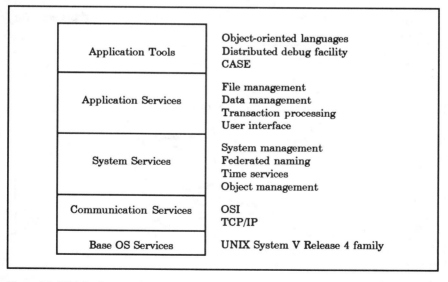

Figure 8.8 UI-Atlas framework

- UI has provided DCE support in the UI-Atlas framework but DME/DCE can be incorporated into non-UNIX operating systems.

UI-Atlas is expected to base much of its distributed applications and management environment around the Object Request Broker and the Object Management Architecture from Object Management Group. The next version of UI-Atlas expected in mid-1993 will focus on system management applications for object management. UI will then layer the ORB and OMA services on top of UNIX System V Release 4 (see Section 2.5, The Server, for more details) with a GUI on the desktop.

8.4 Network Computing Environments

Architectures that support the distribution of applications among heterogeneous platforms and software are being developed. These architectures are also referred to as network computing environments. The middleware software that supports these environments makes multivendor networks appear as one seamless environment.

8.4.1 Distributed Computing Environment

OSF's standard for providing services for distributed applications in heterogeneous hardware and software environments is Distributed Computing Environment (DCE). It is an open system that can run on any platform or operating system. Its layered architecture, illustrated in Figure 8.9, supports an integrated approach to distributed processing

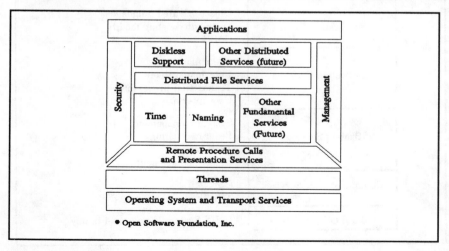

Figure 8.9 Distributed Computing Environment architecture

and offers flexibility for future enhancements. Each layer provides its own security and management.

DCE supports OSI standards and protocols and Internet standards (such as TCP/IP), network protocols, the Internet Domain Name System, and the Network Time Protocol. The Domain Name System supports a global naming system. It provides a name-to-resource mapping scheme for networks. The Network Time Protocol is a time control system.

DCE uses standard interfaces, such as X/Open and POSIX. DCE can be ported to OSF/1, USL's UNIX System V, Digital's Ultrix, HP's HP-UX, IBM's AIX, and Sun Microsystems' SunOS. It can be adapted to IBM's VMS and OS/2.

DCE is placed between applications and networking services on both the client and the server. DCE includes:

- Basic distributed services that support the building of applications
- Data-sharing services that require no programming

These services are discussed below.

Remote Procedure Calls

DCE's remote procedure calls (RPCs) allow a program within an application to execute on more than one server in the network, regardless of the machines' physical locations or architectures. The DCE RPC is based on the Network Computing System from Hewlett-Packard and Interface Definition Language (IDL) compiler-generated C program files. The RPC specifications include semantics for network transport independence and transparency. The information transfer between different platforms is transparent.

A DCE RPC can specify communication with a specific file server or with any file server offering the required service. Servers can be identified and located by name. The IDL is used to specify server-to-client operations. Because DCE's RPCs support connectionless and connection-oriented transports, an application does not have to be rewritten to use different transport services.

The integration with DCE's Threads Service component allows client machines to simultaneously interact with multiple servers. Integration with DCE's Security Service provides communication privacy and integrity.

The RPC services represent a major difference between OSF's DCE and Sun's Open Network Computing (ONC) architecture, as discussed later in this chapter. Remote procedure calls are discussed in more detail in Section 6.2.2.

Distributed Directory Service

A single naming model is supported throughout the distributed network. Servers, files, or print queues can be located and accessed by name rather than physical location, even if the network address changes. The Directory Service includes a local directory service and a global directory service, which supports the X.500 standard directory service or the Internet's Domain Name System name space.

The Directory Service can support small and large networks and can easily incorporate expansion. Using transport-independent RPCs, the Directory Service can operate in LAN and WAN environments.

Time Service

This software-based service synchronizes system clocks among servers in both LAN and WAN environments, thus providing an accurate timestamp for files that must be stored in sequence. The Time Service also supports time values from external services used for distributed sites that are using the Network Time Protocol.

Threads Service

The Threads Service supports multiple threads of execution in a single process and synchronizes the data access. One thread can be executing an RPC, while another is processing user input. Application programs are not concerned with whether threads are executing on one or several processors.

Thread management becomes an important consideration as organizations begin to incorporate symmetric multiprocessing machines into the enterprise network. A process can be split into multiple threads *and* dynamically assigned to any processer in the enterprise network. Symmetric multiprocessing is dicussed in Section 3.5.3, Mulitprocessing.

The Thread Service, used by the other DCE services and its file system, conforms to Draft 4 of the emerging POSIX standard for multithreaded programs. POSIX (Portable Operating System Interface) from IEEE is discussed in the Windows NT portion of Section 2.5.1, Server Operating Systems.

Security Service

This service provides authentication, based on the Kerberos Version 5 standard from MIT, authorization, and registry functions. The user registry ensures that user names are unique across the network. The registry also maintains a log of user and login activity.

Distributed File System

DCE's distributed file system (DFS) allows users (the client) to access data on another system (the server) via the network. When data is accessed, DCE's DFS caches (stores) a copy of it on the client system, where the client can read and modify it. The modified data is written back to its server.

DCE's DFS uses tokens to keep track of cached information. A read or write token is assigned by the server when the data is cached, depending on the type of access requested. If a write token is assigned, the server informs other clients that a write token for that data has been assigned. If clients have cached the same data with a read token, the server notifies them that the data is no longer current and voids their tokens.

Based on the Andrews File System from Transarc Corp., DCE's DFS allows routine maintenance of servers, such as backup, to be done in real time (without taking the system off-line) and supports replication of all network services. If one server fails, the system automatically switches a client to one of the replicated servers. When diskless workstations are used as client machines, the DFS cache manager can cache files in the diskless client memory rather than on a local disk.

DCE's DFS works with Sun's Network File System (NFS), the current *de facto* standard, but differs in the following areas:

- DFS uses **global file space**, where all network users use the same path names to accessible files, ensuring uniform file access from any network node via a uniform name space. In NFS, each network node has a different view of the file space.
- DFS has **integrated support** for LAN and WAN networks. NFS supports LAN networks only.

8.4.2 Open Network Computing

UNIX International's standard for open computing environments is SunSoft's Open Network Computing (ONC). The major differences in DCE and ONC architectures are RPC-related. These areas are discussed below.

Data Translation

ONC uses canonical data representation, a standard known as External

Data Representation (XDR). The client and server translate all outgoing messages into XDR form and then translate all incoming messages from XDR form to the native format. This occurs even if both the client and server use the same data representation.

DCE RPC tags all calls with a description of the calling system's internal data representation. The called system translates the data only when necessary.

Location Transparency

The RPC methods used by both DCE and ONC provide location transparency through directory services. ONC uses Sun Microsystems's Network Information System. DCE uses a hybrid of X.500 and Digital's Domain Name Service.

Transport Independence

A transport interface API is used to isolate the client requests from the underlying message transport and to provide reliable support to a wide variety of networks. ONC's RPC uses the UNIX SVR4 Transport Layer Interface, which provides its own connection-oriented virtual circuits for reliable message transport, regardless of the underlying network protocol. ONC's RPC can provide equivalent service with TCP, UDP, or OSI protocols.

The DCE RPC implementation achieves approximately the same transport independence using the X/Open Transport Interface (XA), which is the POSIX transport API.

Multithreading

Multithreading allows a server process to handle multiple RPC requests. DCE is based on the multithreaded Mach kernel contained in the OSF/1 operating system. Single-threaded UNIX variants must complete one client request before proceeding to the next one. ONC RPC servers must run multiple agents for each service if they wish to simultaneously handle multiple requests.

Security

ONC uses a hybrid of UNIX access control lists, RPC message encryption, and key passing to authorize and authenticate RPC clients. DCE uses Kerberos authentication, which requires a dedicated security server and enhanced UNIX access control lists.

Other Comparisons

Some other major differences between DCE and ONC are:

- DCE already supports some OSI standards and is evolving toward greater OSI compliance. ONC was not designed to be an open standard and is not OSI compliant.
- DCE is independent of any operating system; ONC is layered on UNIX SVR4.

However, DCE was released in early 1993, and products that comply with its specifications are just now appearing on the market. ONC has been on the market for a while and has a proven track record. It is still too early to tell whether DCE or ONC will emerge as the *de facto* standard.

8.4.3 Tivoli Management Environment

Organizations have the options of using a variety of products that are tailored to individual products and manually consolidating the output or using a third-party tool, such as those discussed in this chapter, that can manage heterogeneous networks of systems. Another third-party product is Tivoli Management Environment (TME) from TIVOLI Systems, Inc.

TME uses an object-oriented framework and provides a GUI interface, resource management, application addressing security, and system configuration. As illustrated in Figure 8.10, TME consists of the following components:

- **Tivoli Management Framework** uses an object-oriented (all resources and operations are encapsulated as objects) system management framework.

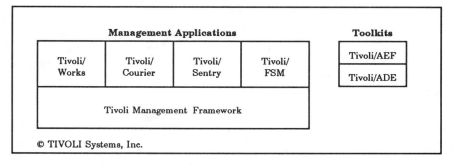

© TIVOLI Systems, Inc.

Figure 8.10 Tivoli Management Environment

- **Tivoli/Works** manages the system resources, including the Management Framework.
- **Tivoli/Sentry,** an optional package, performs resource monitoring.
- **Tivoli/Courier,** an optional package, manages the distribution of software.
- **Tivoli/FSM,** an optional package, manages network file system relationships. Tivoli/FSM can provide a consistent configuration for related groups of machines and change file system access for multiple machines with one operation.

The two optional toolkits are used for building and customizing applications. Tivoli/AEF is used to customize and extend Tivoli Management Applications. New management applications are developed using Tivoli/ADE.

TME was selected by OSF to be part of the Distributed Management Environment (DME) specification and by UNIX International, Inc. (UI) as part of UI-Atlas, UI's distributed systems management framework.

9

Production

Once the applications are distributed and the data is distributed, IS can turn its attention to ensuring that both the data and the applications are available to any user when access is required. But there is a lot that can go wrong from the point when the user decides to start up an application that uses distributed data and distributed processes and the point when the user gets a response from the application.

9.1 Configuration Control

In distributed environments, application software can be distributed to multiple nodes. To provide coordination, there must be some central monitor to keep track of what version of the application software each node is using. In addition, updates from software packages must also be monitored to ensure compatibility among the nodes.

A data dictionary can help control versions of data definitions but does not address source and object code of programs. Organizations have used programming libraries as a means of controlling versioning. At compile time, object code for the application's programs is created by selecting programs from libraries, which contain the latest version of the programs. However, most 4GLs have no compilation step so other means must be followed to ensure that proper versions of source code are run in production.

Maintenance requires changing the system. Each component of the system—hardware, programs, database design, documentation—may exist in different versions at different locations. Configuration control keeps track of the different versions and provides a strategy for supporting the various versions with no incompatibility problems.

For example, the interface used to share data between a distributed site and a central site is modified, requiring a program change at each site. There is no way to guarantee that all the required changes will take place at the same time. During the period that both interfaces exist, the central site must accept both interfaces and know which distributed site uses which one.

9.1.1 Configuration Management Software

Configuration management software allows IS to keep track of an application's components—its objects, modules, interconnected programs, and related material such as documentation. The advantages of configuration management software include:

- Bug fixes and enhancements can be treated as a single unit even if the lines of code are dispersed among several files.
- Even with multiple development teams, code is less likely to be accidently overwritten, misplaced, or changed inappropriately.
- Applications can be built faster (new code for existing code that can't be found is not written unnecessarily) and of a higher quality (bugs have already been worked out of the existing code).
- Tracking changes is automatic and real-time.

Configuration management software requires a powerful command language and a powerful repository. The software should support the tasks of the project administrator who defines the overall process of software management and the developer who works with that process.

The command language should support both a command interface and a GUI, be English-like to accomodate a short learning curve, support alternative development paths, and maintain separate developer work areas while supporting collaboration.

The repository must be able to handle various types of software (such as programs, files, and objects) and nonsoftware (such as documentation sets). The repository must be able to handle multiple changes to multiple files as a single entity, maintain and illustrate relationships between the items, and store changed versions as "deltas from a base" versions (thus saving disk space).

One area in which configuration management software needs improvement is its ability to integrate with other development tools, most notably CASE tools. Without integration, it is difficult to pass information between the tools.

9.1.2 Configuration Management Models

Carnegie Mellon Univerity's Software Engineering Institute has defined four models for configuration management, which are illustrated in Figure 9.1 and explained below. Each configuration management software product uses only one model.

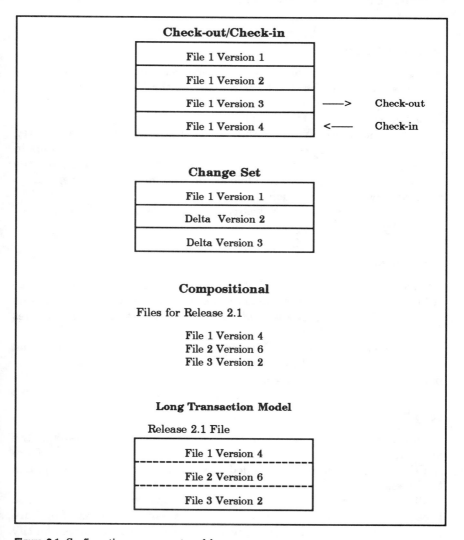

Figure 9.1 Configuration management models

Check-Out/Check-In Model

Products that use the check-out/check-in model manage software as individual file versions. Developers create new file versions as they make changes to the existing file versions. However, there is no way to automatically extract what those changes are.

Only one developer can work on a file version at a time.

Specific releases can be constructed by selecting the appropriate file versions. UNIX shell macros are usually written to accomplish this selection.

Change Set Model

Based on object technology, the change set model identifies every change set in the repository by name and by the list of objects that use it. A change set is a collection of code changes that moves software from one steady state to another.

Every object, in turn, is identified by the change sets that created it. Therefore, an object, which can be lines of code or complete programs, can be extracted from the repository by specifying the change sets that created it. Objects do not have to correspond to discrete physical items, such as files.

Change sets also allow developers to recover any feature, bug, or release by name.

Compositional Model

Products that use the compositional model, an extension of the check-out/check-in model, have built-in mechanisms for selecting file versions for a specific release. The repository maintains version selection rules to indicate which file version goes with which release.

Some compositional model-based products support the use of virtual files. Virtual files combine code segments from several files into one image, providing the appearance of a typical file to the developer.

Long Transaction Model

Under the long transaction model (LTM), developers manage the application software as a version of an entire release. Changes from multiple programmers are handled as a single transaction and applied to the existing release, resulting in a new release.

IS does not have to track which file versions go with which release because all the components represent an entire release. Software updates can be handled in small batches. LTM-based products identify conflicts among updates as the transaction is being completed, leaving IS time to resolve the conflicts before creating the new release.

9.1.3 Software Version Control

Some development tools automate software version control. When a user initiates the application, the server application software checks the version on the user's machine and if the software is out of date, the server application software downloads a current copy.

Software that can manage software distribution is also available. These products can perform scheduled software changes, perform automatic installations, and provide audit trails.

9.2 Shared Data

When data is to be shared, a new focus is required. In distributed environments, the function of data management becomes centralized and data is organized by subject area. If the data is also centralized, the organization could experience performance bottlenecks.

Shared data requires users to work together to agree on definitions and attributes of the data. The concept of a customer may be different in the sales group, support group, and training group.

Shared data also requires the data modelers and database designers to agree on a common strategy. The data modeler is concerned with the business rules, defining business facts in only one place and ensuring that they are placed in the most appropriate place. The database designer is concerned with resource utilization, performance, maintainability of the data structure, and with ensuring that everyone who needs the data can get to the data.

Both groups must work together to design a data structure that balances resource utilization and user access ease and speed. Designers have to understand how data will be used and find mechanisms to support that use. Naming conventions should reflect the users' terminology, not the developers'.

9.3 Networked Systems Management

Systems management tasks in the mainframe world, such as security, performance monitoring, and configuration management, are built-in and, therefore, taken for granted. In distributed environments, this is not the case. There are different platforms and multiple operating systems. Desktop machines are able to access data anywhere in the infrastructure and the data itself could be distributed among the nodes of the infrastructure. Applications run from desktop machines can be distributed among nodes of the infrastructure.

The network takes on a critical role in distributed environments. The term *networked systems management* represents the blending of network management and systems management. The products discussed in Section 8.3, Enterprise Network Management, address this domain.

9.3.1 Systems Monitoring

Capacity planning is difficult when distributed applications divide processing jobs among different computers and when data is distributed among different computers, usually with the computers on different networks. Capacity planning is also very difficult due to the variety of hardware and software used in distributed environments and the very nature of networks. The tools for capacity planning and monitoring that are built into the mainframe and midrange environments are just now appearing for distributed environments.

The first step in identifying bottlenecks is to collect data about the current operations—the computers and the network. Information must be gathered for the network, the server, and the clients.

The level of performance information for servers and clients varies among operating systems. In general, there are more tools—and those tools are more robust—for the mature operating systems. Both IBM mainframes and VAX computers are well supported with built-in features and third-party tools. There are only a few third-party system-monitoring tools available for DOS, OS/2, Windows, and Macintosh. OS/2 is supported by the OS/2 Performance Monitor from IBM. Some products are designed to monitor server performance on a particular network, such as NetWare from Novell.

Historically, there are a few products available for monitoring the performance of UNIX. More products are beginning to appear on the market, but the different variants of UNIX use different formats for system management data. To compensate for these differences, OSF outlined guidelines for consistent system management functions in its DME (Distributed Management Environment) standards announced in early 1993. Due to the newness of the DME guidelines, there are only a few products that conform to those specifications on the market. These include products supporting HP-UX from HP, SunOS from Sun Microsystems, AIX from IBM, and Ultrix from Digital.

The other area of performance concern relates to the DBMSs. There are monitoring tools for mainframe DBMSs, such as DB2, but very few for server DBMSs, such as SQL Server and Oracle. Information is generated by such products, but it is difficult to collect and difficult to interpret.

In addition to the DBMS and operating system, performance measurement is difficult with distributed applications because processing often occurs in background mode. Current monitoring tools can track only one session. When a Windows user opens a second (or third or fourth) window, the applications working in background mode are not monitored. No information is gathered for those applications, even though they may be performing tasks.

Processing could also be split between a number of clients and several servers. A monitoring tool would have to be able to follow the path taken by each task of a transaction, track the performance of each step, and then tabulate the results.

9.4 Network Management

When installations were comprised of relatively homogeneous mainframe and midrange processors on networks that used terminals, systems were managed separately from the network and networks were managed using tools supplied by the hardware vendor. Today, "the system" is comprised of networks and computers (servers and clients) from a variety of vendors. Organizations have to monitor the physical network and analyze performance data to identify bottlenecks, despite the diversity.

Network bottlenecks are hard to pinpoint because the data packets go through a variety of devices, such as bridges and routers. Protocol analyzers can be placed on the line to examine data as it travels across the network and determine how quickly a device is transporting data. Protocol analyzers work with specific types of networks, but distributed applications run over more than one network. The number and quality of analyzers available for each network varies, although vendors are broadening their tools to support multiple networks.

These monitoring tools use proprietary protocols to generate and store the data, which makes it difficult to consolidate the information into a big picture. Standards are emerging for performance information to allow the data to be analyzed by a central system.

IS organizations that feel that capacity planning and performance monitoring is necessary have often turned to home-grown solutions. Other IS organizations take a different route. They decide that buying a new server, which will eliminate most of the performance problems, will cost less than the time and energy required to pinpoint the bottleneck. As more mission-critical applications are moved to distributed environments and written as distributed applications, this point of view may change. But for now, there are lots of obstacles and few complete solutions.

As infrastructures fan out and make increased use of wide area networks (WANs), the organization will actually experience degradation in throughput, due to the difference in capacity between a local area network and a wide area network. As technology improves the capabilities of WANs, by default it improves the capacities of LANs as well. Consequently, barring any technological breakthroughs, the variance in capabilities between the two is likely to remain constant.

9.4.1 Network Management Tools

An effective network management strategy incorporates multiple vendors, network topologies, operating systems, and applications. It must also be flexible enough to support an ever-changing environment. A variety of tools can aid network administrators in cutting through dissimilar products to fine-tune network performance, reduce downtime, and reduce the need for network consultants. These products fall into four categories:

- Protocol analyzers and monitors
- Intelligent wiring hubs
- Network management software
- Network performance monitors

Protocol Analyzers and Monitors

Protocol analyzers and monitors allow network administrators to watch and inspect the packets of a particular protocol within a specific architecture. The functions of protocol analyzers (capture, view, analyze) are divided between the software in the monitor attached to the LAN and the manager software running at the operator's machine.

Protocol analyzers can be dedicated, portable, or remote versions. Remote analyzers plug into a particular segment of the network and allow the data to be read from another location on the network. These are sometimes referred to as *sniffers*.

The products currently in the marketplace range from the software-based LANwatch from FTP Software to hardware/software products from Novell (LANalyzer), Hewlett-Packard (LanProbe II and Probe-View), and Network General Corp. (Sniffer).

Intelligent Wiring Hubs

Intelligent wiring hubs, also called smart wiring hubs, allow the network to be segmented into manageable chunks, making it easier to isolate problems, track configuration changes, and enforce security. Hubs can be run from local consoles or central management stations.

The major vendors of intelligent hubs are Cabletron Systems Inc., SynOptics Communications Inc., Ungermann-Bass, Inc., and Network, Inc.

Network operating systems are appearing as components in smart wiring hubs, which reduces hub cost because the server's CPU runs the hub management software. In addition, wiring hubs allow vendors to ship ready-ro-run networks with preconfigured file servers. Novell's Hub Management Interface bundles low-end hub cards into its servers, integrating the wiring hub and the file server into a single device.

Network Management Software

Network management software allows network administrators to monitor the entire network from a central point. The software can analyze operations at remote workstations and servers as well as the network cabling. Network management software also maintains a topological layout of the network. Vendors of network operating systems are beginning to integrate network management features into their products.

NetLabs, Inc. offers the UNIX-based DualManager family of products for managing heterogeneous networks. Trellis Inc.'s Expose products can be used to manage Banyan's VINES networks. LANlord, from Client Server Technologies, manages and controls resources across multiple heterogeneous LANs, running Novell's NetWare network operating system. HP's PerfView is based on HP's OpenView framework, which supports the management of heterogeneous networks from one location and was accepted by OSF as part of DME. OpenView focuses on managing network resources; PerfView focuses on managing the performance of distributed systems across a WAN.

Network Performance Monitors

Network performance monitors allow a network administrator, from a central location, to analyze network performance and reconfigure resources to bypass problems and bottlenecks.

Current products include Auspex Performance Monitor from Auspex Systems, LAN Administration Manager and NetView from IBM, and LANtern from Novell.

9.4.2 Network Management Information Standards

There are two major standards for network management information—Common Management Information Protocol and Simple Network Management Protocol (SNMP). A new improved version of SNMP (SNMP-2) is currently in the evaluation process and is expected to be ratified by the Internet Engineering Task Force by the fall of 1993.

Simple Network Management Protocol

Simple Network Management Protocol (SNMP) is based on TCP/IP standards and provides a format for network devices to communicate management data to a central machine. A four-year-old standard, SNMP has some major limitations regarding support for today's enterprise networks. These limitations include:

- A lack of security features
- Inability to collect network management data in bulk
- Inability to interconnect different network management applications

Simple Network Management Protocol - Version 2

The Internet Engineering Task Force (IETF), the standards setting body for SNMP, has officially proposed Simple Network Management Protocol-2 as a new standard to replace SNMP. Unlike SNMP, the new version, referred to as SNMP-2, supports the management of applications on hosts and micros and offers secured communications between the management systems and the managed network devices.

SNMP-2 supports manager-to-manager communications, which allows a central management station to delegate tasks to subnetwork managers. Transport mappings are provided for multiple protocol stacks, including AppleTalk, IPX used in Novell's NetWare, and OSI, as well as TCP/IP. SNMP only runs over TCP/IP.

SNMP-2 provides utilities that can be used to send notifications between SNMP agents and managers. SNMP-2 also has richer error codes.

In addition, SNMP-2 can more efficiently retrieve large amounts of data (bulk collection). SNMP-2 also provides security measures including authentication, access control, and authorization.

However, SNMP-2 is not backward compatible with the original SNMP—although it was originally intended to be—making the transition between SNMP and SNMP-2 more difficult.

However, until SNMP-2 becomes an official IETF standard, vendors will remain reluctant to commit resources to commercial SMP products.

In addition, support of OSI standards is critical for some organizations (most notably, the United States Government). Without that support, CMIP/CMIS users are unlikely to switch to SNMP-2.

Common Management Information Protocol

Common Management Information Protocol (CMIP) and Common Management Information Services (CMIS) permit communications among different networks and network management applications. Based on OSI standards, CMIP and CMIS overcome the limitations of SNMP.

Some of the advantages of CMIP over SNMP for enterprise management include:

- CMIP supports peer-to-peer interaction across different network management protocols. SNMP centrally polls remote devices.
- CMIP can provide a centralized view of enterprise networks.
- CMIP, in concert with OSI, can guarantee delivery of data. SNMP with TCP/IP cannot. SNMP-2 is supposed to help the problem, but will not totally solve it.
- CMIP uses common object definitions and object-based systems are viewed as the next wave of integrated network management.
- CMIP is virtually mandated by many European governments.

However, products that use CMIP and CMIS standards are fairly new, few in number, more expensive than SNMP (or SNMP-2) products, and, since they offer more functions than SNMP products, are more complex. In addition, the trade-off for the increased functionality is increased memory requirements.

9.4.3 Standards Implementation

Even if the management information is standardized, each vendor must still supply its own network management application designed to support the devices they sell. This forces operators in the network control center of a large network containing devices from many vendors to monitor multiple consoles. In addition, the data captured in the management information bases (MIBs) are only meaningful to that vendor's network management system. The end result is a proprietary MIB, defeating the purpose of open systems.

IBM's Systems Network Architecture (SNA) supports network management and the NetView family of network management products. But it is a single-vendor solution and does not address multivendor environments or provide an open systems solution.

Frameworks are being developed that support network manageability of multivendor, interconnected information technologies. Some of these products are primarily in the specification stage, although components may currently be available.

OSF's Distributed Management Environment (DME) addresses the lack of standards within network management information. Its CM/API (Consolidated Management Application Programming Interface) is one of the first pieces of DME to become available. Used in combination with the DME data collection architecture, CM/API supports integrated management across the CMIP (Common Mangement Information Protocol) world, which includes telecommunication devices and circuits, and the SNMP (Simple Network Management Protocol) world, which includes routers and LANs.

9.5 Network Security

Desktop machines can access data anywhere in the infrastructure. Unfortunately, micro operating systems and most networking software were not written with security in mind. Yet, these two layers of software are major building blocks in distributed environments.

The level of security must be appropriate for the users and the organization and how they view the value of data. There are costs and additional steps for users associated with every level of system security. These must be balanced against the cost and inconvenience of unprotected or corrupted data.

Network operating systems are beginning to include security functions such as authentication and authorization. The DBMS products usually offer security features such as authorization checking, often down to the field level. Some server DBMS vendors are extending their products to include government specifications for multilevel data security.

In addition, security products are available for this environment. Some mainframe-based vendors, such as IBM and Computer Associates International, Inc., are porting their host security packages to LAN environments. Others, such as Security Dynamics, SunSoft, and Fischer International Systems Corp., are developing products specifically for LAN environments.

Some client/server development tools, such as Ellipse from Cooperative Solutions (discussed in Chapter 11, Client/Server Products for Distributed Environments), are including the capability to build configuration and security management into applications developed with the tool.

9.6 Restart/Backup

It is no longer a matter of just keeping the mainframe or the network up. Enterprise environments are dealing with multiple servers and multiple networks, all of which must be available at all times.

Databases must be backed up and restored while users are accessing the database. Machines are not brought off-line for backup or restart.

In case of a disk drive failure, operations staff should be able to swap in a new disk and restore the data, without taking the machine off-line. In case of a server failure, processing should be able to be switched to another processor, either another processor in the enterprise network or a redundant server.

9.7 Management of Distributed Data

As has been discussed earlier, entire tables or a subset of a table data can be replicated or fragmented. Fragmentation involves splitting the data horizontally, vertically, or both. The resulting subtable is stored at the appropriate node. The DDBMS (distributed DBMS) recognizes that the table is fragmented and how it is fragmented and maintains the integrity of the fragmented data. The local DDBMS treats the sub-table as a complete table. The central DDBMS has control over and can access all the subtables as needed. There is no complete copy of a table that is fragmented.

Data is replicated (copied) for performance reasons. If multiple clients within the infrastructure routinely access the same data, it may be beneficial to replicate it at their node.

Data replication is accomplished by allowing users to make their own copies of a data set. When the users require updated copies of the data set, they copy the new data to their nodes. An alternative to user intervention would be an IS-initiated process. For example, a batch job, executed each time the data set changed, would copy the new data to each user node on an approved list. The weakness in this approach to replication is its reliance on human intervention. Users have to remember to execute the copy instructions. The approved list must be kept up-to-date. The batch job must be submitted and its results checked to verify that every out-of-date copy of the data was rewritten.

A more reliable alternative would be to use a DDBMS's capability to generate snapshots of the data and distribute those snapshots. The timing of the snapshots could be specified by the user. Most DDBMSs do not support transferring updates of snapshot data back to the original source.

Some DDBMSs have the capability to replicate data and handle updates at multiple locations. Using this advanced data distribution method, the DDBMS can:

- Create and maintain copies of the data at multiple locations
- Maintain data consistency among all copies using synchronous or asynchronous processing
- Provide location transparency to the applications accessing the data

The trade-off for replication is the overhead required to keep copies of the data consistent and to maintain the consistency transparently to the user. One approach for managing this process is called the master/slave technique, where one database is designated as the master (primary) database and the others as slave databases. The DDBMS at the primary site is responsible for maintaining the integrity of the slave sites. If a slave site is unavailable when the DDBMS is attempting to update the replicated data, the DDBMS will keep trying that site until it is available and the task can be completed.

The other approach is called two-phase commit. One site is designated as the coordinator. When an application is ready to update replicated data, the coordinator sends a request to every affected site to prepare to locally commit (make) the update. If all respond as ready, the update is made to all sites. If one site responds as not ready, the update is not performed. Two-phase commit is discussed in more detail in Section 8.1.1.

Fragmentation is a more complicated method of distributing data. Relational tables can be fragmented horizontally, vertically, or both. The management of fragmented tables should be the responsibility of a DDBMS. It is a complex implementation. The table segment on each node should be treated as a complete entity by that node. At a central node, the virtual joining of the table's segments must be transparent to the user.

Various methods for distributing data are discussed in more detail in Section 6.6.

Application Development Products

As organizations begin to use distributed environments, they look to automated application development products to facilitate building applications for this new technology. These products include CASE products that organizations may have been using to aid in the specification of their mainframe-based applications; prototyping products that involve the users in the development of requirements and designs for the application; client/server development products that also involve the users in the prototyping process but are also able to generate the screen and logic code for the application; and fourth-generation languages that support prototyping, involve the users to a lesser degree, and focus on the requirements of the application and less on the design of the application.

An IS organization must have a mix of development products, just as they have a mix of applications. A development tool might be more appropriate for one class of application than another. A development methodology might be better supported by one development tool rather than another.

The fourth-generation languages were developed to support end-user requirements and decision-supporting applications and to reduce the IS backlog by allowing users to do more of their computing tasks themselves. As IS worked with 4GLs, their usefulness as prototyping tools also became apparent.

4GLs are nonprocedural—users specify the "what" and the 4GL determines the "how." Their strength lies in their support of semi-structured tasks. Structured applications can be written in a 4GL but the application will lack the security, auditability, and transaction management taken for granted with applications coded in a 3GL.

CASE products support the analysis, design, and implementation of structured applications. These products provide an environment rich in diagrams, cross-reference utilities, development-team support, repositories, and structure. All of these features enhance the communication between the developers and the users. The code for the resulting design can then be generated in a 3GL—depending on the product. Some products are able to generate all of the code, other products only some of the code.

Client/server development products were designed for client/server applications where the presentation logic and most of the application logic are performed on the client and the server handles the data requests and possibly some of the application logic. These products use prototyping techniques to design the interface and the processing logic.

IS organizations have to separate marketing from reality. They have to understand the strengths and limitations of the development tools and carefully match the development tool to the application.

10

4GLs for
Distributed Environments

Organizations are using fourth-generation languages (4GLs) to support the application design and construction phases of application development. These languages support the prototyping methodology and are usually integrated with their own proprietary DBMS. The languages use an English-like syntax which allows developers and end users to work together to build, generate, and test applications.

However, the early 4GLs were designed for decision-support applications and were not robust enough for enterprise-wide production transaction applications. The products reviewed in this chapter have evolved their capabilities to address current issues, such as transaction-based applications, distributed environments, open systems standards, portability, and GUI support.

In order to support today's environments and IS needs, 4GLs have to provide low-level support as well as high-level support. Developers or programmers should not have to drop down to a 3GL to develop applications. The languages must support the concept of a repository or data dictionary, which promotes sharing of code, screen images, and data objects. The languages must use the same interface and syntax within each module or component of the development environment.

The prototyping nature of 4GLs make them appropriate tools for determining application specifications—for presentation, processes, and data. Users react to a working version of their application. The development of specifications identification becomes a shorter and easier process. In some cases, the working specification is then coded into a 3GL for production purposes. In other cases, the working version evolves to become the production version.

If developers intend to evolve a working prototype to the production version of the application, it should be determined in advance that the application under consideration is a good candidate for such a development approach. Applications built with 4GLs are usually not as efficient, robust, or as auditable as those written in a 3GL.

The original focus of 4GLs was end-user support. The languages were relatively easy to use and were intended to be used by business users to perform many of their own information retrieval tasks and build their own applications. The interface was command mode. The languages had their own proprietary data structure. Data retrieval and manipulation are these languages' strengths.

4GLs then evolved into development aids for IS professionals. The development capabilities are accessed using screens and forms. The end-user interface is also screen- and form-oriented. 4GLs usually include a data dictionary or repository. Links are provided to data sources other than the proprietary data structure of the language, which is in most cases relational.

The ability to develop GUI front ends to applications is beginning to be available in development 4GLs. Some of the products reviewed can run under Windows as a DOS application and develop applications that can run as DOS applications. Few 4GLs can create an application that can run as a Windows application or develop applications for a Windows target environment.

The concept of accessing data from a variety of data sources has long been addressed by development 4GLs. The vendors are beginning to address the concept of a client and a server. They are also beginning to address the notion of distributed databases.

It is important to understand that 4GLs are evolving into support for client/server technology. Much of the support still involves thought and effort on the part of the developers and programmers. They do not support event-driven applications by default, nor do they automatically generate GUIs for applications or SQL code for retrieving data.

Some of the areas of differences between 4GLs and client/server development products are:

- Support for Window-based clients
- Support for multiple databases in heterogeneous environments
- Database independence
- Support for stored procedures and triggers
- Support for standard RPCs, network gateways, and (possibly) DCE/DME

The products below are presented alphabetically and were chosen based on their market share, the completeness of their offerings, and the efforts made by the vendor to address the newer GUI-based client/server technologies.

10.1 FOCUS

FOCUS from Information Builders, Inc. (IBI) is a versatile 4GL for mainframe, midrange, and micro computers. FOCUS applications are entirely portable (requiring only system-related modifications) between platforms. FOCUS currently runs on more than 30 platforms and has been optimized for each platform. FOCUS also provides true client/server functionality. The VAX and Alpha AXP platforms (both from Digital) can serve as both clients and/or servers in an enterprise-wide installation of FOCUS.

FOCUS also provides a DBMS that includes integrated features for report generation, graphics, query, screen formatting, and general application development. Users interface with FOCUS via a GUI, menu prompts, a nonprocedural language, or procedural statements.

FOCUS supports SQL as a standard query language. FOCUS can read and write to SQL-driven engines across platforms and across SQL dialects through its SQL Translator. IBI's EDA/SQL (see Section 6.1.4) can be used to provide transparent SQL-based access to relational and nonrelational data on interconnected multivendor systems. Using FOCUS, SQL statements can be used to access non-SQL DBMSs and file management systems. These data sources can be joined using the FOCUS relational capabilities.

10.1.1 User Interfaces

The FOCUS Talk Technologies provide consistent user interfaces to various parts of the FOCUS product. Each module incorporates a menu and windowed interface. The Talk Technologies are:

- **TableTalk,** used to specify nonprocedural report queries
- **FileTalk,** used to select the necessary options for creating a file definition
- **ModifyTalk,** used to generate data entry screens from system defaults
- **PlotTalk,** used to generate graphical output

A natural English interface called English Query Language (EQL), a component of the micro version of FOCUS called PC/FOCUS, provides access to all data sources accessible to the micro—the micro itself, a LAN server, a host, or any computer accessible via the LAN server or host. EQL comes with its own vocabulary, which may be expanded to link synonyms, definitions, and commonly used phases. The vocabulary can be applied globally to all files or to a specific database. EQL issues native FOCUS requests to retrieve the data and produces a formatted display of the data. The user can scroll through the display or use the Hot Screen option, which supports full-screen scrolling, text search, and cut-and-paste.

10.1.2 Support for Application Development

To facilitate the development of applications, FOCUS provides the following tools:

- **Dialog Manager** control statements manage the execution of stored FOCUS requests. They are executed as encountered and support runtime variables. The Dialog Manager also provides access to subroutines in other FOCUS programs and subroutines written in other languages.
- **Screen and window painters** can be used to design and create forms and windows. Screens are automatically linked to the application.
- **Text Editor** (TED) is used to write applications and customize programs created with code generators, such as the Talk modules. This full-screen text editor also includes an integrated screen painter, allowing a developer to design a screen from within TED via a paint mode.
- The **AUTOMOD** facility is used to develop simple prototype applications by responding to prompts and specifying screen formats. FOCUS creates the required file definitions and prompts the user for data to be entered into the database.
- The optional **Application Control Environment** facility is a repository of application entities, such as databases, table definitions, procedures, security, and other information required to set up the application environment. Applications that have been defined to the Application Control Environment can be selected and run as a menu choice. The Application Control Environment restores the user's environment to its original state when the user exits the application. The Application Control Environment uses a windowed interface to establish security, manage test and production versions of an application, and share resources across applications.

10.1.3 Support for Distributed Computing

To support distributed computing, Information Builders offers two products: FOCNET and EDA/SQL. Most of the capabilities of FOCNET, a mature product, are being incorporated into EDA/SQL. EDA/SQL is discussed in Section 6.1.4, Database Gateways.

FOCNET uses a requester/server model (one machine is the requester of services, the other the server of services) and is layered on top of standard hardware and software architectures and products. FOCNET has a layered service structure that features independent protocol subsystems, security interfaces, and a flexible client/server architecture.

FOCNET supports two cooperative processing models for the distribution of data access. These models allow sites to optimize distributed access within their specific hardware environment. These models are:

- **Remote Request Server.** In this model, a user at the requesting node issues a standard FOCUS request that is shipped to the serving node where the data resides and where all access, analysis, and formatting will occur. The formatted results, which may include the data, are returned to the requesting node.
- **Remote Database Server.** In this model, the data selection process occurs at the serving node, and the analysis and formatting occur at the requesting node. This allows (live) data to be accessed in real time at the source.

10.1.4 Graphical Development and Reporting Tools

Information Builders is also providing GUI-based tools. These tools include:

- **PM/FOCUS** is a graphical application development and decision support system running on OS/2. It provides a File Painter, Forms Painter, and Query Painter for building applications without writing code. Application components can be transformed into graphic objects and moved, manipulated, and activated with a point, click, and drag of a mouse. PM/FOCUS also takes advantage of EDA/SQL technology, which provides access to over 50 relational and non-relational data sources.
- **FOCUS/EIS for Windows** is a graphical business reporting system with FOCUS running on the micro and LAN. The micro-based DBMS can link to any database in the enterprise network. The object-oriented environment allows a user to point-and-click on any

area of the screen—text, image, or graphic—to navigate through the data to obtain additional information. FOCUS/EIS for Windows is EDA/SQL enabled as well.

- **FOCUS/DLL** (Dynamic Link Library) allows character-based PC/FOCUS, the micro version of FOCUS, to run in the Windows environment and take advantage of Dynamic Data Exchange and Windows-enhanced memory features.
- **FOCUS/DB Toolkit for Visual Basic** allows developers to use Visual Basic to create GUIs that can navigate and modify FOCUS data. Developers can build and distribute stand-alone or multiuser applications with no change for runtime versions.
- **EDA/COMPOSE** is a point-and-click Windows data extract product that takes advantage of EDA/SQL technology. It provides a simple Windows front end for generating the SQL statements that are used by EDA/SQL to access data. EDA/COMPOSE can also be used to download the retrieved data into micro application programs, such as spreadsheets, word processors, and databases.

10.2 INGRES

In addition to the INGRES Intelligent Database server (which is the foundation of the INGRES product line), Ingres, a wholly owned subsidiary of The ASK Group, offers two development products: INGRES/Windows4GL and INGRES/Vision.

The foundations for these two development products are INGRES/4GL and INGRES/SQL. INGRES/4GL is a fourth-generation language provided by Ingres that has been optimized to work with INGRES databases. INGRES/SQL is the version of SQL optimized for INGRES databases.

10.2.1 INGRES/Windows4GL

Designed to address the development of graphical applications, INGRES/Windows4GL is built around a portable GUI and an object-oriented 4GL.

INGRES/Windows4GL integrates SQL directly into INGRES/4GL syntax. INGRES/OpenSQL, a subset of INGRES/SQL, provides transparent access to data residing in the INGRES Intelligent Database. Using INGRES/Gateways, INGRES/OpenSQL can also access DB2, IMS, Rdb, RMS, and ALLBASE/SQL data. The various access methods supported by INGRES are illustrated in Figure 10.1.

Data Dictionary

INGRES/Windows4GL uses a data dictionary to store and track all components of an application, such as:

- Menu and dialog windows
- Database procedures
- INGRES/4GL procedures
- 3GL procedures
- User class definitions

The dictionary provides a check-out/check-in facility to ensure component integrity. The product also provides an interactive test environment.

Visual Editors

INGRES/Windows4GL offers visual editors that allow developers to paint objects onto a screen. Once the interface is defined, a developer can add INGRES/4GL code behind the screens to increase functionality. In many cases, the prototype evolves into the production version of the application.

The Frame Editor allows developers to:

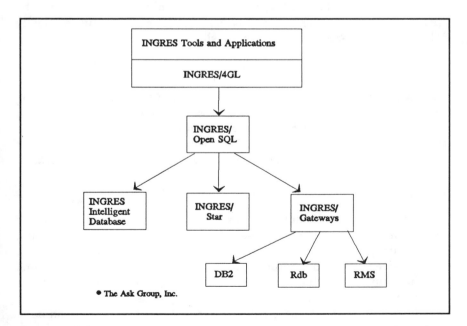

Figure 10.1 INGRES data access

- Interactively place visual elements, such as fields, buttons, boxes, and bitmaps, in a window
- Define menu windows or dialog boxes
- Combine elements into subforms and table fields for multiple record displays
- Access all visual elements through INGRES/4GL as variables
- Encapsulate INGRES/4GL definitions with any visual interface element

The Menu Editor allows developers to:

- Define pull-down and pull-across menus
- Define complex menus
- Include check boxes and radio buttons in menus to indicate status or modes
- Define menu text for international applications
- Encapsulate INGRES/4GL definitions with menu buttons

Developers are able to specify an application once and deploy the application immediately across a range of window managers and platforms, with no modifications to the code. All visual elements of the application will be supported by the target platform, which includes Windows, DECwindows, Motif, and, in the future, Presentation Manager, OpenLook, and Macintosh. When applications are ported, the interface elements, such as scroll bars and radio buttons, automatically take on the look-and-feel of the new window manager.

Interactive Debugger

An interactive, source-level debugger is integrated with the interpreter and development environment. Developers can monitor an application during execution via a source-level display and interactively specify break points or events. The debugger supports stacking, event manipulation, action lists, and object examination and manipulation.

Object Orientation

INGRES/Windows4GL supplies more than 60 system classes, such as frames, forms, menus, and fields, to simplify the task of designing and developing graphical applications. These system classes have attributes, such as size, font, and default value; and services, which are functions used to manipulate objects in the class. These attributes and services are inherited when a new instance of the object is created.

Class definitions are integrated into the development environment and the INGRES/4GL. Developers can benefit from the power of object-oriented programming (OOP) without requiring an understanding of OOP.

In GUI-based environments, an application is made up of event blocks. When an event takes place, the corresponding block of code is executed. INGRES/Windows4GL includes a wide range (numbering about 35) of event types common to graphical applications, such as resizing a window, clicking on a field, selecting a menu button, or receiving a message.

Developers build a series of event blocks behind each window of an application to provide the application's functionality. Developers can build generic event blocks that dynamically take on functionality based on messages to the application, data values, or user-initiated actions. These scripts can be in INGRES/4GL, INGRES/SQL, or 3GL code such as C. The INGRES/4GL code is compiled to an intermediate code, which is run by an interpreter on the target platform.

10.2.2 INGRES/Vision

INGRES/Vision integrates a 4GL and an advanced user interface to generate character-based applications. INGRES/Vision automatically generates all the code typically required for an application. Applications can be customized by adding INGRES/4GL code modules.

The two major components in the INGRES/Vision environment are:

- **Application Flow Diagram** is used to create the application structure visually. The screen layouts (called frames) for the application are created first. The developer then specifies the menu items that will be used to navigate through the frames. As each frame is created, the developer specifies its frame type (menu, update, or append) and which data tables it accesses.
- **Visual Query Editor** is used to define the data to be accessed and the operations that are to be available to the user within each frame.

Based on the frame and data specifications, INGRES/VISION automatically generates the application frames, including forms, menus, queries, and error-free 4GL processing logic.

10.3 NATURAL

NATURAL, from Software AG, is an open 4GL with interfaces that insulate NATURAL applications from the hardware and system software environment, making them independent of user interface, network, DBMS, and operating system. NATURAL evolved out of the IBM mainframe environment, which it continues to support, and is also available under Windows 3.x and OS/2 on micros. The support for GUIs includes all the features found in a particular GUI environment. It is not necessary to change the code to move from GUI to character environments.

NATURAL is available on IBM mainframes, Digital VAX, and UNIX platforms. A large number of DBMS products are supported, including ADABAS (also from Software AG), DB2, SQL/DS, DL/1, Rdb, RMS, and sequential files, as well as ADABAS and Oracle on micros. NATURAL handles the management of database cursors automatically.

To access SQL-based databases, NATURAL supports SAA (IBM's Systems Application Architecture) and ANSI-standard SQL. In such cases, instead of containing NATURAL data manipulation language, the NATURAL programs contain SQL commands which can be executed statically or dynamically, thus guaranteeing portability across heterogeneous database environments.

10.3.1 Integrated Software Architecture

NATURAL is the foundation of Software AG's open Integrated Software Architecture (ISA). The primary role of ISA is to separate the logical and physical aspects of application implementation, making the applications independent of the hardware and system software environment. As illustrated in Figure 10.2, ISA contains four main layers:

- **ISA Common User Access**, which ensures a consistent user interface whether the presentation is via a workstation or character terminal
- **ISA Common Application Solution**, which includes a set of standard applications that address office automation, document processing, and computer operations management
- **ISA Application Development**, which focuses on the tools required to support application development
- **ISA Information Resource and Database Management**, which manages database data and operating system data

Each level of ISA is connected using clearly defined interfaces, assuring upward compatibility.

For distributed environments, NATURAL supports program-to-program communication (cooperative processing), remote database access, and remote presentation (presentation of mainframe screens as GUIs).

10.3.2 NATURAL Development Environment

In addition to its 4GL, NATURAL offers a development environment with features such as intelligent editors, advanced window techniques, and graphic data display, all with a uniform user interface. The NATURAL development environment has the same functionality across all platforms.

Common User Access	Session Mangement		
	Network Connectivity		
	Data Communications Environment Support		
Common Application Solution	Query & Reporting	WHAT-IF Analysis	Graphic Reporting
	Office Functions	Interactive Training	Operations Center Solutions
Applicaton Development	Application Design (CASE)	4GL Development	Expert Systems Development
	Application Generation (CASE)	3GL Development	System Application Development
Information Resource Management	Active Processing Rules	Active Views	Active Documentation
Data Base Mangement and Distribution	Resource Administration	Repository	Migration Management
		Data Base Distribution	
		Complex Information Objects	
		Traditional, Relational, & System Data Base Management	
Multiple Systems Environments	MVS, VSE, CMS, BS2000, VMS, WANG-VS, MS-DOS, OS/2, UNIX		

Source: Software AG

Figure 10.2 Software AG's Integrated Software Architecture

The NATURAL development environment and NATURAL-developed applications can be integrated into existing environments. NATURAL can call or be called from 3GLs.

The NATURAL Engineering Series provides automated support for application development life cycle by combining CASE technology with NATURAL. The Series includes:

- NATURAL application development environment
- PREDICT, an active data dictionary
- NATURAL CONSTRUCT, an application generation system
- NATURAL ARCHITECT WORKSTATION, an analysis and design tool
- PREDICT CASE, an integrated CASE environment

10.3.3 PREDICT

PREDICT is an active data dictionary and repository. It is extensible and can support a variety of methodologies. PREDICT is implemented as an ADABAS database and stores metadata about an application as well as the specifications for relationships between the data.

PREDICT can store four types of objects. They are:

- **Data objects**, which describe data structures
- **Processing objects**, which describe the application logic and rules
- **User Defined objects**, which perform user-developed functions
- **Other objects**, such as development team information and keywords

PREDICT maintains references between objects and can be used to check for consistency, completeness, and correctness.

PREDICT supports all aspects of the life cycle. During the Analysis and Design Phase, PREDICT can be used to create data models and functional specifications and maintain project team information. During the Construction Phase, PREDICT can generate code and database schemas, provide consistency checks, and can be used to create test plans. During the Cutover Phase, PREDICT can forecast the impact of global changes.

Specifications generated with Information Engineering Facility (IEF) from Texas Instruments and Excelerator from INTERSOLV can be integrated into PREDICT via PREDICT GATEWAY. Data flow diagram and entity-relationship diagram information can be uploaded to and downloaded from PREDICT. Data uploaded to PREDICT via the GATEWAY is first placed in a Staging Dictionary, which is maintained separately from the PREDICT dictionary. Objects in the Staging

Dictionary may be browsed and selected for copying to PREDICT.

Data from other CASE products can be imported using PREDICT's migration formats.

10.3.4 NATURAL CONSTRUCT

NATURAL CONSTRUCT is an application generation tool for developing business applications in NATURAL. It supports prototyping and the development of complete business applications. NATURAL CONSTRUCT generates NATURAL applications and uses PREDICT to get information on the fields and views used.

NATURAL CONSTRUCT uses a model concept for its generation process. The standard models, called application templates, incorporate windowing, cursor selection, context-sensitive help, and error handling. Developers add their specifications to the templates via a menu-driven interface.

NATURAL CONSTRUCT extends the existing NATURAL facilities with generation-specific subsystems, which are:

- **Generation** subsystem generates the complete NATURAL source code for the application based on the templates.
- **Administration** subsystem is used to customize the templates.
- **Help Text** subsystem is used to create and maintain help messages for any field, program, or application generated with NATURAL CONSTRUCT.

10.3.5 NATURAL ARCHITECT WORKSTATION

NATURAL ARCHITECT WORKSTATION is an analysis and design tool for developing applications using NATURAL. This Macintosh-based tool uses diagrams to specify application requirements, which are then used by other NATURAL Engineering Series products to build applications based on NATURAL.

The ARCHITECT Data Dictionary is a repository for specifications developed during the analysis and design phases. Every diagram change is automatically reflected in all related diagrams. Dictionaries can be shared across projects or be dedicated to a particular project. A central data dictionary can be located on a host while a local data dictionary is maintained on the workstation.

The Design Compiler analyzes dictionary contents for completeness and consistency. Compiled output is stored in an object file for transfer to the host.

The following editors are provided:

- Data Flow Diagram Editor
- Entity-Relationship Editor
- Program Structure Diagram Editor
- Forms Editor

The NATURAL ARCHITECT Gateway consists of a workstation component and a host interface that reads object files generated by the Design Compiler and distributes the contents to the PREDICT dictionary and NATURAL program libraries. The ARCHITECT Gateway can also be used to download information to a local dictionary. The supported host platforms are IBM mainframes, Digital's VAX, and Wang VS.

10.3.6 PREDICT CASE

The PREDICT CASE methodology uses entity-relationship modeling, functional decomposition, and data flow analysis to support the planning and development of applications. The design of applications is supported through the following features:

- Specification of system configuration
- Documentation of integrity rules
- Generation of the database schema
- Specification and generation of executable NATURAL programs

Specifications developed with PREDICT CASE can generate entries for PREDICT.

PREDICT CASE contains three primary interfaces:

- The MAINTENANCE INTERFACE permits the inquiry and modification of single objects, their attributes, and associations.
- The NAVIGATOR breaks the structure of the development database into manageable subsets for fast navigation.
- The PREDICT CASE WORKSTATION provides similar facilities to the NAVIGATOR via a graphical micro-based interface.

10.3.7 ENTIRE Product Line

ENTIRE is a set of products that support distributed applications. Neither ADABAS or NATURAL are required by ENTIRE, although they do add value to it. ENTIRE is currently available for MVS only, but Software AG has plans to support many UNIX variants, Windows, and Macintosh platforms as well.

The major components of the ENTIRE product line are:

- ENTIRE Broker
- ENTIRE Network
- ENTIRE Connection
- ENTIRE APPC Gateway
- ENTIRE Transaction Propagator

ENTIRE Broker

ENTIRE Broker is the foundation of the product line. It uses object-oriented concepts to manage and access information concerning the location of services and the requirements to communicate with each service. ENTIRE Broker delivers requests for services from clients to servers and returns the results to the clients.

The major components of the ENTIRE Broker are:

- **Name Service**, which links the logical name of a server with its physical address
- **Information Service**, which stores information about a service's availability and requirements for communicating with it
- **Security**, which coordinates access to security systems used within the environment, such as IBM's RACF and Kerberos
- **Administration**, which is used to configure and control the ENTIRE Broker
- **Accounting**, which provides access to system accounting data
- **Monitoring**, which provides a console-based monitoring capability
- **Tracing**, which supports debugging and maintenance
- **Translation**, which provides translation services between different data formats

The ENTIRE Broker includes an API that allows developers to take advantage of the underlying communication protocols without having to deal with the details. The ENTIRE Broker API can be used to shield developers from RPCs, IBM's APPC conversational protocol, network versions of SQL, and queuing systems.

The ENTIRE Broker's messaging mechanism is asynchronous. A message is submitted to the broker with the expectation that the response will be sent later. In contrast, OMG's CORBA API uses an RPC in a deferred synchronous mode to support asynchronous communications. Using this technique, the RPC communications can be spread over time as opposed to being handled in a synchronous request-request manner. To support CORBA, Software AG intends to add support for the OMG's calls and CORBA's Interface Definition Language during the summer of 1993.

ENTIRE Network

The ENTIRE transport-independent networking software provides a common access point to transport services for the ENTIRE Broker. Nearly 40 different protocols and transports are supported, including APPC, TCP/IP, DECnet, AppleTalk, and Novell IPX. The software also supports protocol switching on the fly.

ENTIRE Connection

The ENTIRE Connection provides terminal emulation services, file transfer, and related services to applications.

ENTIRE APPC Gateway

The Gateway uses an API to link to LU6.2 commands to provide access to applications using IBM's APPC protocol.

ENTIRE Transaction Propagator

This component supports asynchronous distributed transactions across multiple databases. In asynchronous mode, distributed databases are linked together as masters and replicas. When an application requires an update of multiple databases, the master coordinates the update, but not synchronously or in real time. Consequently, the updates may occur at various times.

Asynchronous transactions are the opposite of transactions performed by distributed databases using two-phase commit protocols. In two-phase commit, a transaction updating multiple databases is processed as a single unit. Either all of the updates occur in real time or none of the updates occur.

10.4 Oracle

Oracle is a relational database management system (ORACLE) and a set of application development products from Oracle Corp. Individual products are integrated with the ORACLE DBMS through adherence to SQL. The entire Oracle product line is implemented on more than 100 hardware operating system platforms. One reason for such a great diversity of hardware platforms is that the underlying software is written in C.

Applications implemented in one Oracle hardware/software environment are transportable to other Oracle environments without modification. Using the SQL*Star facility, applications can also be integrated across operating platforms supported by the system.

10.4.1 Cooperative Development Environment

A set of tools called Cooperative Development Environment (CDE) is due for release late summer 1993. It is expected to provide tools for transforming character-based applications to GUI-based client/server applications that can run on a variety of workstations. The CDE architecture is illustrated in Figure 10.3.

The first CDE products will support Windows, followed by versions for Motif, OpenLook, Presentation Manager, and Macintosh. All the CDE products will generate Oracle PL/SQL code, which allows the code to be ported across many platforms.

The CDE toolset can be used with the Oracle Glue API and Microsoft's ODBC (Open Data Base Connectivity) interface. Such support eases the transition of Oracle character-terminal applications to client/server applications.

CDE tools use the Oracle Open Gateway Technology to access other relational databases, such as DB2 and Rdb, as well as legacy non-relational databases. This technology accesses non-Oracle databases using servers outfitted with database gateways. However, developers will have to write some database-specific interface code to access non-Oracle relational databases.

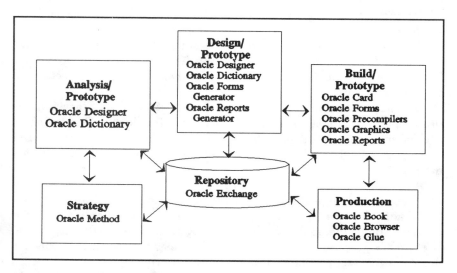

Figure 10.3 Oracle's Cooperative Development Environment

Tools for Production

Oracle Book, a new product, is an end-user tool for creating and viewing shared electronic documents that can include video, scanned images, and sound. It can also be used for context-sensitive online Help systems. It also provides hypertext links, supports word or phrase searches, and provides electronic annotation through text, image, and sound.

Oracle Browser is a database query product that provides a GUI front end to the enterprise databases. Oracle Browser gives users a graphical way to visualize data. Users can click to select conditions and connect related data sets by drawing lines between them. It uses a familiar worksheet interface.

Oracle Glue integrates third-party end user and developer tools into CDE. It provides access from Macintosh and Windows clients to services, such as E-mail and data access. CDE tools use Oracle Glue to access non-Oracle services.

Tools for Building Prototypes

Oracle Card is a development package that runs under Windows and on the Macintosh and can be used by end users or developers. It can be used to prototype, build, text, and deploy graphical client/server applications. Users point-and-click to navigate through data in an Oracle database. Oracle Card's strengths are query and browsing capabilities, as well as interactive data updating. The current version of Oracle Card (1.1) supports the Windows DDE (Dynamic Data Exchange) facility.

Applications are comprised of screens, known as *cards*, that collectively create a *stack*. Cards contain fields of text, paint and draw items, on-screen fields associated with database fields, and objects such as icons and buttons.

Developers use objects to create cards and stacks. The Stack Builder uses a point-and-click interface for the specification of Oracle tables and columns that define a card. The Table Builder allows users to build Oracle tables. The Query Builder allows users to define complex queries.

A run-time version of Oracle Card allows users to run Card applications but not change stacks that have been created by others.

Oracle Forms is used to develop forms-based applications for entering, querying, updating, and deleting data from the database. The WYSIWYG graphical design facility provides nonprocedural tools for developing custom forms, simple menus, and reports.

The applications can run on graphical and character- and block-mode platforms, automatically adhering to the native look-and-feel of each environment and adapting to the capabilities of each interface.

Because Oracle Forms is integrated with the Oracle repository, all rules and restrictions enforced by the dictionary entries are obeyed automatically within the forms. Procedures written in 3GLs, such as COBOL and C, can be linked to and called from Forms applications. Oracle Forms allows developers to generate two types of forms:

- **Automatic forms** are generated by answering a few menu options. Oracle Forms automatically generates all formatting attributes and error message handling. Automatic forms are useful for prototyping. They can also be customized at a later time.
- **Custom forms** allow a developer to change the attributes of the form and precisely define the contents and actions associated with a form. Field attributes that are different than those stored in the data dictionary can be specified for each field of the form.

Oracle Reports, a report writer adapted to support GUIs, uses a WYSIWYG report layout painter and a graphical data model facility to define report flow, relationships, and computations, as well as a preview option. Oracle Reports shares its code and PL/SQL language with Oracle Forms, Oracle Graphics, and the ORACLE7 cooperative server. The CDE modeling tools (Oracle Dictionary, Oracle Designer, and Oracle Report Generator) are integrated with Oracle Reports to provide additional code generation capabilities.

Oracle Graphics is a software layer that can import charts and other images into standard report forms. Oracle Graphics shares data and displays with Oracle Forms and Oracle Reports. Oracle Graphics shares its code and PL/SQL language with Oracle Forms, Oracle Reports, and the ORACLE7 cooperative server. Oracle Graphics can access a wide variety of data sources using Oracle Open Gateway Technology and by accessing popular file formats directly.

Oracle Call Interfaces and **Oracle Precompilers** can be used to link in-house and third-party applications to CDE.

Tools for Analysis and Designing Prototypes

Oracle Designer is a CASE product that supports most major development methodologies and is used to capture requirements and present system specifications. Oracle Designer includes entity-relationship, function hierarchy, matrix, and data flow diagrammers.

Oracle Designer ensures that developed models comply with rules in the Oracle repository. As models are developed, Oracle Designer automatically updates the shared, multiuser repository.

Oracle Designer supports simultaneous access by multiple developers and allows developers to work simultaneously on overlapping models.

Oracle Forms Generator and **Oracle Reports Generator** produce applications that are consistent with the rules stored in the Oracle repository during the analysis and design stages. Oracle Forms Generator automatically creates form and menu layouts and generates the code necessary for database access. System developers have control over application features such as layout and validation control. Oracle Reports Generator automatically creates reporting layouts and logic. Regardless of the development environment, generated applications can run on all Oracle platforms.

Oracle Dictionary provides the interface to the Oracle repository, allowing all the tools in the Oracle system modeling environment (Oracle Dictionary, Oracle Designer, and Oracle Reports Generator) to access the stored business rules. It incorporates features of the ORACLE7 cooperative server, such as data integrity, security management, and support for PL/SQL stored procedures and triggers. In addition, Oracle Dictionary can generate database schemas, with support for the ORACLE7 cooperative server, DB2, and ANSI-standard SQL Data Definition Language.

Repository

The Oracle repository centrally stores the definitions of an Oracle database and developed forms, screens, reports, and rules. The tables are automatically created and maintained as the database structure changes.

Since the dictionary is actually stored as Oracle tables, the contents of the data dictionary tables can be accessed by any of the Oracle end-user products for such tasks as reporting.

Oracle Exchange is used to exchange application modeling specifications between Oracle Dictionary and CASE products from third parties. It automatically consolidates the specifications.

10.5 PowerHouse

The PowerHouse application environment, illustrated in Figure 10.4, is comprised of integrated components that support the entire development life cycle. PowerHouse from Cognos Corp. provides a range of development products and offers the flexibility to manage data in its own DBMS or another DBMS.

The suite of PowerHouse products includes:

- **PowerHouse 4GL** can be used to build interactive screen-based transaction processing and volume processing applications.
- **PowerHouse Architect** automates the maintenance environment by generating documentation (systems, user, and prototype), prototypes and impact analysis information; and providing a screen-driven environment that supports creating and maintaining the dictionary.
- **PowerDesigner** is an analysis and design tool.
- **PowerHouse Windows** allows Windows workstations to act as clients with host applications running on HP MPE/iX and UNIX servers.
- **PowerHouse PC** allows developers to create stand-alone micro applications or work on an application development workbench for midrange machines. PowerHouse PC applications can communicate with PowerHouse host applications and are portable to PowerHouse 4GL on midrange machines.

10.5.1 PowerHouse 4GL

PowerHouse 4GL can be used to build complete interactive applications without reverting to 3GL coding. Nonprocedural syntax can be used to create applications quickly. PowerHouse 4GL will generate defaults based on information stored in the central dictionary and logic for essential functions, such as data integrity control and concurrency checks.

Simple applications can normally be constructed entirely with high-level constructs. More complex tasks can be handled with the more powerful procedural code. PowerHouse 4GL supports conditional prompting, automatic rollback of uncommitted transactions, and a concurrency processing mode.

Menus and data entry screens are easily created, along with the

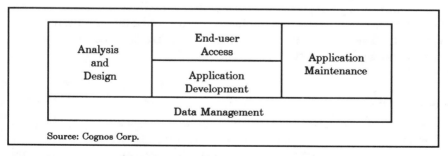

Figure 10.4 PowerHouse application environment

program code needed to link them into a hierarchy that meets the application specifications.

Reporting features include a global join facility, which can join a number of different databases, even if they are formatted differently.

The PowerHouse volume transaction processing module can be used as an interactive *ad hoc* means of editing data, moving data between files of different types, performing global updates, or maintaining files. It can also be used to define regular production batch runs.

Supporting all these features is an intelligent data dictionary which serves as the central storage of data definitions. By using data entity abstractions, known as elements, designers specify the characteristics of a data entity once. The data dictionary is maintained with a set of interactive tools, which include the ability to generate physical files based on the dictionary definitions and online referencing of dictionary definitions.

PowerHouse products store common code for each component as a separate image. The common code is preloaded to optimize resources. Application-specific code is compiled for fast loading and execution.

10.5.2 PowerDesigner

Running under OS/2, PowerDesigner uses a rules-based database and graphical techniques to aid developers in designing applications. PowerDesigner supports a multiwindowed environment. Designers can implement data and process views at logical, physical, and detail levels.

The logical view is created using entity relationship modeling and data flow diagramming techniques. The models can be validated using Normalization and Entity Life History Analysis reports.

A default physical design is created automatically by PowerDesigner during the creation of the logical model. The physical design can then be optimized and refined using Database Design Diagrams, Program Data Flow Diagrams, and Program Call Hierarchy and Access Maps.

When the physical design is complete, PowerDesigner generates an application prototype which includes all appropriate data definitions, screen transactions, reports, volume processing transactions (batch), and menu screens for the target platform.

10.5.3 PowerHouse Architect

PowerHouse Architect can produce cross-reference and application documentation, including full system and user documentation. PowerHouse Architect can also be used to generate a complete and functional prototype application that can be used for testing, generating input test data into the application, and user review.

10.6 PROGRESS

PROGRESS, from Progress Software Corp., provides an application development environment that integrates a 4GL, a client/server relational DBMS, a set of development and end-user tools, and gateway technology. The PROGRESS DBMS is not required for PROGRESS applications; an SQL-based DBMS can be used instead. The platforms supported by PROGRESS are shown in Figure 10.5.

An extended set of tools can be used to expedite the development process. These tools are:

- **FAST TRACK** is a menu-driven, nonprocedural application builder.
- **Results** provides end-user query and reporting capabilities.

However, PROGRESS does not have GUI building capabilities. Interfaces to PROGRESS applications are screens with menu choices. The product can run in Windows, OS/2, and Motif environments but does not produce GUI screens.

PROGRESS	End-User Access		FAST TRACK		CASE Bridges		
	4GL	SQL	Editor	Application Library			
	Data Dictionary/Application Knowledge Base						
User Interfaces	ASCII Terminals	Windows	X Windows		Motif	Presentation Manager	
Databases	PROGRESS	ORACLE	RMS	Rdb	C-ISAM	CT-ISAM	
Networks	TCP/IP	NetBIOS	DECnet	SPX/IPX	OSI		
Operating System	UNIX	DOS	VMS	OS/2	CTOS	OS/400	
Hardware	M680x0	80x86	RISC	VAX	88000	SPARC	AS/400

Source: Progress Software Corp.

Figure 10.5 PROGRESS-supported platforms and features

10.6.1 PROGRESS ADE

The Progress Application Development Environment (ADE) is comprised of the following elements:

- The **PROGRESS 4GL** consists of high-level constructs to support rapid prototyping and low-level modifiers to provide detail control for the application. PROGRESS has ANSI-standard SQL integrated into the 4GL and both can be used in the same procedure. Code written in the PROGRESS 4GL is 100 percent portable among PROGRESS-supported platforms.

- The **Data Dictionary**, the central storage location of all the application's defaults and definitions, provides a centrally managed library of commonly used procedures, messages, and defaults. When used over a network, the Data Dictionary supports location independence by providing each client with its own data dictionary.

- The **PROGRESS Help System** provides full-screen descriptions of errors and 4GL syntax diagrams. Features include context-sensitive help, an online facility that includes explanations for compilation errors, and an online Quick Reference Manual.

- The **Procedure Editor and Compiler** support the creation of clean blocks of code. The Procedure Editor supplies an integrated edit, compile, and test loop. The Editor displays all error messages, provides direct access to the help system and the data dictionary, and provides smooth integration to the PROGRESS Compiler for syntax checking and unit testing.

- The **PROGRESS relational DBMS** (RDBMS) is a client/server database engine that supports distributed processing across a range of operating systems, hardware platforms, network protocols, and multivendor databases. It features roll-forward/roll-back recovery, record-locking controls, online backups, two-phase commit, and a multithreaded, multiserver architecture. The PROGRESS RDBMS allows an application to communicate with any PROGRESS database and many other database managers in a networked environment. A PROGRESS 4GL session can dynamically connect or disconnect multiple databases simultaneously.

10.6.2 FAST TRACK

Using FAST TRACK, developers can quickly create character-based screens, build menus and reports, and compose inquires. FAST TRACK generates PROGRESS 4GL code so applications are not machine-dependent. It is comprised of four modules:

■ **Menu Editor** is used to define the application choices and the associated actions to be performed with each choice. The Menu Editor can generate a menu tree to illustrate the complete structure of an application.

■ **Screen Painter** uses a WYSIWYG approach to screen and form design. Objects can be moved within a form and copied between forms. The screens and forms can be a collection of fields from tables, independent variables, or free-form text. Created forms can be used with PROGRESS procedures, FAST TRACK, or Query-By-Form Generator. These screens are not GUI-based; they have no icons, buttons, or sizable windows.

■ **Query-By-Form Generator** is used to build procedures to retrieve, modify, add, or delete information from the database. It can build a default form or use a form designed with Screen Painter.

■ **Report Writer** automates the production of standard report types. For more complex report generation, developers can include 4GL logic statements.

10.6.3 Results

Using simple pull-down menus, Results gives users an easy interface to view, enter, and maintain database information. Users can perform *ad hoc* queries and build special reports quickly. System administrators still retain full control over the user's ability to access and manipulate data. Results also includes an application programming interface (API) to integrate it into custom systems.

11

Client/Server Products for Distributed Environments

Client/server development products support developers in designing and generating GUI-based client/server and distributed applications. These products use a GUI front end and minimize the requirement for detailed knowledge about GUIs, networks, and relational databases.

These products were designed specifically for developing applications in client/server environments. As such, they are able to generate GUI-code and access multiple relational DBMSs using SQL. They can generate application logic code in either their proprietary scripting language or calls to C. The development tools that can generate GUI-code and provide their own 4GL are referred to as GUI/4GL products. Many of these development products support RPCs (remote procedure calls), stored procedures and triggers, and network gateways.

These development products start with an installed database schema. Developers use the defaults stored in the data dictionary of the DBMS to specify the GUI screens. Events are then identified and code or actions specified for each event.

These tools provide a prototyping-like environment for application development. Specifications are refined as users work with the prototype version of the application.

Client/server development tools can be used to build transaction-based applications but do not provide the same level of robustness achieved by applications coded in a 3GL. They are especially suited for informational applications and low-volume transactional applications that are not mission-critical. (See Section 1.8.1)

11.1 EASEL Workbench

EASEL Workbench from Easel Corp. is an evolution of the EASEL product that is used to build front-end interfaces for existing 3270/5250 host applications. An OS/2 development platform product, EASEL Workbench can generate CUA-compliant client/server applications for DOS, Windows, and OS/2 environments and provides portability between OS/2 and Windows.

EASEL Workbench provides dynamic SQL access to SQL Server, DB2/2, Oracle, and Micro Decisionware's DB2 Gateway, as well as DB2, SQL/400, and SQL/DS via their DDCS (Data Definition Control Support) facility. Built-in EDA/SQL support provides access to more than 45 relational and nonrelational databases. EDA/SQL, a gateway product from Information Builders, Inc., and DB2 Gateway are discussed in Section 6.1.4, Database Gateways.

EASEL-developed applications are made up of objects, events, and responses. The supported object types are the visual and interactive components of an application. The supported object types are:

- Windows (called regions)
- Keys
- Dialog boxes
- Dialog controls

EASEL Workbench is object-based but not object-oriented. EASEL Workbench is based on the earlier EASEL product—in fact, it is written in the EASEL language—and its procedure engine. In 1993, to address the market's need for object-oriented development products, Easel Corp. purchased Enfin Software Corp., whose ENFIN product is an excellent state-of-the-art object-oriented development tool. ENFIN is discussed in Section 11.3.

All functions provided by EASEL Workbench are accessible through a menu in the main Workbench window. These functions are:

- **Workbench Project** identifies the EASEL source code for an application, the most recently compiled version of the program, information about the state of the program, and the program's target platform.
- **Layout Editor** creates the application objects.
- **Drawing Editor** creates images using vector graphics.
- **Attribute Editor** specifies the attributes of an object.
- **Text Editor** creates and edits application logic using text-form objects and responses.
- **WYSIWYG Menu Editor** creates and edits pull-down menus without having to use the Text Editor, and generates menu code.

- **Incremental Compiler** compiles only the modified source code for the application.
- **Program Execution Controls** control the execution of the application, such as start, pause, abort, continue, and restart, within EASEL Workbench.
- **Interactive Debugger** debugs the operation of a program within the EASEL Workbench environment and includes source-level debugging, trace facilities, and a stack window.
- **Parts Catalog** is used to retrieve objects and responses from a central repository of all objects and responses.
- **Project View** groups related objects and responses into logical views to promote code sharing.

High-level support is provided for a variety of host protocols, including 3270/5250, VT100, and asynchronous. Using CommBuilder, developers can create the communications portion of an application using point-and-click techniques to interact with a 3270 host screen display. CommBuilder is a visual programming tool that automates the development of 3270 communication logic for OS/2, Windows, and DOS-based EASEL applications. Peer-to-peer capabilities are provided through APPC and DDE support.

As illustrated in Figure 11.1, EASEL Workbench generates EASEL source code which is compiled by platform-specific production systems, EASEL/WIN, EASEL/2, and EASEL/DOS, for Windows, OS/2, and DOS, respectively. Each production system optimizes the GUI capabilities of the platform, such as windows; dialog boxes; and bitmap, vector, and business graphics. Support for Windows NT will be provided soon after its release.

EASEL Workbench SQL Edition, which includes all the Workbench development tools in addition to SQL database support, can be used to build advanced SQL-based database-access applications. It is available for OS/2 and Windows clients.

11.1.1 EASEL Transaction Server Toolkit

With the EASEL Transaction Server Toolkit (ETS Toolkit), EASEL Workbench developers can create an OS/2-based transaction server with high-speed static access to all Systems Application Architecture (SAA) databases—DB2/2, DB2, SQL/DS, and SQL/400. Using a graphical interface, developers can create entire SQL transactions without knowing SQL or transaction processing. Functionality can be placed on either the server or the client workstation.

With the ETS Toolkit, transaction management is centralized: all

SQL code and related transactions are maintained in the ETS server's dynamic link libraries (DLLs). A single request and reply is sent between the EASEL client application and the EASEL Transaction Server DLL. Complex transactions with multiple SQL statements are executed completely on the server.

All transactions are processed asynchronously, allowing EASEL applications to continue normal operations while transactions are executing. When the transaction is complete, an EASEL event is triggered and the EASEL application begins to fetch the results either by row or in bulk.

11.1.2 Client/Server Architecture Options

Easel Corp. has bundled EASEL Workbench's optional capabilities into groups that support particular client/server environments. These

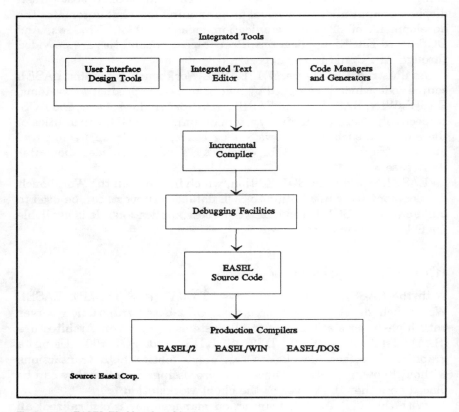

Figure 11.1 EASEL Workbench architecture

client/server architecture options are:

- The **Distributed Presentation** option supports the generation of GUI front ends to existing legacy applications. It includes the CommBuilder visual communications code generator and language support for 3270/5250 and VT100 protocols.
- The **Transaction Server** option supports transaction- and data-intensive applications under OS/2 and Windows. It includes the ETS Toolkit. For OS/2 platforms, it also includes the CICS OS/2 interface.
- The **Peer** option is used to create cooperative OS/2 applications. It includes language support for APPC/LU6.2 communications.

11.2 Ellipse

Ellipse, from Cooperative Solutions, Inc., was developed specifically for distributed client/server online transaction processing applications. Much of the mainframe system software necessary to maintain the integrity of online transaction processing (OLTP) applications is not yet supported by conventional client/server software. To compensate for this deficiency, Ellipse includes the system-level software required to support distributed OLTP applications in client/server environments. Cooperative Solutions refers to these applications as client/server transaction-processing (CSTP) applications.

Ellipse-generated application code automatically includes error handling and process-to-process communication. Ellipse applications can handle transactions that are distributed across multiple LANs and databases. Ellipse's features are listed in Figure 11.2.

Ellipse currently supports Microsoft Windows 3.x and OS/2 Presentation Manager clients on OS/2 or UNIX-based servers. Support for Sun platforms and VMS is due in late 1993.

Developers use Ellipse after a database schema has been prepared and business transactions defined. The application is then broken into activities, which are sets of transactions that share a common user interface. Activities (also referred to as objects) contain the definitions of data types, variables, and constants used by the activity and the definitions for reports and procedures for data manipulation or calculations. All specifications and definitions are stored in an active LAN-based repository.

Applications developed with Ellipse include the following CSTP requirements automatically—no programming effort is required:

- Application partitioning

- Distributed transaction management
- Communications between clients and servers
- Support for multiple DBMSs
- Heterogeneous DBMS transactions

The Ellipse solution to developing distributed transaction processing applications incorporates the Ellipse Development Environment (Ellipse/DE) and the Ellipse Production System (Ellipse/PS) with application life cycle management facilities. Ellipse adheres to current standards to support open systems architectures.

11.2.1 Ellipse Development Environment

Ellipse/DE provides an object-based, repository-based development

---

Ellipse Application

Ellipse Production System

OLTP Services
- Integrity
- Availability
- Security
- Scalability
- Performance
- Concurrency
- Manageability

CSTP Services
- Distributed transaction management
- Multiple database access
- Set-oriented transactions
- Application partitioning
- Graphical user interface
- National languages

Standards-Based Services

Presentation Services
- Presentation Manager
- Windows 3.x

Operating Systems
- OS/2
- DOS
- UNIX

Communications Services
- Named Pipes
- TCP/IP
- Novell

SQL DBMSs
- SQL Server
- DB2/2
- Oracle
- Sybase
- DB2 (via gateways)

Networks
- LAN Manager
- NetWare
- LAN Server
- Vines

Source: Cooperative Solutions, Inc.

Figure 11.2 Ellipse features

environment for defining the activities and their components. It supports team development, testing, and maintenance of distributed applications.

Ellipse/DE provides the following editors:

- An **activity overview editor** illustrates the overall structure of an activity, such as a user interface for initiating transactions, procedures that execute the transactions, and working storage for storing data temporarily.
- A WYSIWYG **forms editor** facilitates the definition of GUI-based interfaces.
- A **template-based procedure editor** is used to specify procedure statements selected from a pull-down menu. Using a template for the statement, the developer fills in the blanks to specify the complete procedure statement. Semantic checking is performed immediately.

Developers build applications using familiar objects such as forms, procedures, and reports. Developers can produce reusable application components, such as GUIs, data elements, and application logic.

Using a feature called Open Transaction, developers can extend the capabilities of Ellipse by adding custom functions, such as special computations and access to non-SQL data, existing mainframe gateways, and specialized hardware devices.

Ellipse/DE includes an integrated, version control and configuration management system. Developers use configurations as manageable views of large volumes of objects. Version control manages automatic version creation and change distribution.

After the activities and related interfaces of the application are defined, the application can be generated and installed on a LAN. As part of the installation process, the installer provides the following information:

- Configuration information, such as addresses for databases and external procedures and locations of printers
- Description of the production environment, such as operating system(s), number of servers, types of DBMSs, and presentation services.

Individual procedures can be coded to execute on the client or the server. The installer can specify where specific application activities, such as stored procedures or reports, will execute on the network. Alternatively, locations can be assigned by Ellipse using an algorithm, designed to reduce network overhead and optimize performance.

Among the headaches that developers of client/server applications (or any distributed applications) have is installation of the same application software on a variety of platforms—different presentation services, operating systems, LAN technologies, and DBMSs. Added to this problem is the lack of standard system services for client/server applications. Even if the application functioned exactly the same way in each installation, customized versions of the application (containing system-level code) would have to be created and maintained.

Using Ellipse, developers are not concerned with the topology of the LAN or the partitioning of the application objects until the application is installed. At that time, the developer specifies the topology for the individual environments and Ellipse generates the code required for each environment.

Consequently, the same application can be deployed at hundreds of different sites, each site possibly configured differently, without customizing application code. This facilitates maintenance, version control, and software integrity, not to mention decreased development time.

11.2.2 Ellipse Production System

Ellipse Production System (Ellipse/PS) provides an environment for deploying distributed applications. Ellipse/PS is installed on both the clients and the servers. Ellipse/PS extends the security supported by the DBMS, LAN, and operating system.

At runtime, Ellipse creates an application process on each server and a process on each client, based on their configurations. The application processes on the servers communicate with the client processes. As transaction volume increases, more application server processes are added automatically. The end-to-end control provided by these processes allows Ellipse to handle application error recovery and transaction management in the distributed environment. To accomplish this, Cooperative Solutions developed Application Procedure Call, its own remote procedure call (RPC).

Ellipse/PS partitions applications intelligently, dynamically, and transparently. Individual portions of an application can be processed on either the client or server, thus reducing network overhead and optimizing performance. Ellipse/PS also provides scalability, insuring that server resources are not dedicated to a particular client but shared among clients.

Ellipse/PS transforms the SQL statements in an Ellipse application to an equivalent set of statements, optimized for the target DBMS. Ellipse can also be used to transform SQL statements into equivalent stored procedures for databases that support stored procedures.

Ellipse/PS includes a transaction manager that works with the DBMSs in the enterprise network. The two major features of the Ellipse transaction manager are:

- It is designed to handle transactions that involve multiple databases and processes that are distributed between client and server.
- It handles aborted transactions using the rollback and recovery mechanisms used by a variety of DBMSs.

The Ellipse transaction manager uses the *optimistic* database concurrency control model. Database records are not locked while data is in use at the client; they are locked only during retrieval and update. Before a record is updated, Ellipse rereads the data to determine if it has been changed. If no change occurred, the update proceeds. If a change did occur between retrieval and update, an exception error is transmitted to the application so the application can determine how to proceed.

The Ellipse transaction manager uses a two-phase commit protocol to support distributed transaction management, synchronizing the state of the client and server applications to the state of all the database servers (which may be on different nodes and may be different DBMSs) participating in the transaction.

Ellipse/PS provides a visual working table. Users can scroll through and potentially update sets of data retrieved from the database and displayed in this two-dimensional tabular area.

The production environment provided by Ellipse/PS provides for online, real-time installation of upgrades or new applications without taking the application system off line. System administrators can centrally manage applications and system resources with all application installation and version control occurring on the server. Facilities for creating user accounts and controlling access to applications for each user are also provided. Access in Ellipse applications can be controlled at the application level, individual transaction level, and for particular fields on forms. Security provided by Ellipse is in addition to existing security mechanisms on the server.

11.3 ENFIN

ENFIN from Easel Corp. provides an object-oriented, visual application development environment for Windows and OS/2 operating platforms. Its open architecture allows ENFIN-developed applications, which are modular and reusable, to integrate with external applications, including 3GL-based applications.

ENFIN is based on Smalltalk, which competes with C++ as the object-oriented programming language (OOP) of choice within businesses. Despite all the focus on object-oriented technology, most businesses are just beginning to explore the technology—how to define their business processes as classes of objects and the cultural change required by OOPs. It is too early to tell when (and if) there will be widespread acceptance of object-oriented technology.

Access is provided to a variety of LAN- and host-based DBMSs, including SQL Server, Oracle, SQLBase, DB2/2, EDA/SQL, Rdb, dBASE, and DB2, SQL/400, and SQL/DS via DDCS. ENFIN supports scrollable cursors, database cursors, and embedded SQL, even if the accessed database does not natively support those features. A built-in local database permits DBMS-independent development work.

ENFIN provides full support for the APPC/LU6.2 and EHLLAPI protocols in mainframe environments. In addition, it can connect to a DB2 database through IBM's DRDA (Distributed Relational Database Architecture, which is discussed in Section 6.5, Distributed Database Standards) and Micro Decisionware's gateways (which are discussed in Section 6.1.4, Database Gateways).

ENFIN incorporates all the standard CUA '91 constructs as well as notebooks, tables, sliders, and business graphics. With ENFIN's open architecture, other GUI controls and language constructs can be added to the environment. Support is also provided for Dynamic Data Exchange (DDE), Object Linking and Embedding (OLE), and direct access to dynamic link libraries (DLLs).

11.3.1 Object-Oriented Features

The ENFIN kernel, which is a portable Smalltalk engine, consists of the following components:

- **Object management system**, which is a pure object-oriented system with support for inheritance, polymorphism, encapsulation, and late binding
- **Incremental compiler**, which supports continuous interactive development
- **Optimized interpreter**
- **Set of classes**, which can be used by the developer as is, or can be broken into subclasses

The object-oriented programming tools include:

- **Workspace Editor**, used to test individual methods and/or parts of a program

- **Method Editor,** used to create methods and their assignments to objects
- **Transcript Window,** where debugging output and error messages are displayed

11.3.2 ENFIN Development Tools

ENFIN includes a WYSIWYG GUI design environment, which uses a point-and-click method for developing interfaces and linking them to databases, financial modeling, and other controls. A WYSIWYG report writer can mix text and graphics and allows reports to be previewed. A financial modeling facility supports the interactive creation of models for applications.

Additional tools for building GUIs include:

- **Screen Layout Tool.** An object is dragged from a palette of visual object templates and positioned in an interface.
- **Data Link Tool.** A visual object is selected and its linkage to a table, an SQL query, a financial model, or an instance variable of an object is defined interactively.
- **Action Definition Tool.** Actions are defined as methods with the Method Editor.

As illustrated in Figure 11.3, ENFIN also provides a variety of tools to support the development of other components of an application and the programming and testing phases of application development.

After the specifications are complete, the ENFIN Application Generator generates a compiled, completely portable application ready for unlimited distribution. Unlike other client/server development products, there are no end-user fees charged for the deployment of ENFIN applications.

11.3.3 ENFIN Development Environments

ENFIN/3 is a 32-bit development environment for IBM's OS/2 2.x. ENFIN/3 support is planned for Microsoft's Windows NT and versions of UNIX. Applications developed with ENFIN/3 can also be deployed under ENFIN/2.

ENFIN/2 is a 16-bit development environment for Windows and OS/2 and offers all the functionality of ENFIN/3. Applications developed with ENFIN/2 can also be deployed under ENFIN/3.

ENFIN SQL Edition includes all development tools as well as SQL database support. It is available in OS/2 2.x and Windows versions.

Category	Tool	Use
Design	**Designer**	Uses a 4GL to create and edit interfaces
Database	**Database Notebook**	Provides a consistent interface to all databases accessible by ENFIN
	Model Builder	Provides a point-and-click interface to build and maintain models
	Report Builder	Allows users to build, maintain, and run reports from database tables or SQL queries
	SQL Editor	Provides a point-and-click interface for specifying SQL queries
Programming & Debugging	**Class Browser**	Provides an overview of the classes and their available methods to the developer
	Class Information Generator	Generates the appropriate operating system help file for the specified classes
	Inspector	Displays instance data for any object in the application
	Workspace	Allows developers to execute Smalltalk code within the development environment
	System Transcript	Displays system messages and errors
	Debug with Trace Facilities	Provides a Trace window for following the path a message took, and can be run in single-step mode
	Profiler	Provides monitoring facilities for performance tuning
	Program Generator	Generates stand-alone applications that can be executed without the development environment

Source: Easel Corp.

Figure 11.3 ENFIN development tools

11.4 ObjectView

ObjectView from KnowledgeWare, Inc. provides an object-oriented development tool for creating Windows and OS/2 Presentation Manager applications. ObjectView has direct support for accessing relational databases, including Microsoft SQL Server, SYBASE, Teradata, Oracle, INFORMIX, and INGRES. ObjectView also supports the major database interfaces, such as Microsoft's ODBC, Pioneer Software's Q+E, and Information Builders' EDA/SQL, as well as the leading gateways, such as Micro Decisionware, Oracle, and Sybase.

ObjectView offers full Dynamic Data Exchange (DDE) protocol and OLE support, as well as Multiple Document Interface support.

KnowledgeWare added ObjectView to its product line when it purchased MATESYS Corp. in March 1993. KnowledgeWare plans to integrate ObjectView and ADW (Application Development Workbench, KnowledgeWare's CASE product which is discussed in Section 12.1) in two phases.

The first phase, expected by September 1993, will allow developers to import Data Definition Language information from ADW/Design Workstation to ObjectView. Developers can model and change SQL databases supported by ObjectView, such as Oracle and Sybase, via ADW tools. The second phase, expected by the end of 1993, will expand the link to be bidirectional with both ADW/Design and ADW/Analysis workstations.

ObjectView offers three development modes: visual programming, ObjectView Basic, or C and C++ languages. The ObjectView Basic language is very similar to Microsoft QuickBasic. The ObjectView proprietary functions can be embedded in application script files.

ObjectView's user interface is graphics- and object-oriented. Icons are used for each object. Drop-and-drag functions are supported. A form-based Query by Example feature is incorporated into the product.

Developers begin by specifying screens using default forms or by painting screens using the ObjectView Editor. Objects are painted using a tool palette, which includes tools such as push buttons, background text, multiline text boxes, and pulldown menus. Objects can be placed on the screen, moved, and sized.

Developers can define an unlimited number of nested windows. Windows can be traversed using ObjectView's hypertext-like navigation capabilities.

Actions are defined for specific objects. Objects pass messages to one another to initiate an action. A set of preprogrammed objects and their methods is available. Developers can extend the features of the product with procedural language code, either ObjectView Basic or C.

A method (code routine) is associated with the object in its dialog box via script in ObjectView Basic, C, or C++, by using the built-in high-level functions, or a combination of both. Scripts can also use the library of commands and functions available in ObjectView.

A report writer is used to paint reports which are presented in WYSIWYG format. ObjectView supports scalable fonts, bitmap or Windows Metafile graphics, and conditional breaks.

In addition, ObjectView includes the following features:

- A panel object provides built-in, data-aware access to data models and SQL databases.
- A spreadsheet object with powerful spreadsheet functions can be used to combine and present data.
- There is built-in support for eleven types of business graphs.
- The product includes an interactive code debugger and trace facilities.

ObjectView can also be used to generate a default application using point-and-click operations. Default forms and screens are created from the database definitions.

ObjectView run-time versions are created after the screens and scripts have been created. The accompanying Player product is used to generate and execute application run-time files.

11.4.1 Object Manager

Object Manager, an object librarian, is an ObjectView application that is used to store all "standard" objects for an application. Objects stored in the Object Manager can be used (pasted) in other screens.

The next version of ObjectView, expected by late 1993, will include an object repository, which will support inheritance at the object level, and check-out/check-in version control.

11.5 PowerBuilder

PowerBuilder from Powersoft Corp. combines object orientation with GUI, 4GL, and CASE techniques to provide a client/server development environment for building production-quality distributed applications.

PowerBuilder can be used to build multiuser, transaction-oriented, high volume database applications that take full advantage of a GUI and the installed DBMS. Applications can be built to use particular features of a particular DBMS or can be independent of the target DBMS. PowerBuilder can also be used to create *ad hoc* query and reporting applications.

The characteristics Powersoft uses to describe the PowerBuilder tools are explained in Figure 11.4.

The software was written for and extensively uses the Windows environment. Currently, there is no support for the Macintosh, UNIX, or OS/2, although Powersoft is moving toward support for the Macintosh and UNIX environments.

Complete support is provided for the Windows interfaces:

- **DDE** (Dynamic Data Exchange) for communication with other Windows applications, both sending and receiving
- **OLE** (Object Linking and Embedding) for launching other Windows applications, performing processing within the other application, and returning results and control to PowerBuilder

SQL Smart	▪ Supports a number of relational DBMSs on a variety of hardware and network systems ▪ Minimizes code requirements through the use of DataWindow objects, which are intelligent SQL objects for manipulating data from SQL databases ▪ Supports embedded SQL ▪ Provides a point-and-click environment for database administration
Object Easy	▪ Provides the benefits of object orientation without the complexities of object-oriented programming ▪ Allows custom user objects to be created from other objects ▪ Allows an object to be used in an unlimited number of windows and applications
Windows Rich	▪ Provides complete support for Windows objects, events, functions, communications, and windowing styles ▪ Does not require knowledge of Windows SDK to create GUI applications ▪ Allows applications to use the Windows Help engine to provide context-sensitive help to users
MIS Friendly	▪ Offers a robust set of painters and tools for managing the development process ▪ Supports development by project teams ▪ Allows application objects to be shared among project team members

Source: Powersoft Corp.

Figure 11.4 PowerBuilder characteristics

- **DLLs** (dynamic link libraries) for calling external routines

PowerBuilder applications provide transparent access to several back-end databases—Oracle Server, SQL Server, SQLBase, XDB, INFORMIX, DB2/2, INGRES, and ALLBASE/SQL. DB2 can be accessed using Micro Decisionware's DB2 Gateway.

One of PowerBuilder's unique features is its DataWindow object. This intelligent SQL object can manipulate data from a relational database, without requiring user-coded SQL commands, and manages database interaction and manipulation directly. DataWindows objects can be created and modified dynamically during an application's execution.

PowerBuilder creates an extended attribute repository in the DBMS that stores default definitions for data validation rules, display formats, column headers and labels, initial values, and type fonts and styles. These defaults can be overridden.

After development is complete, an application run-time file is prepared and delivered to the users together with a run-time version of PowerBuilder. The file is an .EXE file which contains all the application's objects, as well as other resources such as icons, cursors, and bitmaps. The application can be launched via the File Run command in the Windows Program Manager or File Manager, double-clicking on the application's icon within Program Manager, or at the DOS prompt by typing "WIN [application-name]".

PowerBuilder 3.0, currently in beta test, includes the following new features:

- A built-in relational database engine for creating stand-alone applications or for working on server-based application without accessing the server
- Dynamic creation of custom user objects
- Report painter
- Support for print preview and print preview zoom
- Query painter
- Support for placement of Bitmap or graph objects in reports
- Ability to call PowerView, the new end-user reporting tool discussed below, from within a PowerBuilder application
- Configurable toolbars
- An open API to the library management system for importing PowerBuilder objects from front-end modeling and design tools and export them to software distribution systems
- An enhanced Application painter which allows developers to view an entire application object hierarchy graphically

In concert with PowerBuilder 3.0, Powersoft is releasing two new graphical development products:

- **PowerMaker,** a Windows-based development tool which is built around a query, report, and form-based development metaphor
- **PowerViewer,** a tool that is similar to PowerMaker but more appropriate for end users and is built around a query and reporting metaphor

PowerSoft is also expected to unveil a scaled-down version of PowerBuilder aimed at end users by the end of 1993. The slimmed down product will compete against micro database and development frameworks, such as Microsoft's ACCESS.

11.5.1 Application Objects

Application objects respond to events by executing PowerScript routines that define the function(s) to be performed. PowerScript is the 4GL provided with PowerBuilder.

PowerBuilder applications consist of four major types of objects:

- **Windows,** application windows created in the Window Painter
- **User objects,** custom user objects
- **DataWindows,** intelligent SQL objects that manipulate data
- **Menus,** independent objects created in the Menu Painter

PowerBuilder supports *inheritance*, which allows subclasses to inherit attributes or services by default, and *reuse*, which allows an object to be used more than once in an application and by more than one application. These characteristics of objects speed up development effort and provide consistency within an application and among applications in the organization.

Developers specify and control information about an object, such as:

- **Attributes,** such as size, position, current status, colors, text fonts and sizes, and tab sequence
- **Events,** such as the Windows Clicked and Modified events, as well as user events within user objects
- **Functions,** which define the application behavior and transaction logic

Scripts (code) are written for specific object/event or control/event relationships. Attributes can be referenced and modified from within PowerScript routines. Functions can be either PowerBuilder built-in functions or user-defined functions.

Window Objects

PowerBuilder application windows are created in the Window Painter. Within a window, a developer uses a mouse to position and manipulate user objects, menus, DataWindows, and any of the standard controls that Windows 3.1 supports, such as radio buttons, check boxes, and drop-down list boxes. User objects, DataWindows, and menus are unique window objects created in other painters and tied to a window in the Window Painter.

User Objects

Custom user objects can be created from other objects. User objects contain attributes, events, and functions. After a user object has been created and saved, it can be associated with one or more windows in the Window painter.

There are three types of user objects. They are:

- **Standard**, created by a single standard control to perform generalized processing
- **Custom**, created from two or more standard controls and other previously defined user objects to perform specialized processing
- **External**, created outside of PowerBuilder and accessed through a DLL (dynamic link library)

DataWindow Objects

A DataWindow object, which is an intelligent SQL object that can manipulate data from a relational database without user-coded SQL. A DataWindow object can retrieve, update, insert, delete, scroll, print, and save data in any of ten file formats. DataWindows can establish validation criteria and display formats and use internal and external code tables. After a DataWindow has been created and saved, it is tied to a window and associated with a DataWindow control using the Window Painter.

DataWindow objects can be created and modified dynamically during an application's execution and can act in response to PowerScript routines.

When an application requires more control over database processing than DataWindows can provide, a developer can paint SQL graphically and embed SQL statements in a script or user-defined function. The embedded SQL is converted into the equivalent SQL requests for the target database server. Both static and dynamic SQL are supported.

Menu Objects

A menu is an independent object created in the Menu Painter. Menus, both action bar menus and pop-up menus, can be organized into any number of cascading levels. Shortcut keys can be assigned to menu items. After a menu has been created and saved, it can be associated with a window in the Window Painter.

11.5.2 PowerBuilder Painters

PowerBuilder provides a set of painters and tools designed to support developers who work in project teams and produce large-scale business applications. The painters can be used in a workbench environment with multiple painters open at the same time.

PowerBuilder's painters are accessible through a central menu called the Power Panel, which displays each function, called a Painter, as an icon. The Power Panel can be customized for each installation.

The PowerBuilder painters are:

- **Application Painter** defines the application environment, including the application name, scripts for application events, and search libraries.

- **Window Painter** builds windows and the objects and controls that are part of a window, such as Window's standard controls, user objects, and DataWindows. The interface allows users to initiate activities by dragging a control and dropping it on another. Multiple Document Interface (MDI) windows can be created.

- **Menu Painter** creates menus that can be attached to any window, either when the window is defined or dynamically from a script at run time. It supports pop-up menus and top-level action bar menus with drop-down lists.

- **DataWindow Painter** builds DataWindow objects that can be placed into a window. The DataWindow objects present and manipulate (including update) data in the application database without directly coding SQL statements into scripts. Static and dynamic SQL is supported. The DataWindow provides three automatic presentation styles: tabular, grid, or freeform.

- **Structure Painter** defines structures (arrays) from one or more related variables (same or different data types), allowing the group to be referred to as a single unit.

- **Preference Painter** establishes default information to provide a customized development environment.

- **Help System** contains context-sensitive PowerBuilder Help.

Additional PowerBuilder Help, particularly for user objects, events, and functions, can be added by a developer.

- **Database Painter** creates and maintains database definitions in a point-and-click environment. The SQL Painter graphically performs most DDL and DML functions. Developers can create tables and views, define extended table and column attributes, maintain security, and edit data in the database.
- **Picture Painter** launches a graphics package of choice (it must be able to save files in the .BMP format) for drawing pictures.
- **Function Painter** allows developers to define functions that extend the capabilities of PowerScript language.
- **Library Painter** creates and maintains libraries—the repository for PowerBuilder applications and objects. Available facilities include check-out/check-in, browsing, impact analysis, and detailed reporting. More than one PowerBuilder library, such as the application library, the test library, and the developer's personal test library, can be used during a PowerBuilder session.
- **User Object Painter** creates user-defined objects by specifying their attributes, events, scripts, and functions.
- **Script Painter** is a full-function text editor used to write scripts in PowerScript and includes facilities such as block move, cut-and-paste, search, replace, and undo. Its Browse-and-Paste facility will display all objects, controls, and data in the application. When the developer exits Script Painter, the PowerScript compiler is automatically called to compile the script and store it in the application library. If errors are detected, the compiler works with the Script Painter to pinpoint the errors. Error messages can be scrolled up and down. When a particular error is selected, the Script Painter scrolls the script window to bring the erroneous script statement into view so that the problem can be corrected. Since each script is independently compiled, an entire application does not need to be recompiled if a change is made to only one script.

11.5.3 PowerScript Language

A developer creates *scripts* to define the response to a specific object/ event occurrence that has been specified for the application. Scripts are written in the high-level, graphic, object-based language called PowerScript, which has hundreds of built-in functions. Scripts can accommodate external C and C++ code and can link to other application software through OLE, DDE, and dynamic link libraries. Once the scripts are defined, the developer uses PowerBuilder to generate executable code, which executes under Windows.

Integrated debugging facilities support dynamic breakpoints, inspection of values of application variables, single-step execution, and save/restart execution of a debug session.

11.5.4 Client/Server Open Development Environment

Client/Server Open Development Environment (CODE) is Powersoft's vision for an open PowerBuilder environment. CODE enhances the PowerBuilder application development functions and provides links to other components in the client/server platform.

The components of CODE include:

- **Database interfaces,** to connect to a variety of back-end database servers
- **CASE interfaces,** to integrate with CASE products, such as those from INTERSOLV; LBMS, Inc.; Bachman Information Systems, Inc.; and Popkin Software & Systems, Inc.
- **Host interfaces,** to provide access via a variety of terminal emulators
- **Object library interfaces,** to manage application objects
- **Other server interfaces,** to access other servers through APIs
- **Desktop application interfaces,** to provide dynamic integration among applications

11.6 SQLWindows

SQLWindows from Gupta Technologies, Inc., is a development system for Windows or OS/2 Presentation Manager applications. As illustrated in Figure 11.5, SQLWindows offers a diverse set of integrated, object-

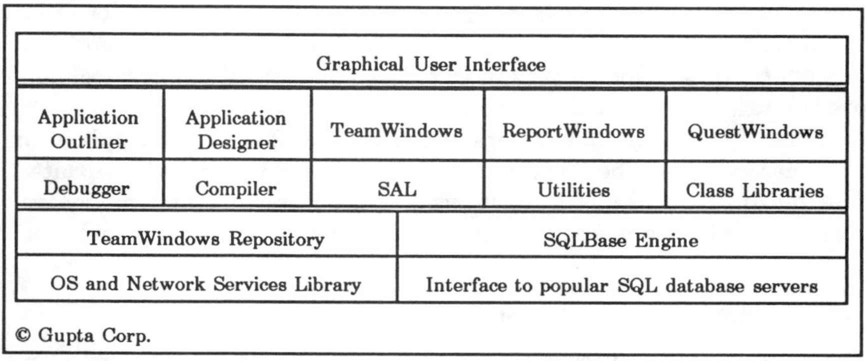

Graphical User Interface				
Application Outliner	Application Designer	TeamWindows	ReportWindows	QuestWindows
Debugger	Compiler	SAL	Utilities	Class Libraries
TeamWindows Repository		SQLBase Engine		
OS and Network Services Library		Interface to popular SQL database servers		
© Gupta Corp.				

Figure 11.5 SQLWindows architecture

based tools and services for developing GUI front-end client/server applications.

SQLWindows supports multiuser access to data stored in any SQL database on the network and supports simultaneous access to multiple data sources by a single application. Messages drive SQLWindows applications and are triggered when an action occurs on the screen.

Object-oriented programming (OOP) is supported via the three rules of object orientation: encapsulation, inheritance, and polymorphism. SQLWindows allows programmers to learn OOP as they go by putting all of the OOP facilities in a specific section of the SQLWindows outline and giving programmers the option to keep the section closed. When the programmer wishes to start taking advantage of the OOP features, the section can be opened. Object classes can be used directly from the tool palette or browsed via a class browser.

11.6.1 Application Designer and Application Outliner

Development in SQLWindows is performed using the Application Designer and Application Outliner components of the product. The Application Designer provides a visual environment for creating and modifying screens, forms, and objects, such as data fields, multiline fields, push buttons, radio buttons, check boxes, lists of values, and BLOBs (binary large objects). Objects can be customized using the Object Customizer. Code can be shared among applications as objects that are public and can be included by any application. When an includable object changes, applications using that object can be manually or automatically refreshed.

SQL database access is controlled in the TableWindow, a component of Application Designer. TableWindow displays relational tables in row and column format. From within a TableWindow, a user can display a query, browse through rows of data, and insert, update, or delete rows of data. Any actions done in the TableWindow automatically generate procedural code, which can be modified. An intelligent editor checks the procedural code for syntax errors.

When application objects are added or modified in the Application Designer window, the Application Outliner is automatically updated. The outline provides a flexible way of documenting and navigating through applications and facilitates maintenance and enhancements.

11.6.2 SQLWindows Application Language

To augment the facilities in the SQLWindows Application Designer and

Outliner, developers can use the SQLWindows Application Language (SAL) to program custom application actions and object methods. SAL is a full-featured 4GL and can access externally developed C and C++ code.

Connectivity to data sources, such as Oracle, SYBASE, SQLBase, DB2, DB2/2, ALLBASE/SQL, and Teradata, is provided through Gupta's family of SQLRouters and SQLGateways. Client support is provided for both Windows and Presentation Manager.

SAL supports both internal functions written in SAL and external functions via dynamic link libraries. In addition, SAL supports declared variables and one-dimensional arrays and accepts values from called functions and procedures. SAL also supports the DDE and Clipboard Windows interfaces.

Run-time versions of an application are distributed in compiled form. Gupta uses an application registration service that eliminates run-time fees.

11.6.3 TeamWindows

TeamWindows supports collaborative programming, which enables teams of programmers to work together to build large, enterprise-wide applications. The TeamWindows repository stores all information concerning the application, from the forms and reports to programming standards and staffing information. It also includes project management utilities for tracking development and performing impact analysis.

TeamWindows supports template development using predefined templates for quickly generating SQLWindows screens and applications using data dictionary information.

Once the SQLWindows application is complete, it is stored in the repository and managed with the TeamWindows source-code controller, which provides a check-out/check-in facility that allows sharing but ensures that only one programmer works on a component at a time. TeamWindows also tracks and updates version numbers for application modules throughout the entire development cycle.

11.6.4 QuestWindows

QuestWindows, which incorporates the facilities of Gupta's Quest product, allows developers to use a point-and-click interface to quickly develop forms, reports, and queries for SQL databases without knowing SQL. Applications built with QuestWindows can be enhanced with SQLWindows and the SAL language.

11.6.5 ReportWindows

Windows-based ReportWindows has an on-screen, object-oriented WYSIWYG designer for specifying report templates, which may then be produced with data accessed from SQLBase Server or any SQL database supported by Gupta's SQLNetwork.

It offers a full selection of fonts, colors, and other formatting options. Reports created with ReportWindows are fully compatible with reports created with Quest.

11.6.6 SQLWindows Debugger and Compiler

The SQLWindows debugger enables interactive application testing using multiple break points, single-stepping, watch values, and code animation. Applications can then be compiled into executable form for deployment on multiple workstations.

11.6.7 SQLBase Server for Windows

SQLBase Server for Windows is a single-user multitasking copy of the full-function SQL database server from Gupta, SQLBase. The single-user database enables application testing and debugging on stand-alone micros.

11.7 UNIFACE

It is difficult to categorize UNIFACE from Uniface Corp. as a 4GL or client/server development product because it contains many important features of each. UNIFACE provides a fourth-generation toolkit that supports most presentation interfaces, database engines, operating systems, and networking environments. The product provides an open technology-independent application development environment, which is illustrated in Figure 11.6. The product is an appropriate tool for rapid application development as well as an ideal product for developing applications that need to access different databases and run on a variety of platforms.

The product's openness is based on the ANSI/ISO three-schema architecture, which separates the data definitions from the data manipulation and storage, and the UNIFACE Central Application Dictionary. The three-schema architecture consists of:

- **External** schema describes how the information will be presented to the user, such as forms, menus, windows, and reports.

- **Conceptual** schema describes the definitions and assignments for entities and fields, and for the relationships between entities. UNIFACE uses this information to drive both external and internal schema design and implementation.
- **Internal** schema describes how the data is actually stored and accessed—the logistics for handling the data once it is stored.

Developers build a data model and implement specific application functions with the external schema. UNIFACE handles the data logistics automatically.

The product is object-based. Developers maintain entity (object)

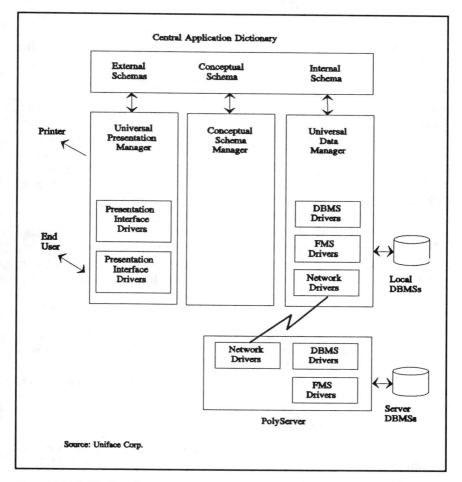

Figure 11.6 UNIFACE architecture

definitions in the conceptual schema (data dictionary). An external schema inherits the attributes and procedures (Uniface calls them Procs) associated with the entity. Entities are manipulated through triggers associated with events, the triggers themselves associated with Procs.

All UNIFACE code is written to be portable across the supported platforms, which include VAX/VMS and UNIX. To redeploy a UNIFACE application, a backup copy is made in ASCII format, loaded onto the new platform, and recompiled.

User interfaces are managed through a standard layer called the Universal Presentation Interface (UPI), which ensures that applications developed under one supported user interface can be deployed under another without modifications to the application. UPI currently supports Windows, Presentation Manager, Motif, OpenLook, and character-based terminals. At runtime, the native look-and-feel of the GUI is established automatically by the particular Interface Driver.

In addition, the drivers allow applications to take full advantage of the graphic environment. For example, a UNIFACE application running under Windows supports the environment's cut-and-paste, DDE, and DMI capabilities.

Uniface Corp. offers CASE Bridges that are used to move data dictionary information between UNIFACE and CASE products. Current CASE Bridges include links to Digital's Common Data Dictionary (CDD), KnowledgeWare's Application Development Workbench, INTERSOLV's Excelerator, and Interactive Development Environments' Software through Pictures.

The UNIFACE application development environment is composed of two major components: Information Engineering and Design Facility (IDF) and UNIFACE Runtime Manager (URMA). The product also includes a 4GL called the Proc Language, which supports a debugging mode.

Two additional tools are:

- **UNIFACE Reporter,** an end-user report writer with a windows interface whose use does not require the user to know the details of the data or the relationships between items
- **Report by Form,** a forms interface for creating professional reports

11.7.1 Information Engineering and Design Facility

IDF, the UNIFACE application development environment, has a menu-driven, windowed user interface. Most of the work done in IDF is performed in one of three workbenches:

- SQL Workbench
- System Administrator's Workbench
- Application Designer's Workbench

SQL Workbench

This workbench is used to enter and edit SQL statements. It presents a split screen with the top portion used for user input and the bottom portion used for displaying results, status, and messages from the accessed DBMS.

System Administrator's Workbench

This workbench is used to define and analyze the conceptual schemas— the definitions and assignments of entities and fields, and the relationships between entities. Conceptual schema information is stored in the Central Application Dictionary.

Application Designer's Workbench

The Application Designer's Workbench deals with the external schemas. Its External Schema Editor is used to define and modify external schemas. Its Form Paint Tableau is used to define forms and frames.

Frames are sections of a form that are used for data entry and display. A simple frame per entity creases a dialogue-box effect. Entity frames can be places within entity frames to reflect the relationships between entities. Within an entity frame, field frames are used to control display and entry of individual field data. Entity frames can be created by defining an external entity or with the FastForm facility if the entity is defined in a conceptual schema.

11.7.2 UNIFACE Runtime Manager

The UNIFACE Runtime Manager (URMA) is used to run applications. It manages access to compiled objects and makes calls to the DBMS drivers using the UNIFACE Runtime Library. Both the target data source and the network protocol can be determined at runtime.

Uniface Corp. offers drivers for a variety of data sources, including ADABAS, C-ISAM, dBASE, FOCUS, INGRES, INFORMIX, Microsoft SQL Server, Oracle, Rdb, RMS, and SYBASE. Uniface also offers a DBMS Driver Cookbook that documents how to build custom DBMS drivers to nonstandard or proprietary data sources.

In addition, Uniface recently released an interface between its 4GL and Micro Decisionware's Gateway for DB2. The UNIFACE MDI/DB2 Interface supports full read and write access to DB2 data and supports the entire DB2 feature set.

11.7.3 Proc Language

The Proc Language, the UNIFACE 4GL, can be used to manipulate fields, entities, and registers. Proc code is also used to define triggers, which are automatically invoked based on an event, such as selecting a menu or leaving a field. The four types of triggers are:

- Application level
- External schema level
- Entity level
- Field level

Procs are compiled to a tokenized form which is interpreted at runtime. Procs can be placed in libraries and used by multiple applications.

The Proc Language also contains a debug statement that puts the application in Debug mode. The developer can then monitor the Proc execution as the application runs, using break points, status requests, single-step execution, and a trace function.

11.7.4 PolyServer

PolyServer, an optional product, allows UNIFACE applications to access multiple DBMSs on remote machines via multiple network protocols. A variety of network protocols are supported including TCP/IP, Novell NetWare, LAN Manager, and DECnet.

A standard UNIFACE application consists of two logical components on the same machine: the application with the UNIFACE Runtime Library and one or more DBMS Drivers. With PolyServer, one or more of the DBMS Drivers is replaced with a protocol-specific Network Driver. The Network Driver allows UNIFACE to communicate with the server where the PolyServer Runtime Library and DBMS Drivers are running—in effect, putting a network between the UNIFACE Runtime Library and the DBMS Drivers. This process can be chained by substituting a Network Driver for a DBMS Driver on the PolyServer platform.

Two-phase commit is managed by PolyServer in a multiple DBMS environment when transactions involve multiple DBMSs.

12

CASE Products for Distributed Environments

Computer-aided software engineering (CASE) products are evolving rapidly to react to the changes in information technology. The shift toward client/server networks and distributed computing has created new application requirements, such as distributed data, distributed processing, and object-based development. Rapid application development (RAD) tools and techniques, such as prototyping and Joint Application Development (JAD) methodologies, must now incorporate contemporary graphical interface requirements. In addition, IS organizations need products to help them migrate legacy applications to the "rightsized" platform.

GUIs have changed how users interact with computer applications. GUI-based systems require more functionality than CASE products have provided in the past. Applications should be developed independently of the target client interface and the server, and must be more graphic-oriented, using a WYSIWYG approach. In addition to producing the code for GUIs, CASE products have to support the client/server computing paradigm.

CASE products have been used by IS professionals to improve the quality of their applications by formalizing communication between developers and users in the early stages of development. (The term *life cycle* will be used to represent the entire systems development life cycle.)

High-end CASE products use intelligent workstations as development platforms and the host or LAN-based server as a central repository for specifications created with the development products, as illustrated in Figure 12.1. Specifications are expanded during each phase of development and are shared among developers.

High-end CASE products use data flow diagrams, entity-relationship diagrams, and functional decomposition diagrams to implement structured design methodologies. Low-end CASE products, such as screen editors and application generators, support rapid prototyping and automatic code generation.

Conventional CASE products assume that the application and the data are on one machine and the user interacts with it via character-based screens on terminals. Client/server environments are not that simple. Client/server applications take advantage of distributed

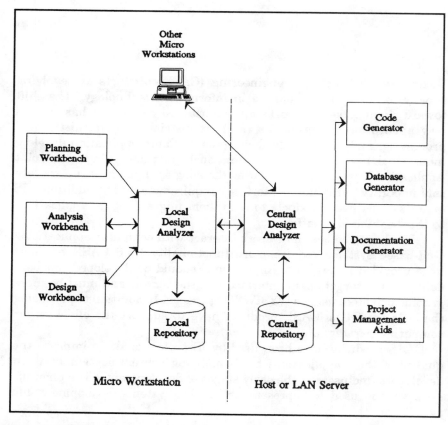

Figure 12.1 High-end CASE tool architecture

computing, use GUI front ends, and run on programmable machines. In addition to the presentation logic, the client machine can perform some database access and application processing.

However, CASE products are beginning to provide limited support for client/server computing. Most CASE vendors have announced plans to have full support for the client/server paradigm in the next release of their product. In addition, most CASE vendors are providing links to client/server development products. Vendors are recognizing that they each provide a very important piece of the development effort and that they should work as partners in the effort, rather than individual players.

CASE products should be considered for applications that are very process-oriented, such as transactional applications. CASE products support structured analysis and design methodologies and enforce a very structured approach to design which fits well with the structured orientation of process-oriented applications.

CASE tools themselves are not difficult to use; the learning curve is more involved with the methodology enforced by the product than the product itself. But it is the learning curve that has often been the stumbling block for successful implementations of CASE products.

There are hundreds of products available that call themselves CASE products and provide development and construction support. To chose among them, organizations should insist on a trial installation. Every product looks great in a demonstration presented by vendor personnel. A short list of CASE products to be evaluated should be generated based on the product's ability to generate 100 percent (or at least close to 100) of the code for the application in the desired target environment. Final selection should be based on a careful evaluation of the products on the list and the results of the trial project with the product.

The products discussed in this chapter are presented alphabetically and were chosen based on their functionality and/or market share.

12.1 Application Development Workbench

KnowledgeWare's integrated CASE product, Application Development Workbench (ADW), combines integrated, graphics-based modules, called workstations, with optional host-based products. Information collected during development is stored in an encyclopedia, ensuring consistency among specifications and designs.

Features of ADW include:

■ Multitasking

- Graphics-based diagramming
- Open architecture
- Central and local encyclopedias
- Data consistency checking
- Reusability

A new release of ADW, scheduled for the third quarter of 1993, will include:

- ADW/Encyclopedia Expert, a utility from third party developer Model Software that manages ADW's repository via micros
- A work group tool that allows up to 10 developers to work on a project simultaneously
- Easier exchange of information among modules that cater to different parts of the development cycle
- An updated ADW/MVS generator

The ADW architecture is illustrated in Figure 12.2. The ADW development engine runs under OS/2 with a Presentation Manager GUI. All ADW components look and function alike and their interfaces conform to the IBM guidelines of Systems Application Architecture (SAA) and Common User Access (CUA).

Design specifications are independent of the target platform. When the design is complete, the code for the application is generated for the

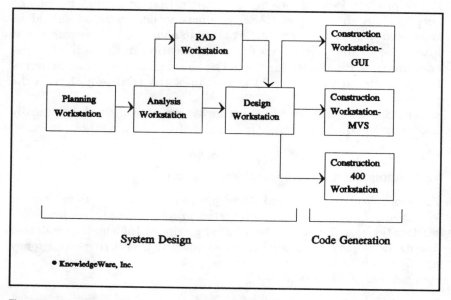

Figure 12.2 Application Development Workbench architecture

appropriate hardware environment, which includes stand-alone micros, workstations accessing servers, and micros connected to hosts.

The heart of ADW is its host- or LAN-based encyclopedia, which is used for centralized information storage. All the information collected throughout the application development life cycle resides in the ADW encyclopedia, which allows the information to be shared by the development products used during the phases of the life cycle, ensures consistency among all specifications and designs, and provides real-time error checking to maintain the quality of the design.

12.1.1 Planning Workstation

The Planning Workstation is used to establish a framework for system development throughout an enterprise and to identify the enterprise components and model how they interrelate. For each organizational unit, the enterprise model defines its:

- Organizational structure
- Business functions
- Goals
- Critical success factors
- Information needs

The Planning Workstation can also provide exception analysis and traceability reporting throughout the life cycle, allowing an organization to review how business requirements are addressed in every phase of the life cycle. The framework developed in the Planning Workstation can be used to determine candidate projects, prioritize them according to the organization's critical success factors, and suggest project scope.

The Planning Workstation can accommodate many planning methodologies, including Information Engineering (for developing enterprise modeling) and those developed internally by an organization. The methodology used in the Planning Workstation assumes that key employees will be involved in the planning process.

All the information generated by the Planning Workstation is stored in the ADW encyclopedia. The stored information is modified as the needs and goals of the business change. All process and data models developed in the planning phase are available for further definition and refinement in the other ADW workstations throughout the life cycle.

12.1.2 Analysis Workstation

The Analysis Workstation builds on the information defined using the

Planning Workstation to create detailed data and process models for each business area and define how the models interrelate. The Analysis Workbench facilitates the identification of the data involved in each business area, the sources and receivers of all data, decision points, and data transformation during a process. All information is presented in diagrams, such as reports and entity-relationship, data flow, process-decomposition, and action diagrams.

Consistency is automatically maintained among diagrams as updates are made. The logical data and process models constructed by the Analysis Workstation are used directly by the Design Workstation as the basis for physical design specifications and by the RAD Workstation for application prototyping.

Scheduled for release by the end of 1993, Model EDA, an EDA/SQL-enabled product, allows data administrators to expand corporate data models in ADW with relational and nonrelational information from multitiered platforms. In addition to data in structures currently accessible by ADW (DB2, DL/1, VSAM, and IDMS), users will be able to access legacy data and reach data residing in structures accessible by Information Builders' EDA/SQL product (See Section 6.1.4, Database Gateways).

12.1.3 Design Workstation

The Design Workstation ensures application quality while automating many of the tedious and time-consuming design tasks, such as high-level program logic, design data definitions and databases, and create screens and reports. Working from the information in the ADW encyclopedia, the Design Workstation maintains information consistency, adherence to business rules, and the integrity of design components. The database tools support multiple data sources, including DB2, DL/1, VSAM, and IDMS.

Applications are illustrated graphically to facilitate understanding. Graphical diagrammers can quickly "paint" screens and reports based on the data definitions stored in the encyclopedia. A preview feature allows examples of the screens and reports to be reviewed by the end users for approval.

From the design specifications, the Design Workstation generates SQL Data Manipulation Language (DML) and Data Definition Language (DDL) code, including any required referential integrity rules.

12.1.4 RAD Workstation

The RAD Workstation supports interative prototyping methodologies by providing screen prototyping based on the information collected using the Analysis and Design Workstations. Using a screen painter, developers create screen templates and hierarchical screen models. Screens can inherit attributes from other screens. Screen prototypes are created to be independent of technology. Detailed design constructs are generated from the application prototype and stored in the ADW encyclopedia. They become the basis for the physical design structure in the Design Workstation.

The prototypes can be animated to allow users to verify the interface and screen flow before design work is started. Users can run prototyping diskettes on their own OS/2 machine, independently of the ADW software.

12.1.5 Documentation Workstation

The Documentation Workstation automates the production of systems documentation by managing the diagrams, reports, and text files collected and produced by ADW workstations and stored in the ADW encyclopedia. The Documentation Workstation can also incorporate text and graphic files from external sources, such as word processing packages. Documents can be organized, formatted, and viewed on the screen prior to printing.

The Documentation Workstation can also be used to facilitate project management through the use of document templates, which allow an organization to enforce procedural guidelines, methodologies, and standards.

12.1.6 Construction Workstations

Construction workstations use the specifications for screen layouts, physical file and database definitions, report layouts, and procedural logic developed with the Design Workstation to generate application code.

Another construction workstation is scheduled for release by the end of 1993. Construction Workstation-EDA will enable developers to generate applications based on Information Builders' EDA/SQL's API from business requirements and design specifications stored in ADW's central encyclopedia. The generated applications will use EDA/SQL's

API/SQL-based 3GL and SQL tools rather than COBOL tools, and will be able to be distributed in multivendor, multiplatform environments.

Construction Workstation-GUI

The Construction Workstation-GUI is used to define the following:

- **Windows and dialogs** using a layout diagrammer
- **User events** (such as a button click or mouse move), which are tied to the business logic created in the Design Workstation
- **Help files** using an online help diagrammer

The Construction Workstation-GUI generates GUI resource files, COBOL programs, and supporting help files. It generates ANSI-standard COBOL that supports Presentation Manager GUIs for client/server applications. The next release will support Windows and a future release will support Motif.

Construction Workstation-MVS

The Construction Workstation-MVS is used to generate COBOL applications (and their user and application documentation) for IBM/MVS environments. The workstation generates ANSI-standard COBOL or COBOL/2 source code that supports CICS and IMS in a variety of database environments, including DB2, DL/1, VSAM, and IDMS.

Construction Workstation-400

The Construction Workstation-400 is used to generate AS/400 applications. The workstation automatically generates the COBOL source code, screen maps, and data definitions. Applications can be compiled and unit tested on the micro. It automatically transfers programs to the AS/400 and initiates compiles.

12.1.7 ADW/MVS

ADW/MVS, a host-based toolkit for encyclopedia management, provides a central point of control for encyclopedia development and works with micro-based ADW workstations. ADW/MVS tracks and records all objects checked out of encyclopedias and allows for analysis and review of all proposed changes as each object is checked back into an encyclopedia. ADW/MVS coordinates with MVS security packages and IBM's DB2 to provide object-, encyclopedia-, and system-level security.

12.1.8 Redevelopment Products

KnowledgeWare also provides three redevelopment products that were originally offered by Language Technology, Inc. These products allow developers to analyze existing applications, determine problem areas, and restructure those areas. These products are:

- **Knowledge Inspector** analyzes a portfolio of COBOL applications for conformance with structured programming standards. Using categories of measurements and different metrics, it estimates the scope of effort needed to improve a program's quality.
- **Knowledge Pinpoint** identifies potential problem areas in a single COBOL program, accesses the program's complexity and quality, and provides insight into what the program is doing.
- **Knowledge Recoder** generates structured code that is functionally equivalent to the original code but easier to read, review, and maintain.

KnowledgeWare is also developing a micro-based common user interface to these three products.

In addition to these products, KnowledgeWare is developing products for extracting information from existing applications and reengineering them into a forward engineering CASE environment, which would fill in the gap discussed in the Software Redevelopment section of Section 4.2.1, Update Implementation.

12.2 APS

Unlike traditional CASE products, APS from INTERSOLV, Inc., uses a painting approach, rather than the generation of structured diagrams, for developing application specifications. Screen, report, data structure, and scenario mock-up painters are used to enter the specifications of an application. This approach is suitable for using prototyping methodologies to develop large and small applications.

The APS family of tools provides an integrated CASE environment for building COBOL applications that will operate in IBM SAA production environments. Supported platforms include MVS, DOS/VSE, AS/400, PC-DOS, OS/2, and LANs. APS can be used to generate multiple production platforms from the same design specification.

APS has two versions:

- **APS/MVS** for MVS, DOS/VSE, and OS/400 platforms
- **APS/PC** for OS/2, PC-DOS, and LAN platforms

  Testing is done at the specification level. APS/PC uses Micro Focus

Advanced Animator; APS/MVS uses Via/SmartTest from VIASOFT, Inc.

The components of APS are illustrated in Figure 12.3 and discussed below.

12.2.1 Application Repository

The application repository is used to centrally store all specifications of an application, including entity definitions, relationships, and rules to create program code. It can also automatically generate project reports and documentation for the application. In a LAN environment, the application repository can be accessed and shared by a project development team.

12.2.2 Application Painters

The Application Painters are used to develop screens, reports, data structures, and application mock-ups. The painters support the use of prototyping and allow the developer to define repository entities during

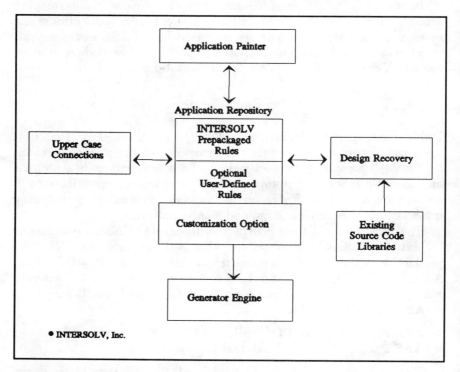

Figure 12.3 APS architecture

the painting process. All elements developed using the Application Painters are stored in the application repository. APS painters operate identically in the host and micro versions. These prototypes can be run with or without data.

A special painter, the APS/DB2 Database Painter, can be used as an optional stand-alone data-administration tool. It can also be integrated with APS products to support the management of DB2 applications.

The APS GUI Painter supports the design and development of CUA-compliant, OS/2 Presentation Manager-based GUI applications. The APS GUI Painter uses a WYSIWYG editor for specifying the visual appearance and related properties for each of the application's entities. It generates COBOL/2 source code for the applications.

The APS GUI Painter also supports design-time object testing. The developer (and end users) can test the performance of each window's controls and presentation specfications before generating code.

INTERSOLV has announced plans to expand APS's GUI support to take advantage of the features of OS/2's WorkPlace Shell and Microsoft Windows 3.1.

12.2.3 CASE Connections and Importers

The APS CASE Connections and APS Importers are used to link existing applications and code to the APS development environment. The APS CASE Connections can also be used to link to other front-end design products and CASE products, including Application Development Workbench from KnowledgeWare, Inc., and Excelerator from INTERSOLV, Inc.

The APS Importers scan source programs to recover database specifications, such as CICS/BMS and SQL/DDL, and store them in the application repository for reuse.

12.2.4 Application Generators

The APS Application Generators use a dynamic rule base, rather than a static one. Each generator operates on a set of rules required to generate source code from high-level specifications. These prepackaged rules can be tailored to individual sites through user-defined rules, which allow an organization to enforce local standards and share reusable rules and algorithms.

The APS Application Generators combine the design specifications in the application repository with the specified rules and can generate standard COBOL with no run-time modules. APS generates 100 percent of the code required for the application, and the generated code is cleanly disconnected from APS and the development environment.

12.2.5 Customization Option

APS application generators can use prepackaged INTERSOLV rules or locally defined rules. This allows local standards, special target considerations, and reusable logic to be defined and used at a project or site level. The APS Customization Option allows a developer to enter or modify the prepackaged rules or user-defined rules stored in the application repository.

12.2.6 APS/PC

APS/PC provides multiuser support to LAN-based developers with a centralized point of installation and control. APS/PC software and the application repository reside on the central LAN server. Developers can share data, entities, code, and documentation and perform joint development. Concurrent updating of the application repository is allowed, with APS/PC ensuring integrity at the entity level.

12.3 CorVision

CorVision, an integrated CASE product from Cortex Corp., includes a front-end design workstation (an IBM PC/AT, or higher compatible, running DOS) and an application generator on the host capable of creating complete working applications. CorVision supports traditional structured-engineering methodologies as well as the interactive prototyping methodology.

Applications are developed by entering specifications via graphical editors that generate diagrams. The specifications are checked against the host repository for consistency and completeness. CorVision also includes screen and report painters. The intelligent Guidance System informs the developer of any application components that remain undefined and logical specification steps that should be performed.

Once the specification process is complete, the application code and the application documentation are generated using the CorVision generator. A production-ready prototype can be generated at any point during the development. Modifications to the application are made by changing diagram specifications, *not* by changing source-code statements. The product produces executable machine code.

The CorVision architecture is illustrated in Figure 12.4. As the specifications are entered into the workstation using graphical diagrams, they are automatically stored in the host-based Central Repository, which checks them for consistency and accuracy.

Code for windows (for Windows and Digital's Pathworks) is automatically generated from the specifications as a set of default windows with all the navigation functions provided. CorVision can generate POSIX-compliant, ANSI C code for Ultrix, AIX, SCO, and HP-UX and SVR4 UNIX server platforms. CorVision is also available on VAX/VMS platforms with direct read/write interfaces to Digital's RMS and Rdb data structures and CDD/Plus repository.

12.3.1 Diagramming Techniques

The diagramming techniques use icons, pop-up menus, symbols, and windows. The four available diagramming techniques are:

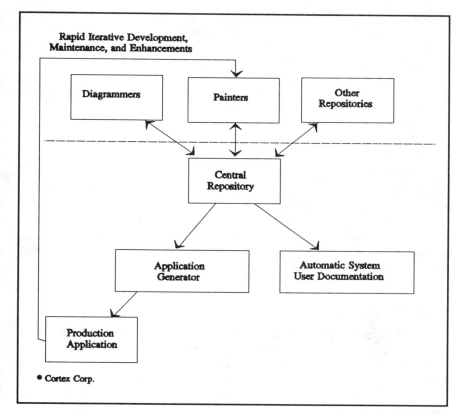

Figure 12.4 CorVision architecture

- **Data Entity** diagrams are used to represent the structure and form of the data used in an application. Data sets, which are a logically related group of fields, are identified and specified with attributes. Using the Data Entity Diagrammer, developers define new data sets for an application or access data sets from other applications.
- **Menu** diagrams are used to specify the hierarchical structure and attributes of an application-menu interface. All CorVision-developed applications are menu-driven. The menu diagram, a simplistic form of structured and decomposition charts, illustrates how the user navigates between functions in the application. Icons are used to represent the different menu choices, functions, screens, reports, and custom procedures. An interactive screen painter is used to specify screen and report formats. The specifications are used by CorVision to automatically generate executable screen and report code.
- **Dataview** diagrams are used to specify the elements of a dataview, which is a subset of data sets specified for a screen or report and is comprised of a main data set and subordinate data sets. CorVision automatically determines the optimal unique paths to logically link the main data set to every sub-data set within the dataview.
- **Action** diagrams are used to translate and display the procedural constructs of a procedure. As the constructs are entered, they are checked for syntax and data consistency.

12.3.2 Painters

Application screens are defined using a screen painter. All I/O and data-entry validation needed to produce a screen is automatically generated by the screen generator from the painted specification.

Reports are formatted online using an interactive report painter. Column headings and field attributes are derived from field definitions stored in the central repository. Report code is generated from the painter specification.

12.3.3 Query Facility

The Cortex Query Facility can be used to produce reports and execute queries against data in a CorVision application. A query is specified via a full-screen editor with pop-up windows. Once the query specification is complete, the query can be executed online immediately or stored to be run at a later time. Stored queries can be modified, copied, or deleted from the system.

12.4 Excelerator

INTERSOLV, Inc., provides The Excelerator Series of products to support developers using DOS, Windows, or OS/2 in LAN-based environments. Excelerator Windows combines the power of Excelerator with the intuitive Windows interface and LAN-support for multiple design methodologies.

Excelerator II is an application analysis and design tool that is a re-implementation of Excelerator for OS/2-based LANs. To support teams of software developers requiring shared access to common design components, XL/II for OS/2 is built around an active LAN-based repository. XL/II uses an object-oriented design to combine the original Excelerator capabilities with LAN support. INTERSOLV describes the product as a full multiuser, multitasking, multithreaded, planning, analysis, and design tool.

The Execlerator Series provides an open architecture that supports interfaces to INTERSOLV's APS, SQL Server, DB2, DB2/2, Bachman's Data Anlayst, Micro Focus's COBOL Workbench, and ABT's Project Workbench.

The INTERSOLV LAN Repository provides central storage and an administrative point for Excelerator components. Members of a design team can access the repository simultaneously in read-only and update mode with full integrity. The repository can operate by itself or can be connected to host-based repositories such as Reltech and BrownStone. The LAN-based repository operates on top of OS/2 LAN Server, LAN Manager, NetWare, VINES, and other standard LAN operating systems. INTERSOLV LAN Repository can interface to back-end CASE products, such as code generators.

The INTERSOLV LAN Repository is based on a standard SQL database (currently Microsoft's SQL Server or DB2/2). Users can store and access application development data through standard SQL tools for quick reports and specification lists. By comparison, the ADW Encyclopedia from KnowledgeWare uses a proprietary data storage format that limits users' options for data retrieval into reports.

Upwardly compatible with previous versions of Excelerator, XL/II supports a library of traditional and new methodologies that can be used off-the-shelf, or can be tailored to local requirements by using an expert system called Customizer. Users can choose from a library of popular development methodologies that support data-driven, process-driven, and event-driven design approaches (client/server applications are event-driven). An optional feature authorizes modifications to the graphical objects and rules defined and stored in the INTERSOLV LAN Repository.

Excelerator comes with a database reporting tool from Pioneer Software called Q+E, which allows users to access the repository directly to perform queries or generate reports. A built-in DDE link inserts information from XL/II into Microsoft Word documents.

To facilitate the design of GUIs, XL/II also includes a Graphical Application Workbench tool, which models GUIs for OS/2 and Windows applications, as well as 3270-type data-entry screens. Support for the generation of GUI code, through Intersolv's APS code generator, was made available in late 1992.

Design Recovery for Excelerator scans existing applications to extract design information and import the designs into a common repository. Developers can then resolve inconsistencies and identify the impact of proposed changes. Design information and documentation can also be regenerated.

12.5 FOUNDATION

FOUNDATION, from Andersen Consulting, is a structured application development methodology that supports host-based applications as well as high-end departmental and enterprise-wide client/server applications. FOUNDATION uses a repository to support batch, transaction, and cooperative processing applications. Planning, analysis, design, and installation objects are stored in the LAN repository and are accessible by all developers. The repository supports group development and encourages reuse and sharing of design objects and application components throughout the life cycle.

The FOUNDATION repository uses industry standard technology and is built on an object-based entity/relationship/attribute mode, which allows developers to write business logic rather than platform-specific code. An ANSI-based interface is provided to import and export data between FOUNDATION and other software products. Built-in support is provided for managing multiple versions of repository information.

The FOUNDATION development products for host-based systems are:

- **METHOD/1**, a workstation-based structured methodology that addresses the entire life cycle, supports the strategic analysis and planning functions, offers three alternatives for systems implementation (iterative development, package selection, and custom development), and includes a facility for managing enhancements to the production application.

- **PLAN/1** uses information engineering techniques to assist an organization in planning and modeling applications. It supports top-down and bottom-up methodologies. Workstation-based PLAN/1 automates tasks such as affinity analysis, entity relationship modeling, and functional decomposition.
- **DESIGN/1** is a LAN-based set of facilities that are driven by the repository, and automates the analysis and design of traditional and cooperative processing transactions. DESIGN/1 runs under DOS and OS/2 and facilitates the transition from DOS to Windows and OS/2 environments. DESIGN/1 offers data flow diagramming, data modeling, and prototyping facilities.
- **INSTALL/1** uses the DESIGN/1 specifications to construct traditional, distributed, and cooperative mainframe transaction processing applications. This tool generates partial applications, including screens, reports, database schemas, and a skeleton of the COBOL code required for application logic.

All FOUNDATION tools share these common attributes:

- Methodology drive
- Cooperative processing based
- Repository based
- Multiple-user support
- Graphical user interface
- Reengineering support

12.5.1 FOUNDATION for Cooperative Processing

FOUNDATION for Cooperative Processing (FCP), designed for developing client/server cooperative processing applications, is based on a shared central repository. FCP addresses every phase of the life cycle and provides a framework for managing the development activities.

The platforms supported by FCP are:

- Client: OS/2 PM, DOS Windows
- Server: OS/2, CICS, HP-UX, UNIX, VMS

Client versions for VAX Motif and UNIX are planned for a late 1993 release.

Within FCP, the FOUNDATION methodology is expanded to incorporate issues unique to distributed environments, such as communication standards, GUI design, and the packaging and location of functions among client, server, and message components. FCP also provides location transparency: an application can communicate with another application without knowing the physical location of the application, the underlying communication access method, or the underlying platform environment.

FOUNDATION Design

FOUNDATION Design provides development tools for analyzing, designing, and prototyping client/server applications. It provides a graphical view of FCP's design objects and the relationships between them. FOUNDATION Design simplifies the development process for:

- Client and server programs
- Module definition
- Windows
- Service messages
- Process logic
- Copybooks
- Data layouts

The Window Painter uses a WYSIWYG approach for designing window layouts. Developers can position controls, such as push buttons and pull-down menus, directly onto a window image. Display attributes and event processing rules can be associated with controls and stored in the repository for consistency and reuse.

The Entity-Relationship Diagrammer is used to develop models of entity relationships that define the application. The Data Flow Diagrammer describes information flow. The Procedure Diagrammer captures the business requirements, either at a high level or at the program logic level.

FOUNDATION Design's Rapid Application Builder supports the quick development of prototype applications, using a point-and-click interface, with design objects stored in the repository. At the end of the Rapid Application Builder session, the application design is ready to be generated using FOUNDATION Construction's flexible application generator.

FOUNDATION Construction

FOUNDATION Construction automates the process of generating the application's client and server programs for the target environment. The design information stored in the repository is used to build executable components (but not complete applications) of a working cooperative application. FOUNDATION Construction creates workstation programs or LAN- or host-based server programs, which are portable to other platforms, and workstation-based client programs. Code can be generated in either C or COBOL.

The GUI for an application is automatically generated during the client generation process. The user interface files produced by the generation process contain user interface events with their associated functions and components of the user interface, including windows, controls, and dialog boxes.

FOUNDATION Production

FOUNDATION Production is an open message-based architecture that handles the communications between platforms. By providing a layer between the application and the operating system, FOUNDATION Production shields developers from the network protocols, native window environments, and operating systems. DDE support allows developed applications to interface with other GUI software packages.

FCP Open Architecture

Applications developed using FCP run under its open architecture. The components of FCP are illustrated in Figure 12.5. The Presentation Services provided by FCP simplify platform-independent GUI imple-

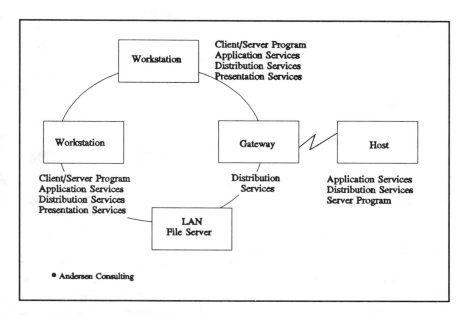

Figure 12.5 Components of FOUNDATION for Cooperative Processing

mentation. Support is provided for OS/2, Windows, and native Presentation Manager.

The Application Services provided by FCP include common functions, such as logon and security facilities, compatibility and version checking, and Dynamic Data Exchange (DDE) interface.

FCP's Distribution Services shield developers from the technical complexities of communication. They handle routing and management of messages and translate data between applications written in different languages (C or COBOL) or residing on hardware with different internal data representation (EBCDIC and ASCII). The Distribution Services also provide a single set of communication APIs for messaging. Distribution Services support several standard networking protocols and operating systems, including LU6.2, Novell, LAN Manager, and OS/2 LAN Server, with support for TCP/IP currently and DECnet expected in late 1993.

12.6 Information Engineering Facility

Information Engineering Facility (IEF), an integrated CASE tool from Texas Instruments that implements the Information Engineering methodology discussed in Section 4.3.4, supports the development of GUI mainframe- and midrange-based applications. IEF was developed with the contributions of James Martin Associates, Ltd.

IEF is installed on intelligent workstations and the host. The host components of IEF include a central Encyclopedia, a code generator, a database generator, a testing toolkit, and a public interface.

The IEF product provides full integration within each stage and across all stages of the development life cycle by way of the IEF Encyclopedia, a comprehensive repository of sharable information. The specifications created with the diagramming tools are stored in both the local and host IEF Encyclopedia. An Information Integrator module on the workstation coordinates the information displayed on the screen and enforces the disciplines of the IE methodology. IEF uses expert-system techniques for consistency checking.

Specifications that have been accumulated in a local workstation Encyclopedia are uploaded to the IEF Encyclopedia on the host, which is implemented as a DB2 database. The host IEF Encyclopedia has configuration and project management capabilities.

Specifications in the host IEF Encyclopedia may be uploaded or downloaded to workstations using a check-out/check-in procedure. When the design is divided among several workstations, IEF guarantees that each workstation has a logically complete subset of the contents of the host Encyclopedia. IEF will only check-out objects that are complete and consistent.

When the specifications have been determined to be sufficiently complete, they are routed to the code- and database-generator modules. These modules generate 100 percent of the operational code and physical databases of an application for the target environment directly from the specifications.

Developers design and build the mainframe/server portion of an application, design and build the client portion, and then tie the two together using diagrams to allocate processes between the client and the server. With each step of the methodology, developers are required to define three models: data, activity, and interaction. The IEF architecture is illustrated in Figure 12.6.

The IEF Toolsets can also generate the required communications components for a client/server application, using industry standard protocols.

The next version of the IEF product, due for release in late 1993, will support run-time specification of the target environment, a LAN-based repository, and additional target environments.

12.6.1 Planning Toolset

The Planning Toolset supports the Information Strategy Planning phase of Information Engineering during which a high-level analysis of the organization, its primary functions, and its major categories of data

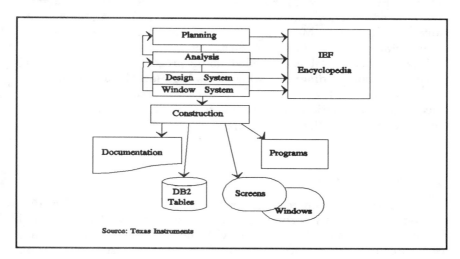

Figure 12.6 Information Engineering Facility architecture

called "subject entities" is developed. To define data, developers use the Data Modeling Tool to build a global, conceptual data model that depicts the data used by the business activity. Other models include interaction analysis, organization modeling, and business area definition. All models are independent of the physical and technical details of implementation.

The activity model is developed using function-hierarchy diagrams and function-dependency diagrams. A function is a set of activities that are independent of any specific department or organization. A function-hierarchy diagram is a decomposition diagram of the major functions of the organization. A function-dependency diagram shows how various functions interrelate with one another (in a sequence) to perform a specific activity.

When the data and activities are defined, an interaction model is built using a matrix that relates entity types to business functions with a weighted pattern of usage (create, read, update, and delete—CRUD) in each cell. The cluster analysis technique is used to identify common business processes and business areas that then become the focus of the next phase of life cycle.

12.6.2 Analysis Toolset

The Analysis Toolset is used to further refine the data, activity, and interaction models specified with the Planning Toolset. The data model is refined using entity-relationship and entity-hierarchy diagrams. The entity-hierarchy diagram is a subset of the entity-relationship diagram and is used to show how a specified entity is broken down into subtypes. The Data Modeling Tool provides numerous panels for detailing attributes and editing constraints.

The activity model is expanded using process-decomposition and process-dependency diagrams, which show high-level business functions and processes as lower-level, more detailed processes. IEF uses a convention called action diagramming to show the interaction between data and activity at the detailed process level, which is referred to as a process-action diagram.

12.6.3 Design Toolset

The Design Toolset is used to generate a logical (top-level) design that is independent of any technology. It is used to refine the conceptual data and activity models developed with the Analysis Toolset, produce user screens, and prototype dialog flows between screens. Action diagrams are used to describe the actions in the procedures and structure charts are used to illustrate how action diagrams interrelate.

The Design Toolset is also used to develop a Technical Design, which introduces environmental constraints into the specification. The output from this step is a complete Data Structure Diagram—the first cut at a database definition.

The Design Toolset also allows animation of the design to illustrate the sequence of screens and user interaction.

12.6.4 Construction Toolset

The Construction Toolset is used to generate complete applications and provides a run-time test environment that simulates the production environment. The Construction Toolset is used to create business system specifications for the data and business activities.

When the specifications are complete and the target environment has been determined, code for the application (COBOL or C) and the SQL DDL (data definition language) to generate the SQL-based database are generated by the IEF Construction Toolset. The Construction Toolset also compiles and links the application and generates the documentation.

12.6.5 Window Designer

Developers create GUIs with Window Designer, which is integrated with the Encyclopedia and the other IEF Toolsets and generates the code necessary to create and manipulate window objects. Current GUI support is for OS/2 PM and Windows with DDE support. Motif support will be available in the next release of the IEF product.

12.6.6 Business Templates

IEF Business Templates, which are application models developed with I-CASE technology, can be used as complete applications or modified to meet specific business needs. The Templates can be as brief as a set of business specifications or as extensive as a complete architecture for transaction processing applications.

12.7 Magic

The Magic family of products from Magic Software Enterprises, Inc. uses an object-oriented approach to design, develop, and maintain SAA-compliant applications. The environments supported by Magic are illustrated in Figure 12.7.

Magic has built-in support for a variety of data sources, such as Rdb, RMS, and dBASE. The MagicGate can be used as a bridge to additional file managers and RDBMSs (such as Oracle) which can be used as back ends to the Magic development environment. Magic uses Novell's Btrieve as its embedded file manager in DOS and LAN environments.

Magic's open architecture combines heterogeneous data from multiple databases and computers into a tightly integrated system. The integration is transparent to users and developers. A Magic application developed on one platform is immediately executable in multiple and/or mixed environments without additional programming effort.

Magic handles data manipulation, programming logic, and user interface. Magic relies on the back-end DBMS to preserve the integrity and security of data and deliver high performance on back-end execution tasks.

Magic applications are table-driven and self-documenting. Applica-

User Interface Environment	MS-Windows Character-based		Motif DECwindows	
Application Runtime	Magic End-User Queries Magic Application Execution Report Generation			
Application Development	Magic Environment and Menu Design Magic Computer-Aided Programming Magic Automatic Program Generation Magic Data Definition Magic Display and Report Design			
Database Management	Btrieve Sybase SQL Server	C-tree Oracle NetwareSQL	INFORMIX INGRES dBASE	Rdb RMS
Communications	Novell NetBios	LAN Manager TCP/IP	PC Network DECnet/PCSA	IPX
Operating Systems	DOS OS/2	UNIX BTOS/CTOS	VAX/VMS	
Hardware Platforms	IBM Unisys	Digital Data General	SUN Hewlett-Packard	NCR

Source: Magic Software Enterprises, Inc.

Figure 12.7 Magic-supported environments

tion design specifications are organized in easy-to-maintain Dictionary Tables. Magic's Relational Development Technology automatically links changes made to any one part of an application to other related parts of an application. Magic organizes the design into an easy-to-manage database of application specifications.

A Magic task is represented by an Execution Table that contains a sequence of programming steps that are built from logical operations. Tasks can support interactive (screens, windows, menus) or batch (reports, import/export, global updates) processes. A task can call other nested tasks, pass parameters back and forth, and call itself for recursive processing. Object tasks are built in modular fashion, allowing the pretested objects to be reused within a single application or by other applications.

Magic steamlines programming operations into four major groups:

- **Global operations**, application-wide tasks such as control and security
- **Task operations**, such as initializing default variables
- **Record operations**, such as transaction processing control, posting records, and updating other files
- **Field operations**, such as pop-up windows and updating field values

The Magic family has two principal components:

- Application Development System
- Application Runtime System

12.7.1 Magic Application Development System

The Magic Application Development System is used by developers and programmers to generate new applications or modify existing ones. The Magic development tool consists of five basic design tasks, which are:

- **Environment and menu design** allows the developer to define the backdrop and structure of the development process and the application.
- **Data definition**, for example data type, files, fields, and keys, is accomplished via tables with a menu-driven front end.
- **Automatic program generation** creates basic tasks quickly and is extremely useful in producing skeleton or file maintenance programs.
- **Object-oriented programming of execution flow** uses 13 non-procedural operations that are specified and arranged in Magic's building-block tasks. These 13 operations replace the functionality

of hundreds of command and code statements used in 3GL and 4GL languages. They are supported by an object-based Expression Bank, a library of over 100 functions for establishing conditionality and utilizing expressions within the application.

- **User interface design** is used to create screen and report formats.

12.7.2 Magic Application Runtime System

The Magic Application Runtime System allows users to execute applications developed with the Magic Application Development System. Users can also design and produce *ad hoc* reports and queries using a Report Generator. The reports can be saved, reused in a report file, and converted into Magic programs for fine tuning by developers.

12.8 PACBASE

PACBASE from CGI Systems, Inc., provides a complete development environment with an active multiuser repository operating on a host connected to interactive workstations. PACLAN and PACLAN/X provide the same functionality for NetWare-based LANs, under OS/2 and UNIX operating systems, respectively. Network workstations can be either DOS or OS/2. Two or more CGI products can operate in combination using automated facilities to share information between host and LAN repositories. Applications developed with PACLAN and PACLAN/X are independent of hardware, operating system, and TP monitor. (PACBASE will be used to refer to features that are generic to all three products.)

This integrated CASE product can be used to partially reverse-engineer existing COBOL-based applications. PACBASE can also be used to reverse-engineer and reengineer existing PACBASE COBOL applications. CGI also offers RE/Cycle, a reverse-engineering product used to integrate existing applications into the PACBASE environment.

PACBASE maintains a corporate-wide repository to store all application and component specifications. The repository provides facilities for multiuser access, security, integrity and consistency checking, version control, documentation, and project management. From the specifications entered, PACBASE automatically generates COBOL programs, screen maps, database descriptions, error messages, application online help, user and technical documentation, and management reports. Figure 12.8 illustrates the integrated PACBASE environment (a LAN-based environment would not support 3270 terminals but would support micros as production workstations). The workstation facilities provide a Windows GUI to the PACBASE repository. The two facilities are PACDESIGN and PACBENCH.

12.8.1 PACDESIGN

PACDESIGN enters application specifications into the PACBASE repository. It supports structured-engineering and diagramming techniques for each phase of the life cycle, including:

- Process decomposition diagrams
- Data flow diagrams
- Structure charts
- Screen flow charts
- Data descriptions
- Conceptional data models
- Logical data models
- Data-access diagrams

12.8.2 PACBENCH

PACBENCH allows developers to enhance and modify specifications entered with PACDESIGN. A prototyping function provided by

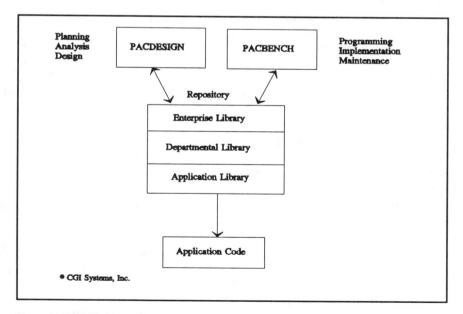

Figure 12.8 PACBASE environment

PACBENCH allows the application, complete with screens and reports, to be reviewed prior to the application-generation step. Procedural logic can be added to an application, either as COBOL source code or as structured routines.

From specifications introduced into the repository, PACBENCH generates complete applications—batch and online programs, screen maps, database descriptions, and hard copy and online documentation. Applications can be generated in COBOL for host environments or Micro Focus COBOL for micro environments.

12.9 Software through Pictures

Software through Pictures (StP) from Interactive Development Environments, Inc. (IDE) is a family of integrated, multiuser CASE products used to develop new applications and maintain and reengineer existing applications. The products support the development of real-time and engineering applications, as well as business applications.

StP products do not generate complete application code; they generate code frames, or skeletons of required code.

Every StP product incorporates an integrated family of graphical editors, a document preparation system, interfaces to version control systems, and an object annotation facility, all sharing a central repository with locking and access control. The basic StP architecture is illustrated in Figure 12.9.

The StP products are built on an open architecture that supports heterogeneous networks of workstations and provides open and published interfaces and user-modifiable templates for code generation, object annotation, document preparation, and SQL schema generation. The StP tools communicate through a shared repository and the use of printing, windowing, and networking standards.

The multiuser, object-based repository is implemented with a relational DBMS and includes a simple front end called the Object Management Library (OML) for accessing the stored information with *ad hoc* queries or for developing applications. In the repository, every object in every diagram, including the diagram itself, has a unique object identifier, an object type, and an object class to which it belongs. Each editor has a Display Definition feature which allows the selection of any object in a diagram and examines its definition. The repository includes a dynamic locking option for multiuser access, with read-write and read-only access privileges.

OML provides predefined views that include a full set of relational operations. Design rule checking and template-driven generation of code and documentation use the OML to retrieve information from the repository.

The StP products are integrated with IDE's Document Preparation System (DPS), a template-driven report generator that combines text and graphics based on the information in the shared repository. All DPS templates are written in a DPS Template Language, which allows users to modify and extend predefined templates or create new templates. DPS supports printing with ASCII text, Device Independent Troff, FrameMaker from Frame Technology Corp., Interleaf from Interleaf Corp., and PostScript.

The DPS also contains templates for Requirements Traceability, Repository Analysis, and DOS-STD-2167A reports. These templates automate tasks that are not supported by graphical editors alone.

12.9.1 C Development Environment

The C Development Environment provides off-the-shelf interfaces between StP products, CodeCenter from CenterLine Software, and

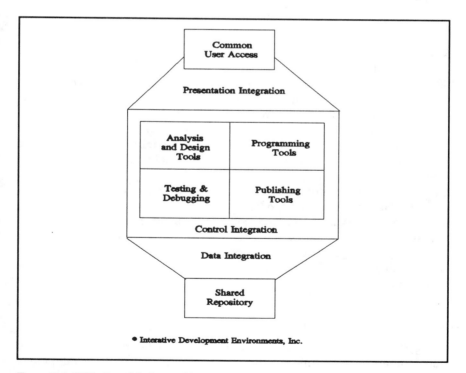

Figure 12.9 IDE's Open Solutions architecture

FrameMaker or Interleaf. It also includes reverse-engineering and code generation modules.

The C Navigator allows a developer to analyze the structure, data types, and parameters of an application. The query facility of C Navigator is used to access the repository, review the relationships between objects, locate unused or redundant code, and assess the impact of proposed changes. The C Navigator automatically generates design and code review documents via interfaces to FrameMaker and Interleaf.

The Design Generator for C generates a complete application design for an existing application, complete with structure charts (with parameters) and data structure diagrams. All the code and design information is stored in the repository.

The Code Generator for C generates standard code frames (skeletons of applications) from the design information stored in the repository. It also includes a facility to automatically synchronize the design and code representations of the application. Developers then use the programming environment to debug and link the code.

12.9.2 Ada Design Environment

Support for Ada development from design through implementation is provided through the integration of Object-Oriented Structure Design/Ada (OOSD/Ada), the Code Generator for Ada, the Verdix Ada Development System, Interleaf, and FrameMaker.

OOSD/Ada supports the architectural and detail design phases, and the implementation, documentation, and reuse of Ada applications. OOSD/Ada includes a design editor, data modeling editors, a reuse library and browser, context-sensitive online help, and template-driven documentation generation.

The Code Generator for Ada generates fragments of Ada source code from OOSD/Ada and data modeling diagrams stored in the repository. It generates specification and code frames for all program objects, including packages, tasks, and subprograms; and the declarations for all data types, objects, and exceptions. Completeness checking routines detect unresolved dependencies and incompletely declared objects before execution.

12.9.3 Integrated Structured Environment

Integrated Structured Environment (ISE) is a language-independent development environment that supports structured development methods and notations. Built-in facilities check design rules for completeness and consistency of diagrams.

12.9.4 C++ Development Environment

Object-Oriented Structured Design/C++ (OOSD/C++) supports the architectural and detailed design, implementation, and documentation of C++ applications, as well as reuse of design components. Its Design Editor is a language-sensitive graphical editor with consistency checking. OOSD/C++ uses the StP Document Preparation System to create application documentation from the repository.

The Code Generator for C++ generates C++ code from the OOSD diagrams stored in the repository. Code is generated for all design components and includes comments entered by the developers.

12.9.5 StP Information Modeling

Software through Pictures Information Modeling (StP/IM) supports the specification of the conceptual model of the data and extracts a logical model from the conceptual model. Developers can define annotations for every object in an information model and diagram using StP/IM's Object Annotation Editor during the modeling process. The information is stored in the repository and used by StP/IM when generating code and documentation.

StP/IM can generate SQL for use with a variety of UNIX and non-UNIX relational DBMSs. It creates the DDL (data definition language) statements from the information models in the repository, the Data Control Language for RDBMS-specific security features, and the DML (data manipulation language) for standard select, update, insert, and delete commands.

StP/IM can create a create/read/update/delete (CRUD) table and do affinity analysis on the CRUD table. Normalization reports based on the attribute dependencies within entities can be generated.

StP/IM also interfaces with the StP Document Preparation System through the use of templates. The report templates can be used as is or changed to support internal review processes.

12.9.6 Graphical Editors

The Software through Pictures integrated family of graphical editors supports popular analysis and design methodologies. The editors are integrated with the StP products described above. The editors include utilities that perform consistency checking such as consistent name usage between editors, undefined data items, improperly labeled nodes and flows, and the balancing of data flows, processes, and data stores.

Graphical editors are available for the following structures:

- **Data flow diagrams**, which provide a functional perspective
- **Data structures**, which decompose data flows and data stores defined in data flow diagrams and structure charts
- **Entity relationship diagrams**, which provide a data perspective
- **Control flow diagrams**, which model the event-driven aspects of real-time systems
- **State transition diagrams**, which model the behavior of event-driven systems
- **Control specification tables**, which show the interactions among discrete-valued control events
- **Structure charts**, which define the interfaces between the models

The Object Annotation Editor is available in all graphical editors. It allows developers to associate structured information and text with symbols, or even the diagram itself, in the diagram.

12.10 Teamwork

The Teamwork software development environment from Cadre Technologies Inc. supports all phases of the development life cycle and includes comprehensive verification and testing throughout the development process. The Teamwork products support requirements analysis, dynamic analysis (predicting system performance, evaluating architectural trade-offs, and verifying functional specifications before the design and coding phases are begun), and rapid application prototyping.

Teamwork does not restrict the development environment to any particular platform. Teamwork operates on workstations using UNIX, Digital's VMS and Ultrix, and IBM's AIX and OS/2 operating systems on heterogeneous networks that are compatible with Network File System (NFS) from Sun Microsystems and TCP/IP networking standards. Teamwork is implemented using the X Window System (see Section 2.4.2 for more details).

Developers use Teamwork intelligent editors as client processes on local workstations. The Teamwork project database, typically located on a networked server, manages specification storage and retrieval. Multiple-user access to the common project database is provided using standard networking protocols for file sharing and communications.

The integrated Data Dictionary in Team*work* enables developers to ensure consistency between phases of development. The Team*work* Data Dictionary is a common repository containing the definitions of all the data objects produced during the creation of analysis and design specifications. Once a Data Dictionary entry is created in the analysis phase of a project, the entry can also be used in the design and implementation phases. Alternate Data Dictionaries can be created to be shared among projects.

12.10.1 Structured Development Environment

The architecture of the Team*work* software development environment is illustrated in Figure 12.10. Each Team*work* module has the same look-and-feel within a common desktop. Checking features within each module assess a specification or design's accuracy, detect errors, and help in final verification of completeness. The Team*work* modules are:

- **Team*work*/SA** supports structured analysis to develop functional requirements using data flow diagrams, process specifications, and data dictionary entries.

Execute and Prototype	Modeling and Analysis	Design and Construction	Re-Engineering and Reuse
ADAS Team*work*/SIM *ShortCut*	Team*work*/SA Team*work*/RT Team*work*/IM Team*work*/OOA	Team*work*/SD Team*work*/Ada Team*work*/OOD Team*work*/Ada Source Builder Team*work*/DSE Ensemble Construction	Team*work*/ FORTRAN Rev Ensemble System Understanding Ensemble Function Understanding
Documentation Generation	**Requirements Management**	**Project and Configuration Management**	**Test and Debug**
Team*work*/DocGen Ensemble Documentation	Team*work*/Rqt	Third Party Relationships/ Integration	Team*work*/TestCase Ensemble Test Case Generation Ensemble Test Verification

Source: Cadre Technologies Inc.

Figure 12.10 Team*work* development architecture

- **Team*work*/RT**, an extension to Team*work*/SA, supports control flow modeling of real-time or event-driven applications.
- **Team*work*/IM** supports information modeling to identify the entities, relationships, and attributes of the application data structure.
- **Team*work*/OOA** supports object-oriented analysis methods developed by Project Technology, Inc., using the strengths of Team*work*/IM, Team*work*/RT, and Team*work*/SA.
- **ADAS** (Architecture Design and Assessment System) offers system-level simulation for combined software/hardware co-design.
- **Team*work*/SIM** is used to simulate the system by dynamically executing specification models, which helps developers verify behavior, estimate performance, and conduct high-level testing.
- *ShortCut* is a rapid applications prototyping tool for requirements analysis and understanding using Team*work*/SA and Team*work*/RT.
- **Team*work*/SD** supports structured design for procedural languages (such as C, Pascal, and COBOL), using structure charts, module specifications, and data dictionary definitions.
- **Team*work*/OOD** provides direct support for the object-oriented design techniques from Project Technology, Inc.

12.10.2 Ensemble

Ensemble is a family of C development solutions that automates the fundamental tasks performed throughout the entire C engineering cycle. The integrated tool set uses a common GUI and an integrated project database. Each Ensemble module performs equally well on its own or with its counterparts. The Ensemble modules can be networked in a client/server environment or used on a single-user workstation.

Ensemble includes the following modules:

- **Ensemble System Understanding** provides design recovery at the physical level from existing C code.
- **Ensemble Function Understanding** accelerates understanding of function logic, as well as function and data complexity.
- **Ensemble Construction** automates the use of structured design for the enhancement of existing as well as new C software.
- **Ensemble Test Case Generation** automates the creation of systematic functional tests from existing C software or designs.
- **Ensemble Test Verification** verifies the completeness of testing activities through test coverage measurements.
- **Ensemble Documentation** automates the creation of design documents from the design/reverse-engineering/testing database.

12.10.3 Ada Development

Cadre also offers Team*work* products to support Ada development. These products support a variety of structured, object-oriented, and Ada-specific methodologies that facilitate quality in development throughout the life cycle. These products are:

- **Team*work*/Ada** supports object-oriented design, using Ada structure graphs.
- **Team*work*/Ada Source Builder** translates Team*work*/Ada designs to Ada code.
- **Team*work* ASG Builder** (Ada Structure Graph Builder) reverse-engineers Ada applications to Team*work*/Ada designs.
- **Team*work*/DSE** enforces the graphic architectural design specified using Team*work*/Ada.

12.10.4 Other Teamwork Products

Additional Team*work* products from Cadre include:

- **Team*work*/RqT** is a requirements management and traceability tool for use throughout a project life cycle.
- **Team*work*/DocGen**, a graphic document layout tool, interfaces with desktop publishing systems, such as Interleaf from Interleaf, FrameMaker from Frame Technology, and VAX Document from Digital.
- **Team*work*/FORTRAN Rev** is a reverse engineering product for FORTRAN programs that graphically reveals the structure of existing software.
- **Team*work*/TestCase** automates the generation of a complete set of software test cases directly from system requirements.

12.10.5 ObjectTeam Workbenches

Cadre Technologies recently announced two development products that support object-oriented programming methodologies. ObjectTeam for Rumbaugh (Paradigm Plus/Cadre Edition) supports the Rumbaugh Object Modeling Technique and ObjectTeam for Shlaer-Mellor supports the Shlaer-Mellor object modeling method. ObjectTeam for Shlaer-Mellor consists of the Team*work*/OOA and Team*work*/OOD products. Both versions are available for UNIX, VMS, and Windows and can generate C++, Ada, and SQL code.

The tools support object, dynamic, and functional models; and object, state, data flow, and event trace diagrams. They can also generate code for a variety of databases including ANSI-standard SQL and ORACLE7, and object-oriented databases such as Versant Object Technology's Versant; Object Design, Inc.'s Objectstore; Objectivity, Inc.'s Objectivity; Ontos, Inc.'s Ontos; and Raima Corp.'s Raima.

Chapter

13

Future Trends

Advances in hardware and new technologies, such as multimedia and pen-based computing, offer new alternatives for how an organization implements its business systems or addresses a new business opportunity. Organizations should rethink their current implementation strategies and plan for the migration to enterprise-wide applications.

Software is quickly catching up. New operating systems that support multitasking on a desktop machine simulate how users really work—on more than one task at a time. The software support for work groups (groupware) removes the geographical and organizational barriers that sometimes exist in a group. Groupware facilitates and formalizes intergroup (and intragroup) communication.

13.1 Hardware Advances

As the hardware technology evolves, so will development technology. There are many hardware advances on the horizon that will have a great impact on how business processes can be implemented, which in turn impacts the development of the applications that automate those business processes.

13.1.1 Microprocessors

The new microprocessor chips are faster—period. What that means to users of computers built with these chips is quicker data transfers, faster interfaces, and accelerated process-intensive applications, such as spreadsheets, graphics, and multimedia. These chips will be able to support new avenues of implementations, such as speech recognition and clear, fluid video.

However, software has to be able to take advantage of this speed. The power of the Intel 386 chip made the usability of Windows 3.0 possible. There will be more of this same type of revolution as software developers take advantage of the power of these new faster chips.

System operating systems and network operating systems will benefit the most from the increased speed of these chips, especially those that can take advantage of multiple processors.

Pentium

Pentium from Intel is the first chip in this new generation of microprocessors to be released, albeit in limited numbers. Hardware vendors, such as IBM, Compaq Computer Corp., NEC Technologies, and NCR Corp., have announced plans to build Pentium micros. Digital, Advanced Logic Research (ALR), Compaq, and Dell Computer Corp. are shipping either Pentium systems and/or Pentium-upgradeable systems.

One reason for slow system deliveries, besides Intel's inability to produce the chips in great quantities, is the chip's potential for overheating—all this processing power generates a lot of heat. However, this is not a new concern with powerful chips. The 486/50 chips were recalled and redesigned for exactly that reason, and the heat problems were solved.

Many of these same vendors are offering 486 systems that can be upgraded by installing a Pentium chip in the micro's OverDrive socket. The socket was designed for an OverDrive version of Pentium slated for release mid-1994. However, hardware vendors must also design their systems to handle the heat generated by the chip.

PowerPC

Apple Computer, IBM, and Motorola have produced the PowerPC RISC-based chip. The first chip, the PowerPC 601, available in 50- and 66-Mhz configurations, is targeted at low-end to midrange desktop systems. Some industry analysts have described the PowerPC 601 as a Pentium with a built-in math coprocessor.

The PowerPC is promised to be available in large quantities (unlike the Pentium which is promised in limited quantities only during its first year of availability), costs about half of Pentium prices, and does not need an air-conditioning system like the Pentium.

IBM is expected to have a workstation by the beginning of 1994. Apple plans to release a PowerPC-based Macintosh in the first half of 1994. The new PowerPC architecture will be 100 percent compatible with Apple's current line of Macintoshes which is based on the Motorola 68000 family of microprocessors. IBM is expected to sell both PowerPC and Intel Pentium-based systems. The PowerPC will be IBM's high-end user RISC line, Pentium will run the more desktop-oriented machines.

The 601 is the first of four planned PowerPC microprocessors. Other models include:

- 603 for portable systems
- 604 for servers and high-end desktop systems
- 620, a high-performance 64-bit microprocessor

In addition to IBM, Sun Microsystems and several UNIX vendors (although currently not The Santa Cruz Operation) have committed to developing for the PowerPC, giving the chip instant presence in the UNIX world.

One note of caution. Microsoft has not announced any support for the PowerPC chip, having already made commitments to Digital's Alpha and the Mips R-4000 processors and having a good relationship with Intel. At best, Microsoft will give in to industry pressures and be forced to port Windows NT to the chip.

Alpha

The Alpha chip from Digital has been shipping (in Digital computers) since late 1992. The Alpha AXP systems are being built to accommodate any operating system or programming language. Digital plans immediate support for three operating systems:

- OpenVMS, a POSIX-compliant version of VAX/VMS, is available now.
- OpenOSF, the Digital implementation of the UNIX-based OSF/1 operating system from Open Software Foundation, is expected to ship by the end of 1993.
- Windows NT from Microsoft will ship shortly after Windows NT begins shipment.

As is true of all these newer microprocessors, the key to success is the number of software products that have been ported to that platform. However, software vendors won't port their software unless there is enough demand in the market and hardware vendors have a harder time selling the new platforms to create the demand in the market without enough software to run on the platforms.

Digital claims that third-party software vendors have promised to port over 1,500 software products to the Alpha AXP platform, but few will begin shipping until the end of 1993.

13.1.2 Mobile Computing

Smaller and lighter machines, developed to support the needs of the mobile worker, are getting more powerful and more portable, smaller and less expensive. The light-weight notebook computers have a full-size configuration (8 Mbytes of RAM, 120-Mbyte hard disk, and 486SX or 486DX processor) and a battery life of nearly eight hours. Clipboard and tablet computers, smaller and less powerful than the notebook computers, are being used to automate forms processing.

Personal digital assistants (PDAs) are hand-held limited-purpose devices aimed at personal management applications, such as address book maintenance, calendar scheduling, note taking, and letter writing. Some are able to transmit files to a host. The PDAs expected from Apple and Sharp Electronics by the end of 1993 will be pen-based (no keyboard or physical buttons) and feature a combination touch and LCD screen interface.

13.1.3 Pen-Based Computing

Electronic pens were first introduced as pointing devices and have evolved into a self-contained architecture. Pen-based operating systems store *ink*, a new datatype that displays the strokes of the pen and stores them as they are created by the user. Pen computing is aimed at supporting mobile field and office workers.

Pen applications currently take a forms approach. A form is displayed on the screen and the user uses the pen to check an item, fill in a box, draw, and write notes to themselves. Notes would be stored as-is in a text field.

Another implementation of pen-based technology is capturing electronic signatures, as is currently done by Federal Express among others. The signature is captured as-is (an image), stored in a text field, and is then retrievable like any other piece of data.

13.1.4 Wireless Networks

Wireless networks allow portable computer users to connect to a network without a fixed address and without a phone jack. Users equipped with portable computers and wireless modems (internal or external) can easily access their organization's host or other computers on the network.

Wireless data messages are sent in digital form over a wireless packet network. Network messages are addressed to individual devices with unique identification codes.

As the wireless infrastructure strengthens and the costs decline, coupled with the advances in hand-held and pen-based computers, wireless communications could impact personal and corporate computing much in the same way cellular telephones revolutionized phone use. The end result will be mobile users who can get data any time, from any where.

13.1.5 CD-ROM and Multimedia

CD-ROM is being used to store gigabytes of data (numbers, text, images, video, and voice) and distribute it at very low cost. CD-ROM is being used as a vehicle for reengineering business processes and how data is provided.

Imaging allows an organization to convert paper files to electronic images that can be searched, sorted, and retrieved. Imaging is also being used to reengineer paper-oriented processes—how documents are processed while they are in active status.

Multimedia applications that include text, sound, and images (such as photographs) are beginning to appear as applications in some organizations and as products to unique markets. Other organizations are evaluating the use of CD-ROM and multimedia as an implementation vehicle—they are looking for the right project for the technology.

13.2 Software Advances

Software is changing to support the new advances in hardware technology. Changes are appearing in the software that allow applications and users to utilize the hardware and also in the software that supports the development of applications.

13.2.1 Operating Systems

Operating systems, both on the server and the desktop machine, will be more robust. The 32-bit operating systems discussed in Section 2.5.1 (Windows NT, OS/2 2.x, UNIX, and Portable OS/2) will spawn off client versions, making the desktop machine even more powerful and the enterprise network more reliable.

Another operating system evolving is the object-oriented one being developed by Taligent (a collaborative between Apple and IBM). Little is known about this system (code name Pink) except that it is very robust, expected to put operating systems in a new light, and is due sometime in 1994.

13.2.2 Integration of Development Products

As is discussed in Section 5.1.4, Integration between Tools, vendors of CASE products and client/server development products are building alliances to support the integration of their products or including the missing functionality into the product itself. The ability to use the best of both methodologies is critical as organizations look for still faster implementation times for applications that use the newer, more mobile platforms—applications that could possibly become a strategic asset of the organization.

With this integration will also come ease of use. If they are to provide quick development (analysis, design, and construction) times, products will have to be easy to use and understand.

The development products will also become more object-based (or perhaps object-oriented). Those development products that do not become object-based will fall behind in market share.

Object-based development products implement the characteristics of object technology—encapsulation, classification, inheritance, and polymorphism (see Section 4.6.1, Object-Oriented Characteristics)—in generating application design specifications (and the resulting code) but does not require the developer to use object-oriented techniques in specifying the designs.

As illustrated in Figure 13.1, FIELD is an object class which is used to build screens, windows, and dialogs. The object class FIELD has a COLOR attribute and two subclasses, INPUT-FIELD and NON-INPUT-FIELD. Subclasses of INPUT-FIELD are VENDOR-NUMBER and VENDOR-NAME. In reality, FIELD would have additional attributes, such as SHAPE and VIDEO DISPLAY, and INPUT-FIELD would have additional subclasses such as INVOICE-NUM and VENDOR-TERMS.

As subclasses of INPUT-FIELD, both subclasses inherit the attributes of FIELD. If a developer overrides the COLOR attribute of INPUT-FIELD, the new value of the attribute is inherited by both VENDOR-NUMBER and VENDOR-NAME.

13.2.3 Object-Oriented Development

Object-oriented analysis and design products are in the trial stage in many organizations. As these organizations begin to understand the theory and the technology and to successfully apply this knowledge toward business issues, object technology (and object-oriented programming) will have a great impact on application development.

As is discussed in Section 4.6.2, object-oriented development has the following characteristics:

- The development process simulates the activity of the application.
- The data and the code that manipulates it is stored together (as an object).
- The data is the driver of the activity.
- Reuse of existing components is a natural by-product of object technology.

Object-oriented analysis is discussed in Section 4.6, object-oriented

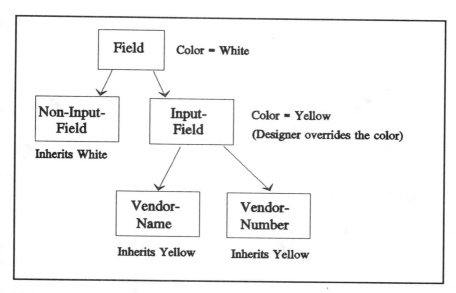

Figure 13.1 Inheritance concept in object technology

development in Section 5.6. Applications developed using object-oriented techniques are coded using object-oriented programming languages such as C++ and Smalltalk.

13.3 What Next?

Predicting how computer technology will be used in organizations over the next ten years, or even the next five years, is not an exact science. Organizations can only look at today's technology, stay informed about current development trends, and try to plan their applications and the manner in which they conduct business to fit the technology's capabilities.

With wireless networks, portable micros with docking stations at the user's desk, and affordable CD-ROM drivers, organizations can focus on their business and the best alternatives for handling their business without being constrained by technology. With so many implementation possibilities, it seems that organizations are limited only by their own imaginations.

List of Abbreviations

3GL	Third-generation language
4GL	Fourth-generation language
ADW	Application Development Workbench (KnowledgeWare)
ANSI	American National Institute of Standards
API	Application programming interface
APPC	Advanced Program-to-Program Communication (IBM)
ASCII	American National Standard Code for Information Interchange
CASE	Computer-aided software engineering
CD-ROM	Compact disk-read only memory
CDIF	CASE Data Interchange Format
CICS	Customer Information Control System (IBM)
CMIP	Common Management Information Protocol
CMIS	Common Management Information Services
CODE	Client/Server Open Development Environment (Powersoft)
CORBA	Common Object Request Broker Architecture
COSE	Common Open Software Environment
CPI-C	Common Programming Interface for Communications
CPU	Central processing unit
CSTP	Client/server transaction processing
CUA	Common User Access (IBM)
DBMS	Database management system
DCE	Distributed Computing Environment (OSF)
DDBMS	Distributed database management system
DDCS	Data Definition Control Support (IBM)
DDE	Dynamic Data Exchange (Microsoft Windows)
DDL	Data Definition Language
DFS	Distributed file systems
DLL	Dynamic link libraries
DME	Distributed Management Environment (OSF)
DML	Data Manipulation Language
DOS	Disk operating system
DRDA	Distributed Relational Database Architecture (IBM)
DSS	Decision Support System
DTP	Distributed Transaction Processing (X/Open)
E-mail	Electronic mail
E-R	Entity-relationship (diagrams)
EBCDIC	Extended binary-coded decimal interchange code

ECC	Error-correction code
EDA/SQL	Enterprise Data Access/SQL (Information Builders)
EDI	Electronic Data Interchange
EHLLAPI	Extended High Level Language Application Programming Interface (IBM)
EIS	Executive information system
FDDI	Fiber Distributed Data Interface
GOSIP	Government Open Systems Interconnection Profile
GUI	Graphical user interface
HPFS	High Performance File System (IBM OS/2)
I/O	Input/output
I-CASE	Integrated computer-aided software engineering
IBI	Information Builders, Inc.
IDE	Interactive Development Environments, Inc.
IDF	Information Engineering and Design Facility (Uniface)
IDL	Interface definition language
IE	Information Engineering
IEEE	Institute of Electrical and Electronic Engineers
IEF	Information Engineering Facility (Texas Instruments)
IPX	Internet Packet Exchange (Novell)
IRDS	Information Resource Dictionary System
IS	Information Systems
ISA	Integrated Software Architecture (Software AG)
ISO	International Standards Organization
IT	Information technology
JAD	Joint Application Development
LAN	Local area network
LTM	Long transaction model
LU6.2	Logical Unit 6.2 (IBM)
MAPI	Messaging Application Programming Interface
MDI	Multiple Document Interface
MIB	Management information base
MIPS	Millions of instructions per second
MPTN	MultiProtocol Transport Network (IBM)
NFS	Network File System (Sun Microsystems)
NLM	NetWare Loadable Modules
NTFS	NT File System (Windows NT)
OBDC	Open Database Connectivity (Microsoft)
OLE	Object Linking and Embedding (Microsoft)
OLTP	Online transaction processing
OMA	Object Management Architecture (OMG)
OMG	Object Management Group
ONC	Open Network Computing (Sun Microsystems)
OOP	Object-oriented programming
ORB	Object Request Broker
OSF	Open Software Foundation
OSI	Open Systems Interconnection
P-code	Pseudocode

PCTE	Portable Common Tool Environment
POSIX	Portable Operating System Interface for UNIX
PTC	Prepare-to-commit
RAD	Rapid application development
RAID	Redundant arrays of inexpensive disks
RAM	Random access memory
RDA	Remote Data Access (ANSI)
RDBMS	Relational database management system
RISC	Reduced instruction set computing
RPC	Remote procedure call
SA/SD	Structured analysis and structured design
SAA	Systems Application Architecture (IBM)
SAL	SQLWindows Application Language
SMP	Simple Management Protocol
SNA	Systems Network Architecture (IBM)
SNMP	Simple Network Management Protocol
SPX	Sequenced Packet Exchange (Novell)
SQL	Structured Query Language (IBM)
StP	Software through Pictures
SVR4	UNIX System V Release 4 (USL)
SWAT	Specialists with advanced tools
TCP/IP	Transmission Control Protocol/Internet Protocol
TLI	Transport layer interface
TME	Tivoli Management Environment (Tivoli Systems)
TPM	Transaction processing monitor
UI	UNIX International Inc.
URMA	UNIFACE Runtime Manager
USL	UNIX System Laboratories
VIM	Vendor Independent Messaging
VINES	Virtual Networking System (Banyan)
VUE	Visual User Environment (HP)
WAN	Wide area network
Windows NT	Windows New Technology (Microsoft)
WOSA	Windows Open Services Architecture (Microsoft)
WYSIWYG	"What you see is what you get"
XA	X/Open Resource Manager
XDR	External Data Representation
XL/II	Excelerator II (INTERSOLV)

List of Trademarks

Trademark or Registered Trademark of

Cooperative Development Environment	Oracle Corp.
Cooperative Solutions	Cooperative Solutions, Inc.
CorVision	Cortex Corp.
Cross System Product	International Business Machines Corp.
Customer Information Control System	International Business Machines Corp.
Data Definition Control Support	International Business Machines Corp.
Database Gateway	Micro Decisionware Inc.
DB2	International Business Machines Corp.
DB2 Gateway	Micro Decisionware, Inc.
DB2/2	International Business Machines Corp.
dBASE	Ashton-Tate Corp.
DBC/1012	Teradata Corp.
DCE	Open Software Foundation Inc.
DECnet	Digital Equipment Corp.
DECwindows	Digital Equipment Corp.
DESIGN/1	Andersen Consulting
Deskset	Sun Microsystems, Inc.
Dialog System	Micro Focus Inc.
Digital	Digital Equipment Corp.
Digital Network Architecture	Digital Equipment Corp.
Direct File System	Novell, Inc.
Distributed Computer Environment	Open Software Foundation Inc.
Distributed Console Access Facility	International Business Machines Corp.
Distributed Data Management Architecture	International Business Machines Corp.
Distributed Management Environment	Open Software Foundation Inc.
Distributed Object Management	SunSoft
Distributed Relational Database Architecture	International Business Machines Corp.
Distributed Transaction Processing	X/Open Corp.
DME	Open Software Foundation Inc.
DRDA	International Business Machines Corp.
DualManager	NetLabs, Inc.
Dynamic Data Exchange	Microsoft Corp.
EASEL	Easel Corp.
EASEL/2	Easel Corp.
EASEL/DOS	Easel Corp.
EASEL/WIN	Easel Corp.
EASEL Transaction Server Toolkit	Easel Corp.
EASEL Workbench	Easel Corp.

	Trademark or Registered Trademark of
EDA/COMPOSE	Information Builders, Inc.
EDA/EIS for Windows	Information Builders, Inc.
EDA/SQL	Information Builders, Inc.
EDA/SQL Server	Information Builders, Inc.
Ellipse	Cooperative Solutions, Inc.
Ellipse/DE	Cooperative Solutions, Inc.
Ellipse/PS	Cooperative Solutions, Inc.
Encina	Transarc Corp.
ENFIN	Easel Corp.
ENFIN/2	Easel Corp.
ENFIN/3	Easel Corp.
ENFIN SQL Edition	Easel Corp.
Ensemble	Cadre Technologies, Inc.
Enterprise Data Access/SQL	Information Builders, Inc.
ENTIRE	Software AG
Excelerator	INTERSOLV, Inc.
Excelerator II	INTERSOLV, Inc.
Extended High Level Language Application Interface	International Business Machines Corp.
FAST TRACK	Progress Software Corp.
FOCNET	Information Builders, Inc.
FOCUS	Information Builders, Inc.
FOCUS/DB Toolkit for Visual Basic	Information Builders, Inc.
FOCUS/DLL	Information Builders, Inc.
FOCUS/EIS for Windows	Information Builders, Inc.
FOUNDATION	Andersen Consulting
FOUNDATION for Cooperative Processing	Andersen Consulting
FrameMaker	Frame Technology Corp.
Gupta	Gupta Technologies, Inc.
Hewlett-Packard	Hewlett-Parkard Corp.
High Performance File System	International Business Machines Corp.
HP	Hewlett-Packard Corp.
HP 9000	Hewlett-Packard Corp.
HP-UX	Hewlett-Packard Corp.
Hypercard	Apple Computer, Inc.
IBM	International Business Machines Corp.
IEF	Texas Instruments, Inc.
IMS	International Business Machines Corp.
Information Engineering Facility	Texas Instruments, Inc.
Informix	Informix, Inc.
INFORMIX	Informix, Inc.
INGRES	Ingres Corp.

	Trademark or Registered Trademark of
INGRES/4GL	Ingres Corp.
INGRES/Gateways	Ingres Corp.
INGRES/OpenSQL	Ingres Corp.
INGRES/SQL	Ingres Corp.
INGRES/Vision	Ingres Corp.
INGRES/Windows4GL	Ingres Corp.
INGRES Intelligent Database	Ingres Corp.
INSTALL/1	Andersen Consulting
Integrated Software Architecture	Software AG
Intel	Intel Corp.
Interleaf	Interleaf Corp.
INTERSOLV	INTERSOLV, Inc.
INTERSOLV LAN Repository	INTERSOLV, Inc.
Kerberos	Massachusetts Institute of Technology
Knowledge Inspector	KnowledgeWare, Inc.
Knowledge Recode	KnowledgeWare, Inc.
Knowledge Pinpoint	KnowledgeWare, Inc.
KnowledgeWare	KnowledgeWare, Inc.
LAN Administration Manager	International Business Machines Corp.
LAN Manager	Microsoft Corp.
LANalyzer	Novell, Inc.
LanProbe II	Hewlett-Packard Corp.
LANtern	Novell, Inc.
LANwatch	FTP Software
Local Area Transport	Digital Equipment Corp.
Lotus	Lotus Development Corp.
Lotus Notes	Lotus Development Corp.
LU6.2	International Business Machines Corp.
MacDraw	Apple Computer, Inc.
Macintosh	Apple Computer, Inc.
Magic	Magic Software Enterprises, Inc.
Messaging Application Programming Interface	Microsoft Corp.
METHOD/1	Andersen Consulting
Microsoft	Microsoft Corp.
Middleware	TechGnosis, Inc.
Mips	Mips Computers, Inc.
MIS Friendly	Powersoft Corp.
Motif	Open Software Foundation
Motif Window Manager	Open Software Foundation
Motorola	Motorola, Inc.
MPE	Hewlett-Packard Corp.
MPE/iX	Hewlett-Packard Corp.

Trademark or Registered Trademark of

MS DOS	Microsoft Corp.
MS Windows	Microsoft Corp.
Mulitple Document Interface	Microsoft Corp.
MVS	International Busines Machines Corp.
NATURAL	Software AG
NATURAL CONSTRUCT	Software AG
NATURAL ARCHITECT WORKSTATION	Software AG
NCR	NCR Corp.
NetView	International Business Machines Corp.
NetWare	Novell, Inc.
Network Computing System	Hewlett-Packard Corp.
Network File System	Sun Microsystems, Inc.
Network Information System	Sun Microsystems, Inc.
NFS	Sun Microsystems, Inc.
Novell	Novell, Inc.
NT File System	Microsoft Corp.
Object DBMS	Versant Object Technology Corp.
Object Easy	Powersoft Corp.
Object Linking and Embedding	Microsoft Corp.
Object Management Architecture	Object Management Group
Objectivity	Objectivity, Inc.
ObjectView	KnowledgeWare, Inc. (Matesys)
OLTP Toolkit	Transarc Corp.
ONC ToolTalk	SunSoft
Ontos	Ontos, Inc.
Open Database Connectivity	Microsoft Corp.
Open Network Computing	Sun Microsystems, Inc.
Open Server	Sybase, Inc.
OpenLook	Sun Microsystems and USL
OpenView	Hewlett-Packard Corp.
Oracle	Oracle Corp.
Oracle Book	Oracle Corp.
Oracle Browser	Oracle Corp.
Oracle Card	Oracle Corp.
Oracle Designer	Oracle Corp.
Oracle Dictionary	Oracle Corp.
Oracle Exchange	Oracle Corp.
Oracle Forms	Oracle Corp.
Oracle Forms Generator	Oracle Corp.
Oracle Glue	Oracle Corp.
Oracle Graphics	Oracle Corp.

	Trademark or Registered Trademark of
Oracle Methods	Oracle Corp.
Oracle Reports	Oracle Corp.
Oracle Reports Generator	Oracle Corp.
Oracle Server	Oracle Corp.
ORACLE7	Oracle Corp.
OS/2	International Business Machines Corp.
OS/2 LAN Server	International Business Machines Corp.
OS/2 Performance Monitor	International Business Machines Corp.
OS/400	International Business Machines Corp.
OS/400 Database	International Business Machines Corp.
OSF	Open Software Foundation
OSF/1	Open Software Foundation
PACBASE	CGI Systems, Inc.
PACBENCH	CGI Systems, Inc.
PACDESIGN	CGI Systems, Inc.
PACLAN	CGI Systems, Inc.
PACLAN/X	CGI Systems, Inc.
PC Storyboard	International Business Machines Corp.
PC/FOCUS	Information Builders, Inc.
Pentium	Intel Corp.
PerfView	Hewlett-Packard Corp.
PLAN/1	Andersen Consulting
PM/FOCUS	Information Builders, Inc.
PowerBuilder	Powersoft Corp.
PowerDesigner	Cognos Corp.
PowerHouse	Cognos Corp.
PowerHouse 4GL	Cognos Corp.
PowerHouse Architect	Cognos Corp.
PowerHouse PC	Cognos Corp.
PowerHouse Windows	Cognos Corp.
PowerMaker	Powersoft Corp.
PowerPC	Apple, IBM, and Motorola
PowerPoint	Microsoft Corp.
PowerScript	Powersoft Corp.
Powersoft	Powersoft Corp.
PowerViewer	Powersoft Corp.
PREDICT	Software AG
PREDICT CASE	Software AG
PREDICT GATEWAY	Software AG
Presentation Manager	International Business Machines Corp.
PROGRESS	Progress Software Corp.
PS/2	International Business Machines Corp.
Q+E	Pioneer Software

Trademark or Registered Trademark of

Quest	Gupta Technologies, Inc.
QuickBasic	Microsoft Corp.
Raima	Raima Corp.
Rdb	Digital Equipment Corp.
Remote Data Access	International Standards Organization
Results	Progress Software Corp.
RMS	Digital Equipment Corp.
RPC Tool	Netwise, Inc.
RS/6000	International Business Machines Corp.
SAA	International Business Machines Corp.
SCO MPX	Santa Cruz Operations, Inc.
ShortCut	Cadre Technologies, Inc.
Sniffer	Network General Corp.
Softbench	Hewlett-Parkard Corp.
Software through Pictures	Interactive Development Environments, Inc.
Solaris	SunSoft
SPARC	Sun Microsystems, Inc.
SQL Bridge	Microsoft Corp.
SQL Server	Sybase, Inc. and Microsoft Corp.
SQL Smart	Powersoft Corp.
SQL/400	International Business Machines Corp.
SQL/DS	International Business Machines Corp.
SQL*Forms	Oracle Corp.
SQL*Star	Oracle Corp.
SQLBase	Gupta Technologies, Inc.
SQLNetwork	Gupta Technologies, Inc.
SQLWindows	Gupta Technologies, Inc.
STREAMS	UNIX System Laboratories, Inc.
StreetTalk	Banyan Systems, Inc.
Structured Query Language	International Business Machines Corp.
Sun	Sun Microsystems, Inc.
SunOS	Sun Microsystems, Inc.
Sybase	Sybase, Inc.
SYBASE SQL Server	Sybase, Inc.
System 7	Apple Computer, Inc.
Systems Application Architecture	International Business Machines Corp.
Systems Network Architecture	International Business Machines Corp.
Team*work*	Cadre Technologies, Inc.
Team*work*/Ada	Cadre Technologies, Inc.
Team*work*/Access	Cadre Technologies, Inc.
Team*work*/DocGen	Cadre Technologies, Inc.
Team*work*/DSE	Cadre Technologies, Inc.

Trademark or Registered Trademark of

Teamwork/FORTRAN Rev	Cadre Technologies, Inc.
Teamwork/IM	Cadre Technologies, Inc.
Teamwork/RqT	Cadre Technologies, Inc.
Teamwork/RT	Cadre Technologies, Inc.
Teamwork/SA	Cadre Technologies, Inc.
Teamwork/SD	Cadre Technologies, Inc.
Teamwork/SIM	Cadre Technologies, Inc.
Teamwork/TestCase	Cadre Technologies, Inc.
Tivoli Management Environment	TIVOLI Systems, Inc.
Tivoli Management Framework	TIVOLI Systems, Inc.
Tivoli/ADE	TIVOLI Systems, Inc.
Tivoli/AEF	TIVOLI Systems, Inc.
Tivoli/Sentry	TIVOLI Systems, Inc.
Tivoli/Works	TIVOLI Systems, Inc.
Tooltalk	Sun Microsystems, Inc.
TOP END	NCR Corp.
Transact-SQL	Sybase, Inc.
Transaction Tracking System	Novell, Inc.
Transarc	Transarc Corp.
Transport-Independent Remote Procedure Call	SunSoft
Tuxedo	UNIX System Laboratories, Inc.
Tuxedo Enterprise Transaction Processing	UNIX System Laboratories, Inc.
Tuxedo/Host	UNIX System Laboratories, Inc.
Tuxedo/WS	UNIX System Laboratories, Inc.
UI	UNIX International, Inc.
UI-Atlas	UNIX International, Inc.
Ultrix	Digital Equipment Corp.
UNIFACE	Uniface Corp.
UNIX	UNIX System Laboratories, Inc.
UNIX System V	UNIX System Laboratories, Inc.
UnixWare	Univel, Inc.
VANGuard	Banyan Systems, Inc.
VAX	Digital Equipment Corp.
Versant	Versant Object Technology
Via/Smart Test	VIASOFT, Inc.
VINES	Banyan Systems, Inc.
VINES SMP	Banyan Systems, Inc.
Virtual Networking System	Banyan Systems, Inc.
Visual Basic	Microsoft Corp.
Visual Planner	Information Builders, Inc.
Visual User Environment	Hewlett-Packard Corp.

Trademark or Registered Trademark of

VM	International Business Machines Corp.
VMS	Digital Equipment Corp.
VSAM	International Business Machines Corp.
VTAM	International Business Machines Corp.
Windows	Microsoft Corp.
Windows New Technology	Microsoft Corp.
Windows NT	Microsoft Corp.
Windows Open Services Architecture	Microsoft Corp.
Windows Rich	Powersoft Corp.
WorkPlace Shell	International Business Machines Corp.
X Window System	Massachusetts Institute of Technology
X/Open	X/Open Corp.
XDB	XDB Systems, Inc.
XENIX	Microsoft Corp.

List of Vendors

PRODUCT	VENDOR
Application Development Workbench	KnowledgeWare, Inc.
APS	INTERSOLV, Inc.
CorVision	Cortex Corporation
Distributed Management Environment	Open Software Foundation
Distributed Computing Environment	Open Software Foundation
EASEL Workbench	Easel Corporation
EDA/SQL	Information Builders, Inc.
Ellipse	Cooperative Solutions, Inc.
Encina	Transarc Corporation
ENFIN	Easel Corporation
Excelerator	INTERSOLV, Inc.
FOCUS	Information Builders, Inc.
FOUNDATION	Andersen Consulting
Information Engineering Facility	Texas Instruments
INGRES	Ingres Corporation
Magic	Magic Software Enterprises, Inc.
NATURAL	Software AG
Object Management Architecture	Object Management Group
ObjectView	KnowledgeWare, Inc.
Oracle	Oracle Corporation
PACBASE	CGI Systems, Inc.
PowerBuilder	Powersoft Corporation
PowerHouse	Cognos Corporation
PROGRESS	Progress Software Corporation
Software through Pictures	Interactive Development Environments, Inc.
SQLWindows	Gupta Technologies, Inc.
Teamwork	Cadre Technologies Inc.
Tivoli Management Environment	TIVOLI Systems, Inc.
TOP END	NCR Corporation
Tuxedo	UNIX System Laboratories
UI-Atlas	UNIX International Inc.
UNIFACE	Uniface Corporation

Andersen Consulting
FOUNDATION
Suite 2010
69 West Washington Street
Chicago, IL 60602
Telephone: 800-458-8851

Cadre Technologies, Inc.
222 Richmond Street
Providence, RI 02903
Telephone: 800-743-2273

CGI Systems, Inc.
One Blue Hill Plaza
PO Box 1645
Pearl River, NY 10965
Telephone: 914-735-5030

Cognos Corporation
67 S. Bedford Street
Burlington, MA 01803-5164
Telephone: 617-229-6600
            800-426-4667

Cooperative Solutions, Inc.
Suite 100
2125 Hamilton Avenue
San Jose, CA 95125
Telephone: 408-377-0300

Cortex Corporation
P.O. Box 9097
100 Fifth Avenue
Waltham, MA 02254-9097
Telephone: 617-622-1900

Easel Corp.
25 Corporate Drive
Burlington, MA 01803
Telephone: 617-221-3000

Gupta Technologies, Inc.
1060 Marsh Road
Menlo Park, CA 94025
Telephone: 415-321-9500
            800-44-GUPTA

Information Builders, Inc.
1250 Broadway
New York, NY 10001-3782
Telephone: 212-736-4433
            800-969-4636

Ingres Corporation
1080 Marina Village Parkway
Box 4026
Alameda, CA 94501-1095
Telephone: 510-769-1400
            800-4-INGRES

Interactive Development
  Environment, Inc.
595 Market Street, 10th Floor
San Francisco, CA 94105
Telephone: 415-543-0900
            800-888-IDE1

INTERSOLV, Inc.
3200 Tower Oaks Boulevard
Rockville, MD 20852
Telephone: 800-547-4000

KnowledgeWare, Inc.
3340 Peachtree Road, NE
Atlanta, Georgia 30326
Telephone: 404-231-8575
                    800-338-4130

Magic Software Enterprises, Inc.
1200 Main Street
Irvine, CA 92714
Telephone: 714-250-1718
                    800-345-6244

NCR Corporation
1700 S. Patterson Boulevard
Dayton, OH 45479
Telephone: 513-445-5000
                    800-225-5627

Object Management Group
Framingham Corporate Center
492 Old Connecticut Path
Framingham, MA 01701
Telephone: 508-820-4300

Open Software Foundation
11 Cambridge Center
Cambridge, MA 02142
Telephone: 617-621-8700

Oracle Corp.
500 Oracle Parkway
Redwood Shores, CA 94065
Telephone: 800-ORACLE-1

Powersoft Corp.
70 Blanchard Road
Burlington, MA 01803
Telephone: 617-229-2200

Progress Software Corporation
5 Oak Park
Bedford, MA 01730
Telephone: 617-275-4500

Software AG
 of North America, Inc.
11190 Sunrise Valley Drive
Reston, VA 22091
Telephone: 703-860-5050
                    800-843-9534

Texas Instruments, Inc.
Information Technology Group
6550 Chase Oaks Boulevard
Plano, TX 75023
Telephone: 214-575-4404

TIVOLI Systems
Suite 210
6034 West Courtyear Drive
Austin, TX 78730
Telephone: 512-794-9070

Transarc Corporation
The Gulf Tower
707 Grant Street
Pittsburgh, PA 15219
Telephone: 412-338-4400

Uniface Corp.
Suite 100
1320 Harbor Bay Parkway
Alameda, CA 94501
Telephone: 510-748-6145

UNIX International, Inc.
20 Waterview Boulevard
Parsippany, NJ 07054
Telephone: 201-263-8400
              800-848-6495

UNIX System Laboratories, Inc.
190 River Road
Summit, NJ 07901
Telephone: 908-522-6555
              800-828-8649

Additional Readings

Atre, Stephen, <u>Distributed Databases, Cooperative Processing, and Networking</u>, McGraw-Hill, Inc., 1992

Berson, Alex, <u>Client/Server Architecture</u>, McGraw-Hill, Inc., 1993

Boar, B. H., <u>Implementing Client/Server Computing: A Strategic Perspective</u>, McGraw-Hill, Inc., 1993

Cerutti, Daniel and Donna Pierson, <u>Distributed Computing Environments</u>, McGraw-Hill, Inc., 1993

Dewire, Dawna Travis, <u>Client/Server Computing</u>, McGraw-Hill, Inc., 1993

Lockhart, Harold W., Jr., <u>OSF DCE: Guide to Developing Distributed Applications</u>, McGraw-Hill, Inc., 1994

Marion, William, <u>Client/Server Strategies</u>, McGraw-Hill, Inc., 1994

Index

ABOUT THE AUTHOR

Dawna Travis Dewire (Wellesley, Massachusetts) has more than 20 years of experience as a programmer, analyst, systems architect, consultant, instructor, and writer. As a contributing editor to the James Martin Report, Inc., she was responsible for preparing such end-user-oriented volumes as *Query, Reporting and Graphics, Decision Support and Financial Analysis,* and *Text Management.* She is an adjunct lecturer at Babson College in Wellesley, Massachusetts, and is president of Decision Tree Associates. She is the author of *Client/Server Computing* and *Text Management,* both published by McGraw-Hill.